YOUTH, EDUCATION, AND THE ROLE OF SOCIETY

YOUTH, EDUCATION, AND THE ROLE OF SOCIETY

*Rethinking Learning
in the High School Years*

Robert Halpern

Harvard Education Press
Cambridge, Massachusetts

KH

Library of Congress Control Number 2013931904

Paperback ISBN 978-1-61250-536-7
Library Edition ISBN 978-1-61250-537-4

Published by Harvard Education Press,
an imprint of the Harvard Education Publishing Group

Harvard Education Press
8 Story Street
Cambridge, MA 02138

Cover Design: Patrick Ciano
Cover Photo: Clerkenwell/the Agency Collection/Getty Images

The typefaces used in this book are Adobe Garamond Pro and Futura

10/6/14

Contents

Dedicated in loving memory to my mother, Martha Halpern

Introduction

This book is about the need for American society to rethink how it educates, socializes, and supports young people. I argue that the central societal task in this regard is to create the means for young people's immersion in the fullness and complexity of the adult world—its places and endeavors, occupations and disciplines, problems and dilemmas. Creating such means will require three related cultural shifts. The first is in how we view and understand young people, what they are capable of, want, and need. The second is in how we feel about young people's presence in adult institutions: young people require an active and welcoming stance from a range of adult institutions and sectors of society. The third necessary cultural shift, and the major focus of much of this book, is in how we view and understand learning. I argue for an expansive view of where and how learning experiences might take place, what the focus and content of learning experiences should be, and what such experiences should lead to in terms of achievement. Our society and its institutions must place greater value on heterogeneity in how, in what directions, and to what ends young people learn.

Cultivating diverse commitments and kinds of expertise is essential to an interesting and enriching culture. If and when our society stops valuing only a narrow range of occupations, roles, and accomplishments, it will help young people learn to enjoy who they are and to see what they can do. Young people need and want to be exposed to a variety of models of adulthood. The adult world is more interesting to them than either school or, frequently, their peer groups because of the diversity of tasks and types of endeavor and, especially, the diversity of people—the engineer, the entrepreneur, the community activist, the caregiver, the poet, the technologist, the antitechnologist, the opera singer, the jazz musician.

I set the stage in chapter 1 with a brief overview of current thinking about learning and an extended discussion of the developmental tasks of the high school years. Learning experiences are most motivating and useful when they support work on the distinct tasks of an age period, and this is especially the case for high school–age youth. Good learning experiences underpin many of the tasks that people have to negotiate, from discovering strengths and limitations to building background knowledge in important domains; learning about, testing out, and preparing for the adult world; and exploring who and what one might become. I argue that work on developmental tasks is best understood as a joint project of individual youth and the social institutions surrounding them, an idea that may sound obvious but one that is strangely neglected in American society.

In chapter 2 and the first part of chapter 3 I explore the nature of and reasons for the neglect of young people's learning and developmental needs. But I then move beyond this critique to give the reader a sense of what good learning for young people looks like, where it is currently located, and how it can be made more available within and beyond the constraints of existing institutional systems. Change in the framework for learning has to start within the school system. It is profoundly problematic that "a high percentage of students dislike the place where they spend most of their learning time."[1] But rethinking schooling is just a start. American society must move away from its historic, school-based vision of learning during the high school years and understand support for young people's learning as a task for many institutions working together.

In enumerating and illustrating the attributes of good learning experiences, I focus on two arenas that hold particular promise: vocational learning—now called career and technical education, (CTE)—and nonschool learning (also called out-of-school learning or nonformal education). I also examine how some other countries conceptualize and arrange learning during the high school years. While faced with the same challenges in motivating young people, finding constructive roles for them, and maintaining their faith in the future, other countries approach these challenges differently than does the United States. Their approaches illustrate how learning arrangements can express such ideals as social inclusion and social citizenship, respect for different kinds of capabilities, the need for adults who can make very different kinds of economic and cultural contributions, and the related need for careful socialization into specific occupations.

In chapter 7 I discuss systemic issues, focusing on how we might make good learning experiences for young people not just more readily available but also more coherent. I consider the society-wide structures needed to help weave together learning experiences and especially what it would take to legitimize nonschool experiences. Our society holds a diverse array of all kinds of *potential* learning opportunities and settings for the diverse population of young people. Yet our youth-serving institutions have hardly begun either the specific the task of helping young people find the domains in which and means through which they learn best or the broad task of creating scaffolding for a coherent set of learning experiences across time and place. Shared—or distributed—responsibility for young people's learning and development will require a shift in perspective in key institutions such as schools and employers as well as some new institutional structures. Most difficult of all, we have to foster a culture of shared responsibility for young people, one that sanctions a broader view of learning during the high school years.

KEY THEMES

A Cultural Dilemma

Rethinking learning for young people means rethinking young people themselves—what they need and want, their role in society, society's stake in their well-being and development. We know that middle adolescence is a time of enormous potential for learning. New cognitive and social capacities open up a wider world for young people and amplify the scope and depth of learning. Developmental imperatives act as a spur for learning, leading young people to seek out new ideas, experiences, and places. In effect, the contours of this age period open up a wider world for young people but also demand that society provide one. It is just this duality that makes the problems with prevailing societal arrangements in the United States so poignant, and consequential, for so many youth.

The very types of experiences that young people most need are the hardest to come by in American culture. Both the learning potential and the developmental tasks of young people are strangely ignored in policy and institutional practices. Key social institutions misread what autonomy and choice mean when it comes to young people, or they let these constructs serve as excuses for keeping them at the margins of the adult world. As a result, too many young people lack access to the kinds of vital, productive learning experiences that would enrich their present lives and provide a foundation for adulthood. Too many cannot find places in which to feel and be productive, to grow, and to do both personal and cultural work. Young people are coping in various ways, but they are not thriving as a whole.

There's a kind of catch-22 at work here. Like every culture, ours needs young people to grow up. But because they are not yet grown up, because we cannot readily see their desire to participate and contribute, and perhaps because we are not fully comfortable with who they are, we deny young people access to what would be most helpful to them. We waste the potential inherent in this age group. Our society is being denied the distinct contributions that those young people would and could make, if supported, to join in our civic, artistic, scientific, social, and economic life.

Although this dynamic affects all youth, it is especially destructive to youth from disenfranchised communities and to those of color. More than any other age group, high school–age youth "sit at the crossroads of social reproduction."[2] Inequity in access to learning and social resources during this life period forces disenfranchised youth onto paths that limit personal and vocational development. Young people can and do push against social constraints. Regardless of background, every young person uses the resources available to her in a distinct way to forge her own path toward adulthood. She even has some role in creating those resources.

Yet many young people also are not being provided even the foundation of knowledge, perspective, and experience that would allow them to be social agents, to know how to be active in particular spheres.

Rationales Matter

As important as it is to create opportunity for young people to join adult endeavors, this societal task requires care. It matters why and how we do so. In the current policy environment, the rationale for any attention to young people seemingly has to derive from market needs. Other possible purposes have been pushed aside by a preoccupation with international economic competition (and a related view that if the United States is to compete economically it has to compete academically). Young people's social worth is tied to their likely ability to generate new or added economic value. We are swamped by rhetoric about "winning the global talent showdown."[3] One prominent business group argues that "governments at the local, state and national level must align their education, economic, labor, technology and commerce functions to support 21st century education from early childhood through higher education."[4]

The rationale for investing in youth and giving them experience in the adult world cannot be construed simply or primarily in instrumental terms. Part of the reason to rethink learning for young people lies in the potential of such an effort to focus attention on societal ideals. The loss of social democratic and liberal traditions in education is leaving young people without the knowledge and inclination for active citizenship, broad cultural renewal, and a sense of participation in a common social enterprise. As young people move gradually into adulthood they will be the ones to hold and remake our country's artistic, scientific, civic, and political cultures; they'll be the ones shaping family, community, and institutional life. Rationales driven by global competitiveness tend to ignore the heterogeneity of young people; the value to our culture of people with diverse talents, interests, and roles; and the needs of many segments of society that reside outside of the market.

It is critical to recognize and attend to the vocational dimensions in learning during the high school years, and vocational education must be responsive to local and regional economies. But the most interesting and compelling role for vocationally oriented learning is personal. It fosters maturity and nurtures a sense of personal competence and of having a place in the world. As one tentatively identifies oneself as a chef or engineer or dancer, one is motivated to explore what this means. For some young people vocationally oriented learning offers a pathway that can continue into early adulthood.

Affordances for learning during middle adolescence thus require a balance. The goals are not—or at least should not be—controversial. Young people need experiences that actualize new cognitive and social skills; that foster curiosity, persistence, and competence; that nurture the will to learn and the desire and the courage to invest in further learning experiences. They need learning settings that are demanding yet also responsive to developmental needs and differences. Learning experience works best for young people when there is room for them to grow and change inside the experience, to take on more responsibility and new roles as they master earlier ones. And they need experiences that provide opportunities to contribute—to a discipline, cause, community, or traditional or emergent cultural endeavor.

The qualities of needed experience reflect the contradictions of the age period. As Tim Ingold puts it, the task of adult institutions is to set up the "developmental conditions within which the next generation can get a feel for things itself."[5] Young people need space for their own individual purposes, space to construct and remake culture. They need to feel a sense of openness and ownership and to have the opportunity to create meaning that is shared rather than imposed. To grow up, young people also need what they cannot create or provide themselves: access to the "shared reservoir of accumulated ideas, skills and technologies" that constitute the richness of culture and provide some scaffolding for maturing.[6] And they need very particular, immersive learning experiences.

The best base for real growth and for expanding young people's sense of the world at large comes from deep inside some particular discipline, set of ideas, or social practice. The ensuing capacities that develop are situated;

they are tied to sustained experience in that particular cultural domain—observing, emulating, practicing, applying, and revising—but not wholly so. Learning and practice in a particular domain provide cognitive, affective, and social templates for other parts of life. Immersion in a particular endeavor also helps foster a sense of belonging, of personal identity, and of continuity in the experience of life, day-to-day and over time. Erik and Kai Erikson observe that there is not only an obvious restriction but a certain freedom in being "firmly told by tradition who one is."[7] That idea is less plausible now than it was in the past, given the weakening of so many specific traditions and of belief in tradition itself. But the instinct behind it remains valid.

Overreliance on Schooling

An important source of the limitations experienced by many American youth is, ironically, the outsized role of schools in addressing developmental needs. Schooling may well remain the self-evident pathway toward productive adulthood in the near future; but as it is currently conceptualized and organized, it is the narrowest of paths. It is a path that fails to hold the allegiance of many young people, one that fails to give them a reason to learn, to nurture the desire and courage to invest in learning experiences, or to foster a sense of identification with the institution itself.

High school learning as typically structured is too fragmented, isolated, and abstract to meet young people's developmental needs. It relies too much on century-old curriculum and pedagogy and is too oriented, in an unreflective way, toward preparing young people for a four-year college experience. High schools continue to take a narrow view of intelligence and to reify a narrow band of knowledge, even as it becomes increasingly clear that there are many kinds of intelligence and that knowledge is heterogeneous and, indeed, even as it is obvious that a healthy culture requires many kinds of talents and skills. High schools have not been responsive enough to the heterogeneity among young people in strengths, interests, and dispositions or attentive enough to the wide range of roles, fields, and disciplines that make up our occupational and civic worlds.

Within the context of high school curriculum, career and technical education is barely hanging on and is often dismissed as obsolete, replaced, instead, by emphases on STEM (science, technology, engineering, math) education and content-free "twenty-first-century skills."

Pressure placed on the historic model of high school is beginning to build. Scores of individual schools and a number of reform organizations are working hard to address problems of curriculum, pedagogy, and learning roles. In a steadily maturing self-renewal effort, CTE has also embraced a variety of promising approaches to young people's learning. Yet the fruit of all this work is hardly seen in national high school reform discourse. The thrust of reform efforts has been to intensify the historic, and prevailing, structure of high school through an emphasis on common core standards, accountability, testing, better data, and sanctions for those deemed to be failing. Government reformers (and their philanthropic enablers) are like losing gamblers who try to recoup their losses by doubling-down. The reform-driven practices experienced by children and youth from disenfranchised communities especially promote habits of mind and dispositions toward knowledge and learning that are just the opposite of what young people will need in the coming years, a problem that has been described as a forthcoming "civic catastrophe."[8]

A significant commitment will be needed by mediating institutions—including community organizations, philanthropies, the academic community, advocacy organizations—to make innovative school-based and school-linked work at the center of reform discussion and initiative. Yet stakeholders also have to be mindful of the American school system's remarkable capacity to absorb new ideas without those ideas leaving a trace. Self-maintenance imperatives are just too strong. And those with the most power to shape school policies too often draw the wrong lessons from the problems of schooling.

Better meeting young people's learning and developmental needs will require far more than a reconceptualized high school experience. It will mean a fundamentally different understanding of where learning can take place and the wholehearted participation of a variety of institutions and sectors of society. These include businesses and nonprofit organizations, cultural, scientific, arts and civic institutions, individual scientists, artists and craftspeople, training and apprenticeship councils, trade-specific groups and workforce development organizations, and institutions of higher education. Some of these stakeholders already understand that they have a critical role in youth development; others do not.

What I will call *nonschool learning* constitutes a diverse, difficult-to-characterize world of settings, opportunities, experiences, and identities. It can be creative or practical, expressive or instrumental. A rich type of learning experience, nonschool learning is characterized by four attributes: its specificity or particularity; the depth to which it engages young people; its heterogeneity, as a whole; and its rootedness in the actual physical, cultural, intellectual, civic, occupational worlds. Because it is a diverse enterprise encompassing a wide range of disciplines, fields, situations, and settings, nonschool learning is able to account for diverse interests and strengths among youth. It also accommodates youth who are at different places within a particular field and in their own overall development. As a base for learning, nonschool learning settings illustrate the enormous variety of what there is to learn and to learn about and why every sector of society has a role, as well as a stake, in supporting young people's development.

In emphasizing the value of nonschool learning, I argue for a different understanding of the sources of individual development and social mobility. Both are rooted not in the progressively narrowing path currently found in schooling but in the multiple, deep, substantive paths created by a range of institutions. We have to believe in and commit to a new social goal with radical implications: providing opportunities for young people who are not thriving in high school and who do not believe they are good at anything to figure out where their talents lie.[9]

This work will require a systematic reconceptualization of learning for young people, especially from age sixteen on. This includes, for example, extended service- and work-based learning opportunities through the last two years of high school and into the postsecondary period. Scholars and proponents of nonschool learning will have to work deliberately to make it better understood, recognized, and accepted by potential and actual partners, including schools, higher education, workforce development, professions, and industries, as well as among young people themselves and their parents. Bridges are being built across settings. Discussions of assessment, certification, and broadening "what counts" are under way. But institutions will have to open themselves up in ways that they have not proved capable of in the past.

Attending More Carefully to the Post–High School Transition

Because this book is about learning and development during the high school years, it is also about the transition to whatever comes next for young people. Transitions are developmentally critical processes, marked by promise and risk, implicitly summarizing growth up to that point in life. As an intern with a program called Inside View at the American Museum of Natural History notes, "Today I realized that one day which is far less than a decade away I will have a steady job, I will have a boss and co-workers . . . Although as a human being you are forced to pretty much spend 18 years of your life going to school, one day it's all over."[10] This captures the seeming abruptness of the transition from high school to postsecondary learning or work and hints at what is so startling and discomfiting about it: the change from a comprehensive structure to an almost complete lack of structure.

Societal responsibility for young people's well-being and growth diffuses dramatically—indeed, it evaporates—as they make the transition from high school to further learning or work. It would seem obvious that it makes no sense to have a support system for young people defined by a single monolithic institution until they reach age eighteen and then, thereafter, the opposite: a fragmented, ill-organized, baffling array of options for further learning, training, and work. But that is the nature of affordance for this time period in the United States. Young people and their families are left largely on their own to make sense of learning options and vocational possibilities; and what advice they do receive from teachers, counselors, and others is sometimes not a good individual fit.

To illuminate the issues involved in this transition, I explore the meaning (the many meanings, really) of aspiring to go to college or choosing (sometimes by default) not to do so. The data are extraordinarily difficult to make sense of in the context of growing rates of enrollment in postsecondary institutions of widely varying quality and authority, stagnating rates of college completion, and a high unemployment rates for eighteen-to-twenty-four–year-olds. Clearly, on average, it makes a difference as to how one decides to proceed after high school. Average earnings may well be higher for those with postsecondary degrees. But averages are hardly helpful for individual youth.

There is now plentiful evidence that young people's aspirations are too global, too often unrealistic, and too frequently not a good fit with their strengths, skills, and life situation. Young people are told over and over that a college degree offers the best assurance of good work and a well-paid future. With no other narrative available, let alone a clear set of supports for alternatives, this has become today's cultural message. Although the great majority of high school seniors intend to enroll directly in college or community college, less than 40 percent actually do so. Of these, fewer than half will graduate within six years from a two- or four-year institution. Types of colleges attended, patterns of progress, and completion rates vary dramatically by social class and race. College-going youth from disadvantaged backgrounds are much more likely than advantaged peers to attend colleges not respected by employers, to attend multiple colleges, to experience disruption in postsecondary learning, and to fail to graduate.[11] A few observers are positing a kind of education arms race, with a "gaping divide" opening up among youth, a "hollowing out of the middle, splitting the country into two tiers."[12]

Yet the noncollege pathway is, if anything, more perilous. A survey of recent (2009–2011) high school graduates not enrolled in a postsecondary program finds 16 percent working full-time, another 22 percent working part-time (most of whom want full-time work), 37 percent looking for work, 17 percent not looking, 3 percent in the military, 3 percent self-employed, and 2 percent volunteering.[13] High school and college educators, government agencies, and the workforce development community have no apparent plan for any of the struggling groups of graduates, let alone for the 30–35 percent of those who do not graduate from high school in the first place.

As with learning during the high school years, there is a clear need for new projects, new spaces, new social tasks for young people finishing high school but not in a position to start formal postsecondary study. It is critical to legitimize applied learning (or worklike) pathways at the edges of and outside of schooling, some of which will lead back to postsecondary education, some directly to types of work that allow for advancement. The lack of a youth apprenticeship system in the United States is especially problematic, given both the urgent need and the international evidence that this is one of the most useful institutions—developmentally, vocationally, culturally, and in every other way—that a nation can organize for young people.

Implications of a Changing Work Context

In the process of writing this book, I discovered what perhaps should have been obvious: reflecting on learning during the high school years requires reflection on work as well. Learning goals and experiences have to be sensitive to the changing nature of work and the structure of the labor force, the changing cultural (and international) context for work, and the evolving role of credentials. As implied above, there is plentiful evidence that historic nonschool pathways of social mobility—primarily through moderately skilled, decently paying blue-collar jobs—have atrophied. Further, the personal and social consequences of dropping out of high school, or barely finishing it, are now more likely to continue playing out over a lifetime.

Starkly different visions of work and economic life provide a backdrop for current debates about young people's learning needs. Some see an emerging high-skill, value-added manufacturing and knowledge-based economy. They envision industrial workers, freed from repetitive assembly line work, using high-order cognitive and perceptual skills to solve non-routine problems and knowledge workers, using technology, focused on the invention, production, and consumption of intangible goods and services. Knowledge economy optimists imagine an "enchanted" workplace where workers are transformed into "committed partners who engage in meaningful work, fully understand and control their jobs," and create new intellectual property for the good of the firm.[14] They imagine a more humane, if not just, economic system, with individuals free to use their creativity toward personal, social, and corporate ends.

More pessimistic observers emphasize that the bulk of available work in coming years will be mundane and service-oriented, require few skills, and provide few avenues for advancement. Such work includes food preparation, low-level retail positions like cashier and store clerk, warehouse work, and back room services in financial and other industries. These observers note a diminution of the next generation's chances of finding a sustaining vocation and forging a meaningful career. Occupational traditions are said to be atrophying and disappearing, taking with them norms, values, and sources of identity.[15]

A middle ground suggests that demand for highly skilled, self-motivating, and creative workers will be strong but narrow—certainly not a model for the majority of those entering the labor force in the coming years. A realistic aim for the majority of youth will be work that is mundane but with technical dimensions, such as that found in licensed practical nursing, allied health fields (e.g., physical therapists, radiology technicians), data entry/management technicians, and, less definitively, skilled manufacturing. While two-thirds of job openings in the coming decade will require some postsecondary learning, half of those positions will require an occupational certificate or license.[16] Even higher-order knowledge work will be subject to "digital Taylorism," with tasks simplified, standardized, and digitally codified.[17]

What seems clear is that the occupational world is more fluid, less easily definable, and less predictable than it was in the past. There will be increased competition for "good work" and the need for personal flexibility in the face of job and occupational discontinuity. Even where occupational traditions continue, experienced workers will be too busy and feel too vulnerable themselves (working freelance or "at will") to mentor a new generation. For the majority of youth, there will be no such thing as a predictable occupational life course. For some, there will be not only little job, occupational, and skill security but little economic security.[18] The personal and social effects of these trends are themselves unpredictable, but they may well further weaken our already frayed social fabric. In effect, the United States, like other nations, is experiencing a broken social contract between generations. As Susan Robertson and colleagues put it, "The opportunity bargain at the heart of the American dream—that investing in education would deliver social mobility, the security of a middle class life—has all but evaporated."[19]

Implications for Learning Regimes

In this fluid and contentious cultural context, the dominant policy instinct with respect to learning has been to stay generic, emphasizing the readiness and flexibility afforded by preparing for college. The notion of choosing depth and specificity as a framework for learning during the high school years has been repudiated. Most of the attributes emphasized in discussions of twenty-first-century skills (e.g., critical thinking, creativity, communication) are treated as content-free, based on the assumption that relevant content will constantly change in the coming years. The exception is the thematic emphasis on STEM fields.

In practical terms, reports that highly skilled manufacturing and technical jobs are going begging for lack of qualified applicants imply some need for clearly defined technical routes through secondary and postsecondary education. The value of applied learning experiences must be made much clearer to parents and policy makers, or we will have more incidents like that in San Diego, where parents recently rose up against a new district policy requiring students to take at least a few CTE courses as part of their high school experience, forcing the school board to rescind the policy. The value of working in the trades has to be revived. As a young man in Illinois who is learning welding and CNC (computer numerical controlled) machine operation tells a reporter, "I know it sounds stupid but I can make just as much money as someone who goes to college once

I'm done with high school.[20] The question is, why does this young man think that his choice sounds stupid?

Our society will have to be ever more careful in considering what learning is for—and good for. It may well be that "it is the capacity to learn that increasingly determines the relative positions of individuals, firms and national systems."[21] But this capacity is more difficult to pin down than would seem at first glance. It is not monolithic; it's rather varied and conditional. Moreover, learning is not neutral; it takes individuals and societies in different directions. Currently, in the United States, learning is viewed through a market lens. Accountability-oriented school reforms are justified by the need keep the United States competitive. It is argued that if we give our young people the right skills, jobs will stay here instead of migrating to China or India.[22] Young people themselves are encouraged to adopt a strongly economic and entrepreneurial perspective on learning. In this, both we and they may be disappointed by an economic system that seeks the lowest-cost workers wherever they may be in the world.

Globalization—shorthand for a range of changes including the creation of one enormous global labor market—has extended itself into American middle adolescence, affecting education, heightening the pressures young people feel from the adult world, and altering what young people see in their families and communities. Young people's freedom to make choices about their lives seems to be shaped in unseen ways by global market needs. Young people are as adaptable and resourceful as ever. But too many are "caught in a gale of creative destruction that makes it difficult to find individual solutions to changing economic realities."[23]

The task of rethinking learning for young people opens us up, then, to a number of concerns. These include the importance of specificity and heterogeneity as well as the consequences for human development of larger social and economic pressures in the United States and throughout the world. They require us to consider—and in some instances reconsider—who we want involved in the public debate about young people's support needs. Not least, these concerns relate to what we value in our culture and how we value young people themselves. Linda Camino and Shepherd Zeldin point out that "adult perceptions of and attitudes toward young people are critical because they provide a foundation for public discourse about adolescents, and a cultural blueprint for policy formation."[24] The ideas, arguments, and examples offered on the following pages should help us rethink how we account for young people and, in particular, how we understand their social role and potential contribution to American culture.

CHAPTER ONE

Foundations of Good Learning in Adolescence

[The teenager is] an exquisitely sensitive, highly adaptive creature wired almost perfectly for the job of moving from the safety of home into the complicated world outside.
—David Dobbs, "The New Science of the Teenage Brain"

Over the past few decades, research from a number of fields has converged to establish a clear picture of the cognitive, affective, and social processes involved in learning and the conditions that best support them. During the same time period, a shift in emphasis in developmental research (reinforced by findings from neuroscience) has created a different picture of middle adolescence. It is beginning to be appreciated as a time not just for grappling with major developmental tasks but as a period of enormous potential for learning. New cognitive and social capacities, combined with pressing developmental imperatives, lead young people to seek out new ideas and experiences. Together, the new capacities of middle adolescence, the biologically and culturally rooted developmental tasks of this age, and society's need for cultural continuity and renewal create fertile ground for learning.

THE MULTIPLE BASES OF GOOD LEARNING EXPERIENCES

Good learning experiences have multiple roots: biological, psychosocial, cultural, and material. They begin (and some would say end) in the brain and extend outward to particular settings with particular attributes, to institutional structures and the culture at large. The human brain is adapted and primed to learn through active, meaningful, socially mediated experiences. It thrives on opportunity for observation, selective imitation, and practice, but especially on tasks and problems that challenge existing mental schema, are somewhat novel, and are partly open-ended. As individuals actively work to connect new ideas and experiences to existing knowledge and understanding, the brain itself is altered. It rewires, builds new neural structures; existing connections thicken, and new ones are created. Emotion plays a critical role in this process, "recruiting a complex network of brain regions, many of which are involved in learning."[1]

Interestingly, the human brain is also oriented toward specialization, an adaptation that derives from living for millennia in societies that needed and demanded different roles and contributions. Human cultures "have a built in tendency to evolve in the direction of producing innovations that unmask and then cultivate the [diverse] talents that naturally exist among a group of people."[2] The tendency toward specialization means that asking every individual to learn the same thing in the same way to the same degree of mastery does not make sense, either personally or for the culture as a whole.

The brain is oriented as well toward learning domain by domain. Cognition is a domain-specific process.[3] The tasks, tools, concepts, language, and forms of representation of substantive domains serve as organizers for internal mental structure, shaping modes of thought, and the brain itself, down to the level of neuronal structure. In learning in a particular domain, the individual is not only elaborating and transforming existing mental structures but, in parallel, connecting discreet bits and pieces of knowledge and experience to develop conceptual structures for that domain. Deep immersion in a particular substantive domain also activates emotions that reinforce critical cognitive processes such as attention and persistence.[4]

In many respects, neuroscience is now validating with its unique technologies what learning theorists (including such foundational figures as Lev Vygotsky and Jerome Bruner) have long argued based on their own tools of observation and experimentation. Recognition of the cognitive and affective value of challenging, detailed, somewhat open-ended learning tasks and the understanding of mental processes as situated have been central to the learning sciences for years. Vygotsky, for instance, argued for the specificity of learning, that it is "more than the acquisition of the ability to think; it is the acquisition of many specialized abilities for thinking about a variety of things."[5] As Bruner put it, "Not only are there many ways of using mind, many ways of knowing and constructing meaning, but they serve many functions in many different situations."[6]

The learning and cognitive sciences have also long emphasized two additional attributes of learning. The first holds that learning is not just an active and adaptive process but a constructive one. What the learner brings—background, goals, interests, motivation, needs, and talents—contributes to and shapes the learning process and modifies the knowledge at hand. The context sets limits, but it is also affected by the learner. Meaning is both "grown," as experiences in a domain deepen pathways in the brain, and constructed, as the learner incorporates and modifies ideas, technologies, and procedures.[7] The second attribute of learning often emphasized by learning scientists is its social nature. Humans learn not just through such processes as observation and emulation but in part through shared thinking and shared attention based on some common ground.[8] What begins as a social process nonetheless becomes internalized at some point. A young person's potential achievements, evoked through observation, imitation, and social interaction, are practiced until internalized as his own.

Building on a social constructivist view of learning, a small but growing group of theorists and researchers argue that learning is about participation, identification, and, ultimately, identity. It is about movement gradually deeper into a particular cultural endeavor, a deepening "relation-ship to some aspect of the world, to an object."⁹ The underlying processes are as much affective as cognitive. As one moves more deeply into a learn-ing domain, a variety of psychological structures grow that are attached to that particular domain: motivation, interest, self-confidence, pleasure, identification, and self-recognition. Emotional associations grow stronger.

In this view, learning is about personal change. The same activities that change the brain—observation, emulation, practice, problem-solving, ad-justing to constraints, reflection, integration, reintegration—change the whole person. The learning domain and the work of mastering it become part of the self, and at some point a matter of identity.¹⁰

There is a narrative dimension to this process. Learning is, in part, about meaning making, about creating a story that involves self and world, purpose and benefit. It is also about developing a story of oneself as a learner, about learning to be and act as a learning self.¹¹ And there is a cultural dimension, too. As the learner changes, her capacity and inclina-tion to contribute to the larger culture do as well.

DEVELOPMENTAL TASKS OF MIDDLE ADOLESCENCE

Insights about cognition and learning take on meaning when tied to the developmental imperatives of any age group. These imperatives shape why and how and what we need to learn. They act as a spur for learning, just as learning settings and experiences provide the material and the scaffold-ing for developmental work. Good learning experiences seem especially valuable during particular life periods, and middle adolescence is one such period. It is a pivotal time for integrating cognitive and affective structure into the singular adult self that is beginning to emerge. It is a time when individuals are no longer just receiving the knowledge that a particular culture offers but are beginning to test and reconstruct that knowledge.

These are the years in which young people begin to set themselves on a path toward adulthood and to forge what Erik Erikson described as an enduring identity.¹² They are loosening ties to family, de-idealizing par-ents, and learning autonomy. At the same time they are seeking out new people, ideas, roles, and institutions from whom they might learn and with whom they might identify. Middle adolescence is a time for building personal knowledge, for learning more about strengths and limitations and for discovering or developing interests. At this age, young people are beginning to find their own voice and to forge personal goals. They are testing, reflecting on, and evaluating the larger culture, its values and value conflicts, and taking the first steps toward finding a place in that culture. And they are beginning to see how the specific parts—gender, race, social class, goals, interests, talents, feelings—might fit together to create an integrated self.

In middle adolescence, young people are beginning to choose what to invest in and learning how to do so effectively. They are experimenting and, at the same time, also learning to commit. Experimentation is critical to self-discovery, to the gradual but central task of becoming "a person in one's own right."[13] The young person is exploring possibilities and interests, strengths and limitations. He is playing with roles and stances toward the immediate and broader cultural worlds. He is learning about "the diversity of human work and human knowledge" and beginning to explore what he might want to accomplish in life.[14]

Commitment is critical to shaping the direction and solidity of growth. It allows for deepening participation in valued cultural activities to learn their qualities and characters. It teaches the young person what will be required to achieve mastery in a specific endeavor and reveals that endeavor's less obvious satisfactions and frustrations. Like experimentation, commitment teaches the young person about herself, providing the basis for more specific and accurate self-appraisal. It serves to ground the self amidst the fluidity of this life period. Even if temporarily, commitment to some endeavor provides a cultural home. Seth Schwartz describes it as "an anchor in a sea of possibilities, allowing one to define oneself as something in particular."[15] It helps the young person begin to see herself not only as one who engages in a particular endeavor but as one who belongs in it.

The process of self-discovery—trying to figure out who I am, what makes me unique, where I fit, what my passions might be—can be exciting or painful at different moments in time. A seventeen-year-old young woman reflecting on her hard work as an intern for eight weeks in an elementary school classroom notes, "I feel horrible about the fact that even though I know I am doing something good for others, I don't feel fulfilled. How will I know what it really is that will make me happy if everything I try soon becomes dry and unsatisfying?"[16] She expresses worry over the impossible task of coming up with a plan for the rest of her life, calling this task "terrifying," yet she also notes that "maybe I will find something that will give me answers."

ACTUALIZING NEW CAPACITIES

Experiences of exploration and commitment afford young people a chance to practice using and, through that practice, to actualize a wide range of new cognitive and social capacities. While childhood and youth are marked by periodic cognitive shifts, the middle adolescent years present a distinctly important shift, a kind of second critical period for brain development. David Dobbs notes that "as we move through adolescence the brain undergoes extensive remodeling, resembling a network and wiring upgrade."[17] A variety of biophysical processes, including myelinization, dendrite growth and differentiation, synaptic pruning, stronger links between the left and right brain and between different brain regions, and generally thicker connections, create a potentially more powerful physical mind. These changes bring undifferentiated new potentials to be developed and refined through experience.

The seemingly unbalanced quality to middle adolescents (e.g., deep thoughtfulness combined with impulsive decision making, deep empathy combined with utter disregard) reflects both different areas within the brain maturing at different rates and the need for experience to catch up with new capacities. At the same time, new cognitive capacities, interacting with heightened emotions (themselves activated by a range of biochemical processes), yield an openness to experience and an intensity of experience and response to it that are unique to this age period.

During middle adolescence almost every quality that will be important in adult life begins to take shape. Capacities that emerge include, for example, being able to grasp abstract concepts, to reason more complexly and systematically. High school–age youth have new capacities to plan, think through, self-monitor, self-correct, and use prior experience. They have new abilities to size up situations, examine assumptions, coordinate actions, find information, and know when to seek help. They can sustain attention and motivation for longer periods. They are beginning to be able to read situations, weigh alternatives, and reconcile competing demands. Critically, young people are more capable of monitoring and controlling their own learning processes.[18] Thomas Bailey and colleagues provide the example of a young woman doing an internship as a tour guide in a museum. In the early weeks, "her supervisor and the veteran tour guide decided when she was ready to undertake specific tasks . . . As she gained expertise, she made decisions more on her own, about when she needed to do additional research on a particular historical issue, about style of speech she should use during the walk through the exhibit."[19]

New social, self-regulatory, and emotional capacities contribute to, and at times complicate, learning experiences. Reed Larson points out that high school–age youth have a growing capacity to manage emotions: on the one hand, not letting emotions "mess with . . . perception and reasoning" and, on the other hand, using them to "direct energy and attention" toward accomplishing goals.[20] They become better able to hold mixed emotions in mind and cope with seeming contradictions. Middle adolescents are better able to take others' perspectives and understand other minds, how to learn from them and that different viewpoints may be valid and helpful. They can better read and understand others' behavior, too. In this age, young people are developing the capacity for deeper and more complex relationships with both peers and adults, relationships with a degree of mutuality.[21]

Growing self-awareness brings potential for patience with oneself and others, for coping with frustration and unforeseen difficulties. A high school senior doing a month-long internship in an elementary school classroom describes her struggle to remain patient with a child who seemingly cannot stay with a learning task. She sits with him, imploring and encouraging him to focus, to simply get going; finally, "I cannot help it. My patience is slowly slipping away from me. I was asked many times before I chose this internship whether I had the patience for it, and I always answered yes. Who would have imagined that eight hours a day dealing with paperwork and children with learning disabilities would be [such a struggle]?"[22]

Middle adolescents have new tools to exercise agency in the world. They can formulate and follow through on personal goals and link work on tasks to them. They are learning to invest in their own learning experiences, productivity, and creativity.[23] New capacities allow for a deeper examination of social realities and for initial efforts to relate how things are to how they ought to be. Young people are beginning to develop social imagination: the capacity to rethink society and one's place in it. This new understanding interacts with growing self-knowledge to lead to larger questions: how adult society really works, whether that society is worthwhile, what they themselves value, and where their place in adult society might be.[24] As Larson argues, the questions of this age period can, potentially, beget cynicism and alienation from the adult world. But under the right conditions, they can be a powerful motivator of engagement.[25]

More Complex Motivational Foundations

During the high school years, young people begin to construct the more enduring motivational structures that will carry them into adulthood, including values and ideals, goals and aspirations. Even as the peer group remains central in their lives, young people understand that they have to begin to loosen its grip and develop their own internal compass for engagement and growth. This is both an integrative task, as young people draw on old and new sources of identification, and a creative one, as they forge their own distinct approach to the world around them.

Staying involved with learning becomes a more volitional act and therefore represents an important task in itself. Young people have to develop their own personal identity as learners. That includes developing a more mature version of what Bruner calls "the will to learn."[26] It means recognizing that learning requires a certain amount of courage and risk taking. As one youthful apprentice tells a researcher, "It's the willingness to learn, and not be frightened of learning, not be frightened of trying things differently, not being frightened of assessing what you're doing."[27]

Young people have to develop a self-narrative in relation to school that supports engagement, persistence, and risk taking and that gives school personal meaning. They have to find a way to understand school as a resource, not a passport or a set of externally imposed obstacles. They have to find the disciplines in which they are most at home. More generally, they have to maintain or renew an identity as a learner both inside and outside of school. For some young people that means coming to view nonschool settings as learning resources and being deliberate about using those settings for learning (e.g., applying ideas and information acquired in school to community or work settings).

Preparing for Transition and Vocation

Middle adolescence is a pivotal time in the long and increasingly unpredictable transition from childhood to adulthood. Though living in the present, young people have to ready themselves for further learning and vocation and, more generally, for pursuing personal goals in a complex, often opaque adult word.[28] They have to begin planning for a path or paths beyond high school, whether it's more schooling, commitment to a vocation, or both. The transition is not linear, but it is ineluctable. The processes underlying it are partly hidden, partly ritualized, as young people move from grade to grade, from one requirement to the next.

Regardless of their plans, young people have to begin to learn about vocational possibilities, to tentatively confirm and disconfirm vocational interests, to think about vocation in deeper and more differentiated ways, and to learn about (and perhaps seek opportunities to practice) the skills and dispositions that the work world will demand. Whether or not they enjoy it, young people know the social role of student. Most young people know far less about what it means to be a worker—the nature and structure of tasks, the daily rhythm, the dynamics of workplace relationships. And most know little or nothing about what it means to work in a particular vocational field.

Young people have to come to understand what it means to be prepared for specific kinds of work, how one prepares, the length of time involved, and the types of credentials and prior experiences most valued by employers. Young people have to explore for themselves, and with others, the roles of work and vocational knowledge in forging a sense of personal competence and integrity.[29] They may begin to explore how personally important work will be for them, what they think they want to get out of it, and what kind of work will fit with their sense of who they want to become, in other words, their "guiding vocational narrative."[30]

THE TASK FOR SOCIETY: PROVIDING EXPERIENCES THAT SUPPORT GROWTH

Although developmental tasks are usually viewed as belonging to individuals, they are better understood to encompass both what young people need to work on and what society needs to provide. As Erikson describes it, forging identity is a joint project "in the core of the individual and yet also in the core of his communal culture."[31] Identity is built with culturally available resources and materials and through participation in and validation by significant sociocultural settings. To support this process, society has to be more than accommodating; it has to be active. Social institutions have to provide young people connections to interesting settings and cultural resources, meaningful roles to play, scaffolding, and social recognition for their efforts and achievements. They have to work jointly with young people to discover, bring out, and develop latent talents.

In a broad sense, experience per se, in specific settings and across settings, provides the ingredients for work on the tasks of middle adolescence, from locating new sources of identification, testing ideas, applying knowledge, discovering talents, experimenting, and making commitments to learning how to do and to make things, contributing and taking responsibility. Concepts and skills are mastered through their use. As one young person observes, "Until you have a chance to apply knowledge you don't really know what it pertains to."[32] Young people may have the beginnings of such new capacities as evaluating alternatives or holding lightly on to (and letting go of) ideas and approaches as they are working on a problem, but converting these to actual cognitive practice is a matter of use.

Young people need a variety of learning and contributing experiences in part because the value of a particular experience is a matter of timing and also because young people are diverse and will find a good personal fit in different settings. Yet, at some point they also need to immerse themselves in a domain, to actively seek mastery in it; to acquire, examine, and apply knowledge in it; to feel productive; and to develop a grounded sense of efficacy and a sense of affiliation with that domain, its goals and activities. Sustained experience in a domain provides the grist for transforming abstract capacities to actual skills, habits, and judgments. Interests and proclivities, often considered innate, are just as likely to develop and grow through sustained experience in some endeavor.[33]

COMMON QUALITIES OF GOOD LEARNING EXPERIENCES

Across domains, a number of qualities of learning seem helpful in stimulating personal development. For instance, learning experiences must be moderately challenging, have clear maturity demands, and be psychologically safe. Challenging tasks create opportunities to develop the new thinking and executive capacities described earlier, such as foresight, planning, sequencing, different kinds of reasoning, or multiple modes of representation. For instance, young industrial designers and animators learn to use hand sketching to express initial ideas and plans. Also, a project may call on (and build) knowledge and skill in a variety of domains. By way of example, a group of young people working as a team to build a small bridge across a creek call on knowledge of "geometry, strength of materials, planning and sequencing, cooperativeness, structural design, spatial relationships, aesthetics, mechanics."[34]

Complex tasks demand, and therefore create, opportunity to develop different kinds of resourcefulness: patience and endurance, the capacity to examining one's own beliefs and ideas, the learning of a particular skill needed to complete a task or project. Engaging in challenge and facing practical difficulties ground young people, decenter them, and open them up for growth. Such experiences modulate a "sense of self-importance, can lead to an increase in curiosity, lower defensiveness and judgmentalism . . . open the mind to new ways of doing and being."[35]

Learning tasks and problems support growth when they are both adequately structured and partially open-ended. This balance of qualities helps young people learn that some choices are better than others. In trying different modes of reasoning, they learn that some are more effective than others for particular kinds of tasks or particular stages in addressing problems. Learning tasks support growth when there is detail to work through. A young woman apprenticing with a plant ecologist is tasked to grow seedlings for varying lengths of time (i.e., one day, two days, three days, etc.) and then press them into a binder that will later be used to measure the age and growth of the seedlings planted as part of a prairie restoration project. There are all kinds of lessons in this task—about measurement, scientific process, the importance of care, the connection between the laboratory and the problems of the outside world.

Young people are motivated toward learning and mastery when they have an opportunity to be genuinely productive. They must believe that tasks and products have meaning and value, be it personal, familial, or cultural; they must believe that their own roles are real, that they are counted on. The plant ecology apprentice, for instance, is part of a team conducting research on the best ways to renew and reclaim prairies. The team's findings will be useful for public agencies and nonprofits all over the country. When young people are working on real tasks and take on real roles in some field, the learning that takes place feels organic, like a by-product of the activity itself.

A good learning and developmental setting must support young people's agency while accounting for their inexperience. Young people must be treated as capable and responsible. They must have opportunity to offer ideas, try out their own strategies, connect things in unexpected ways, acknowledge struggles, and surprise themselves and others. Learning experiences must help reassure young people that adult culture is not a fixed or finished product. Yet young people should not be put into positions for which they are not prepared. They need some external structure deriving from the responsibilities of the task at hand, adult support, and the established norms and traditions of a discipline.

FROM THE PEER WORLD TO THE ADULT WORLD

Some important experience will—and must—take place in young people's self-defined spaces, away from the constraints and pressures that adult institutions embody. Such spaces, both virtual and real, are developmentally and culturally critical. Dobbs describes young people's strong peer orientation as an investment in the future, both personal and shared; in evolutionary terms, it's an important survival mechanism.[36] Among other things, a focus on peers provides an opportunity to learn to develop mature peer relationships and to learn about intimacy. Peer worlds create space for young people's creativity in "developing new learning and life strategies . . . new combinations of formal, non-formal, informal and peer learning."[37] They allow young people to use cultural tools in their own ways, to create and own some space within the larger culture. Young people learn from and energize each other and feed off each other's ideas. They sometimes prefer to master new ideas, procedures, and disciplines informally, using their own self-generated resources and one another.

Yet peer worlds can also be constraining. In reflecting on the distinction between peer culture and the adult world, the director of a youth center observes, "I've got the feeling that when young people join a [peer] group, it's more like they're buying a ready-made box, thoroughly equipped. They do not discover anything new. We have a group at the center that likes acting punk. And everything should be punk, from music to clothes, ideas, books . . . it's all packaged."[38] Pressure to conform explains why, when young people are with peers, they feel happier but less in control and less able to focus on any task at hand.[39]

The desire for autonomy and self-responsibility during these years is, in some measure, an act of resistance as well as a desire to be free from adult controls. Yet the results are not always what young people expect, and they are sometimes the opposite. The more powerful and complete the peer world, the more it is detached from pathways toward adulthood. For instance, when young people are in school, surrounded by peers, they are powerfully sensitive to and influenced by peer priorities and norms and views of the adult world, accurate or not. Peer pressure (especially when combined with difficult personal histories) can make it more difficult for young people to bring true feelings and actions together and to work on finding an authentic self. As Michael Zuckerman writes, "Youth culture may provide a safe haven for teens who are tired of being incessantly tested and found wanting. But the expressive freedom it allows them does not typically provide them preparation for the roles and skills they will require in later life. Such freedom is a token of adolescent marginality . . . the privileging of peer culture actually impoverishes American adolescent life."[40]

If young people need a measure of autonomy, then, they also need developmentally appropriate entry points into the adult world and into the culture at large. The most organic vehicle for connection to the adult world is some recognized tradition or social practice. A young person might be investigating a scientific problem, exploring a vocation, providing a service, working with others to address a societal problem, committing to a cause, or working to master technical, physical, or creative challenges. What is important is the opportunity to enter into a tradition, its norms, rules, practices, language and understandings, physical settings, and tools; to try on specific adult identities, experiencing what it is like to be an architect, chef, photographer, actor, or director; and, where appropriate, to stay with some endeavor in order to acquire a deeper sense of it.

The common language, tools, and activities within a particular tradition promote a sense of shared experience among participants. This translates into a feeling of belonging, especially of belonging to something particular. The desire to belong motivates the young person to master the demands of the field or discipline involved. The feeling of belonging in turn allows the young person to learn to trust the community, opening it further as a learning setting. It allows him to experience the otherwise abstract idea that there are particular places in the larger culture that are internally coherent, "distinctive ethical worlds" that offer ideas about "what is worth striving for."[41]

A Critical Role for Adults

It is within the context of specific traditions and substantive settings that young people get to know adults who can provide the support, guidance, modeling, and sources of identification that move them forward. This is, at once, one more predicament and the answer to at least some of the predicaments of middle adolescence. Young people may not want to be predefined or pigeonholed; they may want and need some control over their own decisions and choices. But they also need—and, as they mature, increasingly want—exposure to a range of adults and a variety of kinds of adult support.

Adults can encourage openness to new experience and help broaden young people's sense of who they can be and perhaps whom they want to learn from. Through example and feedback adults can show young people how to approach tasks and problems. For instance, young people (especially in the United States) tend to think about ability in ways that undermine motivation to master a new field; they overestimate how far aptitude can take them and generally underestimate the importance of effort. Adults can play a critical role in countering these perceptions by encouraging young people to persist, assuring them that, for most learning tasks, effort and persistence will get them through the most difficult periods. As Lauren Resnick notes, adults can help young people learn to see that "effort actually creates ability."[42]

Young people are sometimes not sure what they can do or what they need to do in particular settings. Adults can help them learn to identify the critical features of tasks and to create some constraints or limits so that the young person will not be paralyzed by too many possibilities, while at the same time ensuring that there is space for agency. They can put learning tasks in context, explain their purpose and where they fit in the larger field at hand. Some adults can help young people begin to understand how a particular discipline works and exemplify for young people how professionals in a particular discipline "see things," how they approach tasks and problems. They can help young people see what is important within or about a particular experience, or that an experience itself holds value.

Beyond such mediation, adults (and adult institutions in general) play a critical role in helping young people think about, plan, and prepare for the next steps, during and beyond high school. Adults provide important background information for decisions. Young people may need adult help to see more clearly what they are and are not prepared for, even to see that not everything is possible. Extended contact with individual adults skilled in and passionate about some area of life provides initial vocational narratives, key sources of identification, and models for possible future selves. As Deborah Meier argues, "Young people must be surrounded by grown ups whom [they] can imagine becoming and would like to become."[43]

Fundamentally, adults serve as models of personhood. What young people learn from them—perhaps what they learn most—is how one relates to other people, listens, thinks, responds, formulates questions, handles conflict, provides feedback, reconciles differences in perspective. In a discussion of mentoring during adolescence, Belle Liang and colleagues note that "older adolescents may not only be more accepting of mentors' flaws but may also need to see some aspects of their mentors' personal struggles to realistically balance strengths and weaknesses in the face of life's challenges [that] shortcomings and adversity are inevitable parts of life and need not stand in the way of personal and professional achievement."[44]

CHAPTER TWO

The Limitations of Current
Supports for Young People

In school, students remain students until they leave.
—Jill Adler, "Lights and Limits"

If development is indeed a joint project, the societal side of the equation is problematic in American culture. The experiences, guidance, and ideas that young people need to learn about and sort through are hard to find. The channels young people need to have in order to move back and forth between childhood and adulthood are absent. The "work" that we have assigned young people—do well in school and stay out of trouble—is not compelling to many youth. Success in school is too narrowly defined, as is the social role of "student" itself. And avoiding trouble is simply too negative a goal to strive for. Neither task offers young people opportunities to place their energy and idealism in the service of some valued social purpose, to explore specific social roles, and to test themselves against adultlike demands. It is hardly surprising that young people themselves report that "something is missing," though they are not sure what it is or how to find it.[1]

For at least some, and perhaps a majority, of young people, high school is a weak vehicle for identity work: developing a sense of agency, identifying and nurturing emergent capacities, exploring alternatives, making meaning of activities, and maintaining the sense of an open future. Agency remains in the hands of teachers and the institution itself. The cultural domains attended to are limited, predefined, and unchanging. By their very physical structure, schools isolate young people from the larger world. The wide range of other potential supports, both individual and institutional, either remain latent or are not visible or accessible enough to young people. Neither schools nor other key institutions have a sense of responsibility for students' participation in, and potential to contribute to, adult endeavors. As Botstein observes, "At 16, young Americans are prepared to be taken seriously and to develop the motivation and interest that will serve them well in adult life, yet adult society is too rarely ready to take young people up on this developmental offer."[2]

Young people growing up in disenfranchised communities are especially vulnerable to the present societal context for youth development. They are both more likely to experience schooling as problematic and less likely to have access to the nonschool learning opportunities that might provide other meaningful pathways through middle adolescence. Their development can be constrained by what they have observed of the world and by what they themselves may have experienced in it. Young people's reasoning and decision making are inherently limited by lack of experience. Growing up in or near poverty, in a devalued and neglected neighborhood and perhaps a devalued group, complicates what is an already fragile reasoning process. It changes the perceived value of both experimentation and commitment. It increases the perceived costs of curiosity and ambition. It alters the balance between day-to-day preoccupations and long-term goals. The perception that one has limited "degrees of freedom . . . become[s] naturalized, becoming part of [one's] sense of reality."[3]

The problem is not an absolute lack of social resources for youth; most cities are full of them. Rather, it is lack of connection between youth and those resources. Disenfranchised youth lack access to varied kinds of adult mediation and support as well as to experiences that might counter fears, ground free-floating fantasies, and offer a nuanced picture of the adult world. In other words, disenfranchised youth lack access to ingredients for changing the stories they have already begun to tell themselves about how their lives should and most likely will play out, stories that "work at a quite deep and often unconscious level" to shape learning and social experiences.[4]

Erica Swinney of the Austin Polytechical Academy (APA) in Chicago told me how difficult it is to get young people growing up in one of the most disenfranchised communities in the country to take up entry-level opportunities (created by APA staff) in solid local manufacturing firms, firms with challenging jobs, carefully developed internal training programs, postsecondary tuition reimbursement, and other supports. These young people do not understand that this is how one begins a career, nor do they understand how important it is to stick with such opportunities, which can take years to bear fruit. The students tell APA staff that they want to keep their options open, without understanding that committing to hard work is one important way to do so.[5]

Disenfranchised neighborhoods like Austin in Chicago continue to be characterized by many adult models of how to approach education, work, and other life tasks. Young people themselves have a variety of beliefs about what is worth striving for. But when friends, family, and neighbors approach education or work in widely varying ways, young people get weak signals about the value of pursuing any one path and the possibility of success in doing so. They are less likely to follow through on a specific goal and are more likely to give up when faced with obstacles, seeing that some who made other choices seem to be surviving and doing well.[6] Under such circumstances, young people begin to narrow educational and interpersonal horizons and refrain from making ambitious plans. Or they adopt a position of grandiosity, telling themselves that the world will come to them. They double-down on peer relationships, responding to the consequences of exclusion "by stereotyping themselves, their ideals and their enemies."[7] The forms of resistance adopted by young people are often immediately adaptive and ultimately maladaptive because they are rejecting the very tools and ideas that might serve as sources of transformative experience.[8]

These personal and interpersonal processes among youth lead to the kinds of labeling, dismissal, and efforts at control by adult institutions that are the just the opposite of what youth need in the way of supports. APA succeeds with at least some youth served because it refuses to dismiss young people, accept their claims (e.g., of disinterest in a particular opportunity) without evidence, or accept self-defeating actions at face value. Rather, it sticks with young people, testing and prodding their thinking, seeing them through struggles, and hammering home a consistent message in the classroom, in the machine shop where young people learn advanced manufacturing skills, through internships where mentors in local firms reinforce the message, and in long conversations with skeptical parents. APA continues to welcome its former students after they have graduated from high school because its staff recognizes that development is a long process, full of stumbles, especially when it picks up steam late in childhood.

In a secular sense, most young people today face a more difficult societal context for growing up, one with seemingly more choices and models of adulthood but also less clarity about the meaning and consequences of choices. They perhaps have fewer socially imposed constraints, but they also have less certainty about the benefits of particular commitments. And they have both greater opportunity and greater responsibility for self-definition. The inherent fluidity of the middle adolescent self now interacts with a fluid, fragmented, unpredictable social and occupational world. Young people seem more directly vulnerable to decisions made in financial markets and to events occurring far away from their daily lives, from global labor markets to recessions in countries continents away. For many youth, movement toward and into post–high school life is defined by an extended search for a constructive pathway, including relevant learning experiences and the beginnings of an occupational identity. It is becoming "increasingly difficult for youth to pursue wholeheartedly the wisdom, practices and arts the previous generation offers them."[9]

In the context of this change and flux, young people have more responsibility than ever for making their own way in the world, both for their choices and for the results of those choices.[10] A recent National Association of Manufacturers report notes that "individuals must take responsibility for their [own] employability."[11] The societal shift toward individual responsibility for learning, educational planning, and career development is especially fraught for disenfranchised youth and youth of color, who have the additional responsibility of coping with inequitable social structures.

LIMITATIONS OF HIGH SCHOOL AS A LEARNING AND DEVELOPMENTAL SETTING

Societal support for the developmental work of middle adolescence begins (and sometimes ends) with high school. This is not a monolithic institution, not least because teachers can and do create distinctive learning worlds within the larger world of the school. In their broader critical work on high schools, scholars often have included descriptions of unusual teachers as a reminder and perhaps to soften their critiques. Theodore Sizer describes many such teachers in his writings, providing one example of a biology teacher with a passion for studying the reproductive life of red-wing blackbirds who dragged his students "before dawn into a mosquito-infested swamp to watch and record the movement of birds."[12] In research on high schools in Texas, Linda McNeil observed many gifted and committed teachers in different kinds of settings. Of one valued history teacher "there was no wall between [his] personal knowledge, the content of his courses, and the invitation he posed to students to engage with him in thinking about things." And she observed an English teacher who fought for students to recognize themselves or the life they knew in the works they read.[13]

As with individual teachers, there are scores of wonderful high schools scattered around the United States. A moderate percentage of young people invest in and master the rich course work offered in specialized urban magnet schools and some suburban high schools. Yet, as a type of developmental and learning setting, with certain characteristic attributes, high school does not work well for a sizable percentage of young people (if not a majority, then close to it). The bulk of high school learning affordances do not reflect what the cognitive and learning sciences agree are the attributes of powerful learning environments, what developmental science tells us about how high school–age youth learn best, or what youth tell us about good learning experiences.

Evidence of a mismatch is found in patterns of attrition from ninth to twelfth grade, particularly among young people of color. It is found in disaffection among many youth who stay with school. It is apparent as well in reports of little college and work-readiness among nearly a majority of those who do graduate and in the lack of appropriate or informed choices made even by many youth who are better prepared for college or work, with sometimes irreversible consequences. Data on high school education tell a story of social waste and personal loss, with effects that reverberate through the post–high school years.[14] Of 4 million youth who enter high school each year, 1.3 million will drop out. (In some large cities, losses from grades 9–12 are especially dramatic, with no more than 50–60 percent of young people graduating.) Another 1.3 million youth will earn a high school diploma but go no further. They will probably begin looking for work, but too often they lack a sense of direction and/or a solid foundation of knowledge, skills, and habits to bring to initial employment. (The typical result is years of underemployment and floundering, moving from one job to the next with little progression.) The final 1.3 million youth will directly enter postsecondary education, but about half of these will not complete a two- or four-year degree due to some combination of lack of basic skills, lack of academic structure and social support, lack of purpose or focus, and/or lack of resources.

Regardless of whether they stay or leave, young people typically describe high school as both boring and anxiety provoking. Half of all youth are chronically disengaged from school, and another 25 percent intermittently so.[15] Surveys of young people and school-based studies that have tracked young people over time find a decline through the middle adolescent years in investment, interest, and motivation to learn across subjects and a related decline in willingness to take on challenging learning tasks.[16] It is not that high school never provides the ingredients that young people need to grow, but it does so too intermittently. In a study of daily life in high school classrooms, Kim Pierce found that "episodes of learning about life, others and self emerged rarely during our study; but when they did, a sense of active, well defined individuality bursts through participants' descriptions."[17]

Schools are constrained in many ways, but especially by their isolation from the adult world—its tools, technologies, tasks, situations, diversity, and general complexity—at just the moment when young people need to begin learning about and participating in it. Young people spend almost four thousand hours observing teachers at work and their peers responding—but no one else. It makes little sense to take large numbers of inexperienced individuals who are the same age and relative maturity, place them in an isolated setting, and ask them to use that particular setting to grow, mature, gain knowledge, and experience. When young people are in a peer-oriented setting they are naturally more sensitive to and focused on peer priorities than when they are in adult settings. Ironically, though schools (and classrooms) are self-contained, physically isolated environments, "non-school preoccupations constantly intrude on students' attention."[18]

Curriculum, and the knowledge purveyed through it, typically feels fixed, finished, inert. As Stephen Downes puts it, schools reflect "the failure of the transmission model [of learning] writ large."[19] Schools lack adequate variety and dynamism in what young people might learn, how they might learn, or what the goals of learning should be. These limitations make it more difficult for many young people to find a learning home somewhere in the school curriculum and thereby alleviate fears that they are somehow not smart enough. They make it more difficult for young people to develop a grounded sense of their strengths and limitations.

School too often feels like someone else's institution. Elliot Washor, one of the nation's most experienced high school educators, observes that "young people feel that who they are and what they want to become does not matter much to schools."[20] Youth have no voice in shaping their learning experience and, ironically, only modest opportunity to contribute to it. A young person's growing skill and knowledge in a discipline are rarely the basis for a more responsible role in the school context (e.g., contributing to the design of learning activities, guiding less experienced peers, playing a role in assessment). Young people therefore have little opportunity to experience a sense of mastery and ownership or a deepening participation in a goal-oriented community.[21] Their largely passive position leads (or perhaps requires) them to depend on teachers "to organize their attention and motivation," limiting the self-development of these critical learning attributes.[22]

The same dynamic holds for school as a social community. Young people are rarely asked to help define and enforce norms of behavior or meet expectations for community maintenance. Adult approaches to these issues are infantilizing and sometimes destructive. Michael Zuckerman observes that forty-nine states have instituted

> theatrically punitive policies of zero tolerance that put surveillance cameras, metal detectors, biometric scanners, random police sweeps, search-and-sniff dogs, and undercover agents in the school and make plain to the young that their elders are more anxious to police and discipline them than to educate them and more concerned to instill fear among them than to nurture them or prepare them for productive citizenship.[23]

Fragmented Learning Experience and Unclear Purposes

Learning tasks have to be complex enough and meaningful enough to engage young people individually. Yet the structure of the school day, combined with the large amount of material to cover and the absence of a strong rationale for mastering material, weakens the foundations of engagement. Even when daily lessons are sequenced to build on and continue those of prior days, young people tend to treat each day and each week as new. The sense of fragmentation derives partly from the division of time into multiple short units of disciplinary content, creating (and communicating) a norm of discontinuity. It derives in part from the pressure teachers face over coverage. Material is presented and teachers are then forced to move on quickly to the next unit. This creates a sense of skimming across the surface of learning and prevents students' continued practice and deepening application of new ideas, information, and procedures, the means through which the material is internalized, mastered, and gains meaning. Not least it derives from a lack of any connection among disciplines.

The effects of fragmentation are exacerbated by the difficulty young people have making meaning of school learning experiences. High school youth report struggling to understand the significance and relevance of discrete learning experiences.[24] Adult explanations tend to beg rationales: you are in high school, this is your work. It is difficult, then, for young people to make a connection between present and future. The payoff from investing in academic tasks, and for some youth persisting in school itself, seems remote and uncertain.

Young people note having to work hard to stay engaged. In one "beeper" study a diverse sample of youth reported being engaged with classroom learning about half the time. They were most engaged when working in small groups and lablike situations, less common learning situations, and least engaged when teachers lectured, the most common situation.[25] Young people in another study told Kim Pierce that they try to keep up the appearance of being interested because they do not want to hurt teachers' feelings, even though "you're bored out of your mind." Pierce observes that "acting one way and feeling another seems characteristic of classroom relationships."[26] Those young people who do stay engaged try to reduce learning-related risks by trying to discern what the teacher expects and by providing responses least likely to draw attention, either positive or negative.

Teachers seem well aware of all these problems but too often have little flexibility to work around them, or they simply do not know how to address them. The pressure to cover too much material, together with the large number of students to be taught, leads teachers to lecture more than they might want to and leaves them too little time to build trust and credibility or, in larger schools, to get to know students well. This last factor contributes to a misreading of students' behavior and self-presentation; for example, passivity is too often interpreted as disinterest and not caring.[27] In a vicious cycle, teachers themselves respond by teaching defensively, asking little in order to elicit compliance and avoid resistance, which just makes the problem worse.[28] The emphasis shifts gradually from hard work to "the absence of negative behavior," the opposite of what young people need in the way of support.[29]

A Limited Experience of the Disciplines

The way in which disciplines are conceptualized and introduced to young people exacerbates motivational issues. Schooling too rarely exposes young people to the questions, problems, tasks, or practices of those working outside the walls of the school, whether in a discipline or field or on social or political problems.[30] Teachers too rarely see their role as modeling the thought processes and strategies characteristic of practitioners in a discipline. Although novices in the discipline at hand, students are expected to solve problems all by themselves.[31] Conversely, they are not put into roles in which they can begin to deconstruct and reconstruct a discipline, thereby making it their own.

It is inherently difficult to master a discipline outside the community in which it is practiced as a vocation. Questions and problems have to be simplified, technologies reduced or "spiraled down."[32] These inherent constraints are exacerbated by the way most American youth experience the disciplines that are emphasized in high school. Complex fields, both their knowledge and practice, are broken up into small, discrete units that reflect the flat, linear structure of commercial textbooks. Theories, principles, and rules tend to be presented with little revision year in and year out. Problems tend to be standardized and well-worn. Answers and solutions to them, and often procedures for working on them, are predetermined. One youth notes that "when you're in school, the teacher gives you the lab manual and says, 'Do what it says. Write the data you collect. Turn it in' . . . It's something that somebody has already done, so the answer is already there."[33] These learning conditions limit young people's opportunity to see different fields as growing and changing, to gain experience (and confidence) in finding solutions to open-ended problems, or to use the tools of a discipline for their own purposes. In effect, young people acquire only a limited sense of what it is like to work as scientist, historian, or mathematician.

Disinvestment as a Consequence

In the context of lack of opportunity for ownership, lack of clarity about relevance, and limited opportunity to enter deeply into one or more disciplines or to use what is learned in them, social (i.e., peer) issues become disproportionately central in the school setting. Young people shift their preoccupations to surviving—fitting in, moving along, or staying invisible. Ruth Paradise notes that "instead of getting caught up in learning . . . students often spend their time, energy and concern handling face-saving interactions, or developing social identities that are, paradoxically, both revolutionary and self-defeating."[34] In effect, they are too busy coping to do the work that will help them both get ready and begin to give them some direction. The irony in this is that there is room for varied identities and self-presentations in the educational domain: young people growing up in disenfranchised communities may be bullied, belittled, or ostracized by peers for social reasons but rarely for academic effort; that choice is tolerated, if not always respected, by peers across the social spectrum.[35]

The correlate of disinvestment in the school's learning agenda is "school weariness," when young people become fed up with school.[36] Having to contend with curriculum and pedagogy that do not make much sense in a setting that may not recognize one's individuality is exhausting, or least can exhaust one's self-identity as a learner. And when youth become largely disengaged from learning and school, adults in the school setting (paradoxically) disinvest in them. Laura McCarger, a youth advocate who works with vulnerable youth in Connecticut, reports being told by many that they were "strongly advised" to leave high school because they would do better in a smaller alternative setting, or they were told (falsely) that they would soon be too old to graduate. She noted that many of the youth in alternative settings, whose numbers reach close to 20 percent of the enrolled high school population in a few cities, have fallen into an "educational black hole" with no one responsible for their progress or well-being. In 2010 only 32 percent of youth enrolled in Connecticut's main alternative diploma program actually finished the program and received an alternative diploma.[37]

LACK OF SUPPORTS IN PLANNING
AND PREPARING FOR THE FUTURE

Present and future are intertwined during the high school years. Planning for the transition from high school to postsecondary learning, training, or work moves gradually into the foreground in young people's minds. Yet learning experiences throughout the high school years play a role in helping young people plan and prepare for the future, as fluid and shifting as that future may be. Such preparation includes formulating personal goals and acting on them; learning about, and perhaps experiencing, vocational possibilities and beginning to understand a vocation as part of oneself; and, more generally, thinking about what one might do with one's life. It sometimes includes grounding self-expectations and sometimes struggling to revise them. It also means cultivating learning and work habits that will be helpful in postsecondary education and work.

The need to anticipate and attend to the future is embedded in day-to-day learning experiences. Therefore, the degree to which that need is met is strongly affected by those day-to-day experiences. Encouragement (or discouragement) of the young person as a learner; recognition (or a lack of it) of a young person's distinct qualities and support needs; and the basic awareness among adults that a young person is moving toward decisions with outsize, life-altering consequences will all shape the transition. The task of helping young people stay motivated and engaged in learning is partly about connecting present and future. As David Yeager and Matthew Bundick point out, "The length of time between school and a future career, as well as the perceived disconnect in the relevance of their school work to their career aspirations, can make it difficult for adolescents to find personal meaning in their studies."[38]

In other words, the problematic qualities of high school as a learning setting come at a particularly bad time for young people: as they are beginning to get organized for adulthood. The effects of high schools' core problems on young people's learning selves are multiplied by an institutional context that is ill-equipped to support young people through the critical processes of planning, preparing for, and choosing next steps.

Young people (and their parents) are often left too much on their own, without the concepts, guidance, information, and preparatory experiences to underpin good decision making. A young person cannot make mature decisions if she has not had experiences that foster maturity. A young person cannot explore occupational roles if she is unconnected to the means for exploration. For instance, she may dismiss an occupation that on the surface looks mundane but is deeper than it looks and actually contains many attributes that are a good personal fit.[39]

Young people may or may not recognize the significance of choices to be made about post–high school steps, especially the importance of beginning to plan during the high school years. Many young people have no idea how to make choices or act on them. They choose—or fall into—next steps for what sounds like marginal reasons or by default. For instance, they like the name of a community college or its location. They start an application to a school they really want to attend but fail to complete it. They choose a school that does not offer courses in the discipline in which they are interested. They choose an occupation to pursue based on something they saw on television.

STAGES IN A LONG-TERM PROCESS

Planning and preparing for the future begin with high school placement processes that make sense, continue with pathways through high school that support growth, and culminate in a thoughtful transition from high school to college or work. None of these steps, however, is managed well in the American school system. A young person's path into and through high school is shaped by variables that typically are not transparent and that too often yield idiosyncratic results. High school reputations, parental preferences (well- or ill-informed), test scores, application lotteries, and eighth grade teachers' biases interact in unpredictable ways to place young people in a particular high school and program. There has been little research on what the effects are when, as is not uncommon, young people do not get into their school of choice. A subtle process of separation from schooling is sometimes set in motion, and it usually remains unrecognized.[40]

High schools themselves "have widely different systems of [internal] mobility," assigning students to courses in different ways and promoting or preventing upward movement.[41] Students are assigned to classes based on scheduling conveniences that do not reflect their learning strengths and limitations and sometimes do not even fit their larger high school plan. Counselors take the path of least resistance with students who are not thriving, assigning them to lower-level courses without considering what is getting in the way of learning, what supports might help a young person, or what the long-term consequences will be. The processes that assign young people to different high schools, course sequences, and tracks within high school have been described as a *sociocurricular structure*, in that they closely mirror social class. All too often "the socio-curricular positions occupied by groups of students within the school reproduce the cultural capital of their parents."[42]

Although students today are less likely to be formally tracked than in the past, many small decisions, omissions, placements, and constraints create de facto tracks. Young people who struggle or fail a class in ninth grade typically never recover their place in high school, one reason they are disproportionately likely to drop out at some point. Young people's own decision making ranges from informed to ill-informed to misinformed by friends, siblings, and teachers. Young people are often unaware of the consequences of choices made about specific courses and course sequences. They can "dead-end" without intending to, losing opportunities for interesting upper-level courses or concentrations. Young people who are struggling through high school are especially likely to end up in a general track that prepares them neither for college or work. This reflects lack of imagination, intent, and attention on the part of adults in the school setting.[43]

PREPARATION FOR POSTSECONDARY LEARNING OR WORK

Young people are both curious and (often) naive about various careers. They report being interested in particular career fields but also doing little occupational research or exploration (in part because they do not know how to do so). A large majority lack even basic knowledge of how much and what kind of preparation they will need for a particular occupation.[44] Career interests often are global and not rooted in either personal experience or opportunities in the labor market. For instance, a survey of youth in California found 22 percent interested in a career in arts/entertainment though only 2 percent of all jobs in the state are in these areas.[45]

Hints and clues about possible futures, both further learning choices and possible occupations, come from a wide range of sources. Some are informal and incidental, part of young people's social world in some way, emulation of parents' or siblings' choices, knowledge gained of parents' occupations. Other sources have to be formal and systematic, provided through key institutions and sectors of society, including schools and future employers. As with information about course choices throughout high school, some information provided about future options is accurate and some is not, some is thoughtful and some thoughtless.

Although high schools do a reasonable job of providing young people information about applying to college, they often lack resources to provide the active, unwavering support necessary to ensure that young people realize tentative plans: help to focus attention, address worries, check on deadlines, and so forth. Most high schools are too large to come to know students well as distinctive individuals and thus to be able to match them to post–high school options. For instance, they do not know the kinds of nonschool (after-school and summer) learning or working activities young people have participated in and the skills they have developed through those activities.

There is very little communication in either direction between schools and employers, except through CTE programs. Yet planfulness—on the parts of both individuals and institutions—has become more critical. The democratization of higher education has resulted in hundreds of new institutions and programs of varying quality and relevance to work opportunities. The labor market has become more differentiated and specialized, making it both more challenging and more important to help young people figure out the kinds of future endeavors in which they would most likely flourish. An observation made by Lauren Resnick some decade and a half ago is still apt: "In friendlier economic times we could largely rely on tossing young people into the economy as a way of socializing them and welcoming them into adulthood and responsibility. That option has now ended."[46]

In general, high schools fail to treat vocation, work, and discovering and building on interests and planning for the future as important curricular issues in and of themselves. Although school curricula cannot possibly attend fully to the enormous heterogeneity of domains and disciplines in the labor market, schools can do far more to introduce young people to that heterogeneity and relate it to their traditional offerings. Work- and career-related discussions woven into day-to-day learning experiences have proven helpful in raising awareness of decisions to be made.[47] Deliberate exposure to work roles and to specific occupations during the high school years would be enormously beneficial to millions of youth, broadening and sharpening awareness of the wide range of occupations (and levels within them) and altering conceptions of what might be interesting and worth testing out. Yet high schools rarely provide such exposure to young people, except for the modest percentage (some 10–15 percent) who take a CTE concentration.

Young people themselves report receiving erratic adult assistance in learning about and thinking through options and decisions. In his interviews with students at a racially and socially diverse California high school, Gilberto Conchas found that low- and mid-achieving students who did have career interests had no idea how to act on them and no help from school staff in learning how to do so. These students felt "invisible" within the school.[48] When asked whom he relies on for such support, a high school junior in one study of mostly work-bound youth noted, "I'm not that involved with the school or with my teachers . . . I keep my space from them. I don't use them because they're teachers. I can't talk to them about my problems. I can't even talk with my parents. The only people I talk with are my friends."[49] In studies asking young adults to look back on high school experiences, the majority report receiving too little guidance with respect to postsecondary options and decisions and gaining too little experience in preparing for further education and work.[50]

Young people are especially likely to get mixed messages about early commitment to an occupation. But even such tasks as simply exploring particular occupational domains and learning about work get pushed aside by the emphasis on preparation for college. Jeylan Mortimer and colleagues observe that "without structural bridges between school and work, [most] youth must rely substantially on their own resources."[51] Youth from disenfranchised families and communities face particular difficulties acquiring the supports they need. They especially lack access to the informal networks that might link them to valuable work-based learning experiences, internships, and jobs.

Other institutions share responsibility with schools for important planning and preparation tasks. But with exceptions in a handful of states and cities, workforce development agencies, too, have thought little about and have provided few resources to attend to the support needs of youth during the high school years. The Workforce Investment Act's youth provisions never developed into a coherent program for supporting young people's preparation for and transition into postsecondary endeavors. Labor unions have demonstrated little enthusiasm for supporting young people's vocational development. And employers of all kinds, though emphatic about young people's erratic learning and lack of work readiness, have done relatively little to help address this problem. Employers historically have made little effort even to partner with CTE programs in the high schools, although that has begun to change in many locales. And they, along with unions, remain reluctant to invest in apprenticeship programs for high school–age youth, a particularly promising way of bringing young people into particular fields and helping them gain important work skills.

FATEFUL CONSEQUENCES

The result of institutional and broader societal neglect is a kind of randomness in how young people move toward their futures. A modest percentage of young people find and begin working at whatever they will do in the future. These youth may have been drawn to a particular field for years or grown up around a particular occupation. The majority of youth, especially those from less advantaged backgrounds, are unclear about where they might fit in the larger world beyond their neighborhood and their parents' own occupational horizons. Studies of youth from disadvantaged backgrounds find that they have less information, and less accurate information, than their more advantaged peers about kinds of postsecondary learning, the range of occupations, and the preparation needed for specific occupations.[52] This affects the diversity of those working in a variety of fields and, thus, the diversity of perspective available in those fields.

Lack of accurate information is critical also because of the strong association between the amount and accuracy of labor market information and persistence in both high school and postsecondary learning. Among youth from disadvantaged backgrounds, fewer than 20 percent of those who start community college receive an associate degree within six years. While there are many reasons, not having a focus and a plan are particularly significant.[53] Even at the front end, young people arriving at community college may not know that they have weak academic skills are thus psychologically and practically unprepared for the remedial coursework they have to do, and about 50 percent of cases never complete that gateway coursework. A community college faculty member observes that "many students appear at the door of community colleges completely clueless about what is required of them, or available to them. They don't know they need to do work outside of class. They don't take advantage of tutoring and mentoring services. They don't know about peer study groups or interacting with faculty."[54]

Young people shape and reshape their lives in relation to what they can see.[55] In some instances, they see with some acuity an adult work world that is changing in ways unattractive to them, a world with greater job instability and less clarity in career progressions. Today, refraining from commitment may be a more adaptive choice than in the past. Many youth simply do not feel ready and able to make good choices. It seems somehow simpler to live one's way into the future day by day than to face that future in a deliberate manner. Yet, uncertainty about career aspirations more often than not reflects lack of knowledge about postsecondary education and the occupational world.[56] Moreover, choices are made all the time—about studies, time use, and future plans—and the reasons for choices are often vague. In an illuminating study of one group of working-class youth, researchers found that, among many in the sample, accounts of their lives and thoughts about the future were fragmentary, shifting, and ungrounded. Typically, they viewed the future in overly simplistic terms: either college success or a dead-end job.[57]

Some youth who should be seeking out more competitive options fail to do so. David Feiner, cofounder of the Albany Park Theater Project in Chicago, describes one ensemble member's reaction to a visit to Macalester College while the company was performing in Minneapolis: "She was angry that no one had ever done this [for her] before. And that she had no idea this [type of institution] was out there. And she was so angry because the woman at Macalister [sic] made it clear she was interested in her." Feiner and his wife, Laura Wiley, the cofounder of the theater, also discovered that ensemble members knew surprisingly little about college in general—for example, the difference between a two- and four-year college.[58]

Other young people have unrealistic goals. Many are less prepared for postsecondary education than they think they are. The majority of adolescents imagine that they will work in one of a handful of highly skilled professions, whether or not it is realistic for them individually and in spite of the fact that those professions make up only a modest proportion of the labor force.[59] Young people are told—or they hear—that they should strive for college, but they are not told why it is a good choice for them individually. When asked, the overwhelming majority of high school juniors and seniors say they plan to go directly to college regardless of grades, class rank, test scores, or occupational aspirations.[60] As Osgood observes, they "mouth the 'I'm going to college' mantra because everyone does . . . Everyone says they're going to college, even kids who hate school."[61]

Skilled and semi-skilled (now called "middle-skill") technical trades continue to bear a stigma, even though they will constitute the majority of good jobs and at least some, if not many, young people might be happiest in them. One recent survey found that although most Americans believe a strong manufacturing sector is critical to the American economy, only one in three would support their children's efforts to pursue a manufacturing career.[62] The chief executive of a precision machining firm in Maricopa County, Arizona, tells a reporter that "many kids are being pushed toward college degrees, and because manufacturing's got a reputation for outsourcing and being dirty and dangerous, there are not a lot of kids going into that."[63]

There is evidence that matching personal predispositions to specific pathways yields the best overall outcomes later. Just considering earnings alone, those who choose a technical concentration in high school are unlikely to have earned more if they had chosen differently.[64] Even a year of community college leading to a certificate of proficiency can be a critical first step out of the unskilled labor market and toward a midlevel technical career. Yet educators have been very slow to embrace a broader frame for understanding what young people need and need to prepare for. Reflecting on the large numbers of students pushed without any thought toward college, James Rosenbaum and colleagues note that "with our good intentions, we actually mislead the youth who most need our guidance."[65]

CHAPTER THREE

Fostering Good Learning Experiences, Starting with High School

. . . things remain the same because it is very difficult to change very much without changing most of everything.

—Theodore Sizer, *Horace's Compromise*

Building a social infrastructure for good learning experiences during the high school years will require both moral commitment and imagination, both work within dominant institutional structures, especially schools, and a concerted effort to create new structures. This broad task has to begin with a fundamental questioning of every element of high school as it has been organized for a century: the goals of and reasons for learning; the nature of learning tasks; where, when, and under what conditions learning takes place; the meaning of making mistakes; what the products of learning consist of; how individual growth is conceptualized and how learning is assessed; the nature of motivational structures; who teaches and how teaching is done; how time is organized (every day and over the years); and what institutions are involved. These questions lead to an alternative vision of learning during the high school years. Consideration of alternative ideas and approaches in policy discussions cannot be put off while we wait for current reform emphases to burn themselves out or be subsumed by the weight of schooling.

QUESTIONING THE "GIVENS" OF SCHOOLING

This would seem an opportune moment in our national history to bring new ideas to the institution of high school. As the previous chapter and a parade of commission reports attest, there is growing recognition among stakeholders that high school is not working well for a sizable proportion of young people. Discussions of high school have begun to describe the large numbers of youth alienated from schooling as "the neglected majority." If it is a majority, or even close to one, that means the problem is systemic, typical of young people's experience rather than atypical of it. Yet the thrust of national reform efforts is not systemic. Rather, it focuses on intensifying the current attributes of schooling and then on using fear and shame (in the guise of neutral numerical scores) to pressure participants—teachers, administrators, students themselves—to change in some unspecified, and unspecifiable, way. Pressure is to be applied through tightened bureaucratic controls; standardization of learning outcomes, curriculum, and even pedagogy; and value-added teacher assessment, performance contracts, and test-driven accountability. As the chief academic officer of the New York City schools noted, "If I'm a teacher, I'm going to look closely at what [an] exam is measuring and key my curriculum and my work to passing that exam. That is the reality of what high stakes exams are designed to do."[1] Yet these reform emphases, reinforced by businesslike management practices and increased competition through chartering and school choice, do not address what is most systemically problematic about the typical learning experience in school.

Placed in their best light, current reform emphases convey a sense that reformers are not sure what education is for, beyond recursive calls for young people who are (better) prepared to respond to the challenges of global economic competition. There is hardly a word, at least in the dominant discourse, about the values, habits, and dispositions we would like to nurture in young people—the kinds of adults we would like young people to become—unless it is nothing more than bundles of twenty-first-century skills and future winners in a hypercompetitive global economy.

There is little about education as an exploration of self and as a test of the adult world. There is little about the kinds of math or history or literature learners we would like young people to be—for example, courageous in certain ways (taking risks when not fully understanding) and modest in other ways (being open to feedback and rethinking positions).[2]

In the absence of a generous debate about what we value in our common life and how education should contribute, it is not surprising that reformers turn to quantitative benchmarks as touchstones for reform efforts. But such benchmarks have little real meaning and invariably undermine engagement. Measuring individual teachers' value added to young people's predicted test scores may be a creative statistical strategy, but it is distracting and reductive. Setting "student against student, teacher against teacher, school against school" does little but demoralize those most deeply involved in education.[3] A Brooklyn high school special education teacher, responding in an opinion piece to being rated a bad teacher, admits that even though his teaching efforts have been mostly successful, "I leave work most days replaying lessons in my mind, wishing I'd done something different. This isn't because my lessons are bad, but because I want to get better at my job."[4] This teacher describes experienced and respected colleagues who have left the field because they could or would no longer put up with evaluation practices that utterly failed to reflect the nature or quality of their work and who could or would no longer listen to constant criticism from politicians, business leaders, and others who have little idea of the daily life of schools.

There are even less flattering analyses of current reform emphases. One holds that they reflect a view that rich, interesting learning experiences are a luxury that low-income youth and youth of color cannot afford (at least until they have mastered basic skills and closed the achievement gap). A second analysis holds that current reform emphases are implicitly intended to undermine societal commitment to public schools.[5] In the latter view, data from accountability-focused reforms, ostensibly designed to hold teachers and schools accountable for educating disenfranchised children and youth, are used to shape a narrative that leads from putatively failing teachers and schools to an argument for "competition," choice, and privatization, to an argument "for setting the market loose on our teachers and children."[6]

Whichever interpretation of motives is true, accountability as currently conceived cannot be the driving force in schooling; it misses the point of teaching and learning. An emphasis on raising test scores distracts educators from the work of making school an interesting place to teach and learn. The Common Core State Standards initiative may tip its hat to habits of mind, but disciplines not part of it are left on the periphery of schooling. Teachers in their everyday instruction now have to fight to put aside test preparation concerns; to provide opportunities for young people to practice, enact, and explore the meaning of democracy; to create space to nurture young people's nascent ability to identify and debate the problems faced by our society today, formulate new questions in a discipline, deeply analyze ideas or data, and use symbols creatively and imaginatively. Young people themselves have become aware of the pressures inside the school building. One, adopting the language of reformers, told an interviewer that "teachers can't find wiggle room in the standards because they are afraid of being punished . . . It's too high stakes to stray away."[7]

The most problematic aspect of current reform emphases may not even be their substance or motives but the fact that discussion about them has been structured in a closed and authoritarian way. There is no opportunity for debate because, as noted above, education has been excised from the civic sphere and placed squarely in the market. It is a reprise of a phenomenon described by Marcus Raskin as the "channeling colony," the limiting of debate and judgment about important societal issues to a small group of elites with financial and other kinds of power.[8] The narrowing of debate about education can be linked also to a process that crystallized in the 1980s with *A Nation at Risk*. As David Hursh argues, that report made a direct (and inaccurate) link between falling behind educationally as a nation and falling behind economically; in other words, it placed our education system in a globalized context as well as an economic one.[9] It set the tone for a theme that continues to the current day in which education systems (like economic systems) are seen in direct, market-like competition.

Young people in school, like workers, are now said to be competing—and to bear social responsibility to compete—with hundreds of millions of peers around the world.

THE MYTH OF A COMMON EXPERIENCE

The kidnapping of educational reform discourse explains why we have skipped over needed debate about the ownership and purposes of learning in the high school years, one that would include young people and their parents, teachers, civic and religious leaders, and representatives from different occupations and avocations. What, though, has kept the defining attributes of schooling in place for so long? How do we reconcile the persistence of a century-old framework with the observation that the design of school learning "routinely and profoundly violates what much of our experience and a century of formal thought and research tell us about effective learning"?[10]

The persistence of high school as historically organized and practiced is due in part to the stubborn ideal of the comprehensive high school, with young people joined in a common curricular and socialization experience. This ideal has proved inadequate as a cultural guide, as a social goal, and as a framework for supporting individual development. The idea that all young people will acquire a common body of knowledge at a common depth in a common amount of instructional time has never made sense. Moreover, as Jim Rury observes, no one has ever been able to answer the question of what a common experience means in a world of deeply segregated schooling.[11] The ideal of a shared educational experience is belied by the role high schools have played in sorting young people in a manner masked by the rhetoric of openness and opportunity. Even as they enter high school students are led into different course levels in all the core areas (with different content and pedagogy). This unacknowledged sorting process is far more damaging to motivation and self-belief than one built explicitly on recognition and valuing of heterogeneity in young people.

Common Core State Standards, combined with top-down efforts to standardize curriculum, have been adopted recently as strategies to address inequality in curricular opportunity. Yet there is evidence that they actually flatten curriculum and exacerbate the effects of curricular differences. The curriculum experienced by the majority of youth is general—in the worst sense of the word. It is neither liberal, in the particular yet rich classical sense, nor vocational, in that word's deeper sense; it has no ready character or coloration. The central finding from a multisite study of top-down standardization in Texas high schools was that, while it narrowed and flattened the curriculum for all students, as teachers jettisoned complex, rich material to make sure they covered what would be tested from a common "core," it did so most for those students who were already receiving a lesser curriculum.[12]

As states and cities have increased the number of core academic courses required for graduation, the effect has been to discourage young people as learners and to push more of them toward the periphery of schooling, both psychologically and literally. In a recent school year in Los Angeles, "only 15 percent of graduating seniors . . . completed the 15 college preparatory courses with a passing grade of C or better."[13] Such an outcome serves no one well. States (and localities) have not even had the courage to acknowledge the conceptual failure of current reform emphases; rather, they have pretended their way to progress by changing the definition of and cut off scores for "proficiency" and in various other ways undermined their professed ideal of equalizing opportunity.

The most problematic aspect of a large common academic core is not even the discouragement it produces in young people or the dissembling. It is the dismissal of heterogeneity as a framework for organizing learning. A large common core, with standardized curricula and pedagogy, not only fails to build on but actually suppresses the distinctive mix of qualities that each student brings to school. In ignoring the heterogeneity of young people in strengths and limitations, passions and dispositions, educators are also ignoring our culture's need for—and need to value—knowledge and skill in a variety of domains, including those with a strong vocational orientation.

The large common curricular core has left schools with less freedom to develop substantive curricular threads in a range of domains that might spark students' interests and less time for students to pursue specific non-core disciplines in depth. (Moreover, the departmental organization of schools adds to the difficulty of organizing learning around domains that do not fit traditional academic categories.) Career and technical education barely finds the space it needs to be an elective, let alone the space that would be required to make it a valuable, substantive pathway for millions of youth. In a recent Washington State effort to expand CTE opportunities, especially apprenticeships, CTE teachers and counselors "continually [ran] into competing academic priorities tied to the Washington Assessment of Student Learning and high school graduation requirements."[14]

Emphasis on a large, fixed academic core constrains openness to incorporating applied learning material even in the traditional core subjects. For instance, some two-thirds of middle-skilled blue-collar workers have to be able to read and create visuals—maps, diagrams, floor plans, graphs, blueprints, and so on. These could easily be integrated into a range of courses and learning activities. High school curricula rarely provide learning tasks that require "integration of cognitive abilities with perceptual and manual skills," a key attribute of much current work.[15]

Applied knowledge, including the principles, problems, procedures, language, and tools that go with it, is not a special kind of knowledge for those not capable of academics. It is a category as rich, principled, and complex as academic knowledge. Vocational learning is full of cognitive content, but of a different kind than academic coursework.[16] In contrast to academic knowledge, which tends to be disembodied, vocational knowing "involves much more situated judgments and tacit understanding," application, and adaptation of knowledge.[17] Yet, applied versions of knowledge in the core subjects needed for graduation are often viewed as too technical or as neither broad enough nor conceptual enough. In a recent debate in Louisiana over a proposed vocational pathway to graduation, critics argued that, by definition, an applied pathway would lower standards and rigor. Yet some new courses that emphasize application of math and science in specific occupational arenas (e.g., engineering and biomedical sciences) have proven more rigorous and interesting to young people than similar basic courses (e.g., consumer math or science skills) designed primarily to allow academically weak youth to meet graduation requirements.

COLLEGE FOR ALL REINFORCES THE PROBLEM

The overarching policy goal of the current high school era, that of college for all, acts as a bookend to the emphasis on standards and a large core of common curricular standards. This goal is beginning to be parsed. The downside of rapid, massive expansion in the higher education market is beginning to be noted. (For instance, the model for profitability in this market requires ever larger numbers of new students each year to fill the places of ever larger numbers who drop out.) Yet college for all continues to serve as an anchoring objective, reinforcing the emphasis on Common Core Standards and curriculum. It is averred that, like the Common Core, this goal expresses our societal ideal of equal educational opportunity, but it can also be plausibly argued that, also like the Common Core idea, it undermines the ideal. Policy makers and administrators claim to understand that preparing young people for college and preparing them for vocation are not mutually exclusive. However, that awareness has had little practical effect on high school curriculum, on counseling for juniors and seniors, or on broad discourse about schooling.

Evidence of inappropriate counseling and directing of young people has been emerging in reports of low college progress and completion rates, especially among young people who did not do well academically in high school. According to one report, for example, among those "in the bottom 40 percent of their classes, and whose first institutions were four year colleges, two thirds had not earned diplomas eight and a half years later."[18] Such outcomes have led one observer to describe undifferentiated college-for-all thinking as the "inadvertent bigotry of inappropriate expectations."[19]

There are three related dimensions to those inappropriate expectations, one based on aspirations, the second on readiness, and the third on disposition. Aspirations among young people are higher today than at any point in recent history, and those high aspirations are both global and untethered—not tied to actual knowledge and skill, self-knowledge, personal disposition, or evidence of the outcomes from particular choices and pathways. With respect to readiness, one observer reads the evidence to conclude that "today, perhaps 20 percent of all youth graduate high school fully prepared for academic college." That means that 80 percent of young people need other options and pathways both during and after high school.[20]

Regardless of whether one agrees with this estimate, the dispositional argument is critical. Rose observes: "It is absolutely true—anyone who teaches and, for that matter, any parent, knows it—that some young people are just not drawn to the kinds of activities that comprise the typical academic course of study, no matter how well executed."[21] Such young people would do better (and indeed might thrive) in structured postsecondary programs tied closely to specific occupational domains or to pathways that begin with apprenticeship and work and lead back to further learning. One *Wall Street Journal* reader argued in a letter to the editor that, in regaining our manufacturing competitiveness,

> lowering corporate taxes and investing in high tech equipment is the easy part. Operating and caring for this machinery will require skill and experience. There are literally millions of young people who are dropping out of high school because they are not interested in academic, college-level studies. [Meanwhile] every day master-level workers are retiring without having passed on their experience to the next generation.[22]

Our ideals have led high school educators and other stakeholders in youth to ignore the hard thinking and planning needed to nurture and sanction indirect paths to postsecondary learning through an active, mixed, diverse, and partly applied set of learning and working experiences. A bachelor's degree from a good college or university unquestionably opens up options within some occupational areas and is a prerequisite for others.[23] It is also the case that some among the large number of young people not immediately ready for a four-year college will be ready later on. But these truths are not an excuse for neglecting learning experiences that will prepare young people for other, firmer first steps after high school.

The argument that those with college degrees earn more is not helpful for many individual youth. Young people themselves (some 90 percent in one survey) accept the idea that going directly to college "is not for everyone," and a large majority believes that getting "some hands on experience" is a useful early step toward adulthood.[24] Employers, already wary of the meaning of the high school diploma are becoming increasingly wary of the meaning of the generic bachelor's degree and are looking for specific knowledge and skills conferred through defined learning experiences, certification, and so forth.

OPENINGS FOR ALTERNATIVE VISIONS OF HIGH SCHOOL LEARNING

I have already foreshadowed the ideas that I believe are critical to rethinking learning during the high school years. For instance, good learning involves direct experience and immersion in a meaningful activity. Learning works best when young people can focus in depth on a few things at a time, when they see a clear purpose in a learning activity, when the end result or solution is truly not available to them until the work is done, and when they have an active role in co-constructing, interpreting, applying, making sense of, and making connections. Learning is often most effective when it is social, when it occurs as a shared activity in a fluid teaching-learning situation with more and less experienced learners, and when it allows for increasingly responsible participation in a social practice, in one's immediate community of fellow learners, in one's culture at large. Even as novices, young people need access to the depth and complexity of a domain or discipline. They need to see all the subtle processes and steps in creating products and how adults and more experienced peers work through problems.

Our culture, like any other, is composed of many kinds and depths of knowledge and skills attached to a diverse array of disciplines, endeavors, and purposes. Each discipline or field has "a conception of excellence that is internal to [its practices] and expresses its ideals."[25] Young people themselves are heterogeneous. In any population of youth there are different kinds of learners drawn to different cultural material, ways of learning, tasks and challenges. These ideas tell us that if young people need a common experience, it is that of being able join a particular tradition or community of practice within the many embodied in our culture. Moreover, very specific and applied learning experiences can provide a good foundation for exploring broad issues of democracy, citizenship, and ethics, not least because they sometimes directly raise those issues.

At its best, learning should feel and actually be like practice in the adult world. It cannot be watered down, oversimplified, standardized, or made inert because young people are different (younger, less mature) or because it is too complicated to immerse young people in adult practice. Assessment of mastery, likewise, should resemble that which takes place in the larger training, professional education, and work worlds. Assessment is not only more appropriate but is more interesting when tied to the professional standards of specific fields and when embedded in everyday tasks and performance.

Implications for Schooling

Applying these general principles to schooling does not require a large conceptual leap. Young people need more ways to feel and be successful in school.[26] As such, variability in what young people concentrate on and how and where they learn and grow should be embraced. Not all students should be expected to immerse themselves in and to demonstrate mastery of the same set of disciplines. Educators should think not in terms of one set of core standards but in terms of many varieties of standards, as many as there are disciplines in which young people might participate. Curriculum should be broadened, extended in many directions, but at the same time defined by clear pathways and sequences. Young people need a clear sense of where they are heading as they move through school. Meanwhile, at the micro-level, learning experiences should be fluid and partly open and pedagogies flexible and discipline specific.

Relevant knowledge and skill have to include the kinds suited to culture making and cultural critique: framing and addressing new problems, looking at old questions in new ways. Where there are critical ideas from traditional core disciplines, these have to be woven into learning explorations that ground and animate them. High schools have to recognize the artifacts of different occupations as potential curricular resources. Relevant knowledge and skill also have to include the kinds rooted in skilled perception and handwork, whether technical or artistic, and in sensory discrimination. Young people should be exposed to the representational tools used in different kinds of occupational settings and practice using those tools to address learning problems.

Young people need time and structure to immerse themselves in particular areas over the course of at least two years. For some youth an extensive and intensive curriculum would focus more on the methods of historiography and include delving into archives. For others it would be focused on reading widely in twentieth-century American poetry. For some it might focus on problems of political economy, like the consequences of regulating or deregulating markets. And for still others it would focus on the knowledge and skills that today's machinists need, such as an understanding of advanced manufacturing processes, a familiarity with the properties of metals, and "a facility for three-dimensional visualization—seeing in your mind's eye what's happening in the machine."[27] Learning to closely monitor gauges and instruments and to record their data, to listen to the sound of a machine to understand what is happening with a particular material or to develop the right touch using lab equipment belong in the high school curriculum alongside the well-worn traditional topics.

An example from a study of the work of machine operators illustrates the range of cultural material young people might be exposed to and the range of demands they might be prepared for. Here two workers are trying to solve a problem with the movements of a machine's robotic arm:

> Based on their auditory and visual perceptions, the workers formed a hypothesis as to the source of the problem (an incorrect feeder setting). They confirmed their hypothesis by measuring components of the feeder. They contested each other's suggestions for adapting a machine part and came to agreement on an optimal solution. Then the measurements were checked against the numbers on the machine's computer screen . . . Throughout the

troubleshooting, the workers referred to various kinds of inscriptions such as a blueprint of the [circuit] board, the customer's bill of materials, and the computer program data; they also made their own inscriptions by measuring objects and modifying numbers in the [computer] program. Work with numerical inscriptions pervaded the activity. The workers recognized these numbers as representations of the tasks to be accomplished by the machine, numbers which require careful assessment by comparing them against other inscriptions and, in particular, against their own perceptions.[28]

My point is not that high school learning experiences for all youth should encompass the knowledge, procedures, and skills underlying every single occupation. Rather, it is that such kinds of material are legitimate objects of learning, and beginning to master them, in chosen domains, should be an option for far more than just a handful of youth. Having a broader range of learning experiences would help young people begin to appreciate the range of qualities that different kinds of work require as well as the heterogeneity of culture itself.

Young people need opportunities for agency in their school life. Individual youth should be free (and be supported) to define some of their own learning goals and experiences, and they should be responsible for the effort, progress, and results of those experiences. They would have to figure out what knowledge, skills, and resources they would need to address a chosen problem and be responsible for acquiring each. Young people also need opportunities to make their own personal meaning of ideas, learning experiences, events, and conditions, weighing that personal meaning against the meaning imputed to these things by the culture at large.

More school learning would involve cooperative work, and more—significantly more—would be based outside the walls of school. High school educators would have to work with youth and outside mentors to identify the substantive domains and pedagogical approaches that might engage particular clusters of youth, including different means of representing learning material to young people and affordances for young people to express and illustrate what they have learned in different ways—through writing, drawing, video, oral communication, simulation, physical demonstration, and so forth. An example comes from New Vista High School in Boulder, Colorado, where, for a history class called Protest and Reform, three students undertook a project to learn and teach others about the sit-down strike that occurred at a General Motors plant in Flint, Michigan, in 1936–1937. After doing research to learn the details and historical context for the strike, the students developed a simulation of it with key figures, including sit-down strikers, outside strikers, police, national guard, etc., and events. The simulation was complemented by a comprehensive narrative.

Assessment has to become more descriptive, and growth must be viewed in a more longitudinal framework. Numbers and letter grades convey little information. In fact, cumulative grade point averages sometimes mask patterns of growth. The emphasis in defining achievement has to shift to descriptions of proficiency at doing specific things. Young people should be allowed (and, again, supported) to complete secondary education with different sets of knowledge and skills, even somewhat different kinds of literacy and numeracy. For some youth, the ability to read and make sense of complex technical manuals might be the equivalent of, and stand for, the ability to analyze fiction passages on a standardized test.

Young people's ideas, thought processes, and framing of and solution to problems would be evaluated through means similar to those used in a particular discipline to evaluate knowledge claims and specific skills. Stages or levels of mastery in specific fields and disciplines should be assessed using evaluative criteria and methods specific to that field or discipline at points in time appropriate for an individual young person. In recognition that the purpose of schooling is to prepare youth for tasks, problems, and opportunities outside of it, some assessment would focus on emergent expressions of lifelong capacities—cognitive, social, practical, civic, identity related.

A Discussion with Many Voices

Ideas about attributes of good learning for young people are beginning to weave together into a kind of tapestry. A range of ideas and proposals form a rich basis for critique and to help spur debate.

- A group of leading learning scientists argue that "educational or curricular work . . . must enlist rich contexts and what is too often treated as non-academic content."[29]

- A leading educational scholar argues that we must educate in a way that each young person "finds something of value on which to build a life while learning to value what others offer as well."[30]

- A leading career and technical education scholar argues for more disciplinary offerings, "multiple programs of study, beginning in the ninth grade."[31]

- Two leading scholars of secondary education argue for a different understanding of rigor in learning, one that emphasizes depth as much as or more than breadth, and the ability to apply learning to new tasks.[32]

- A recent report by a team of scholars at Harvard argues that "it is time to widen our lens" to create and validate a more "richly diversified set of pathways for a diverse population of young people."[33]

- A former superintendent argues the need to "tear apart the school day, the high school timetable, the school year, the four year diploma."[34]

Observers argue the need to reorganize the school environment to make it less school-like—or, put differently, more nonschool-like. They argue that, to break from the classroom mold, spaces within schools should resemble laboratories or even the renaissance artist's studio, with its hierarchy of apprentices, master draftsmen, and masters working on various projects in various combinations. Or schools should consist of "constellations of small communities of practice" in which young people observe, critique, and support each other's work.[35]

Many argue that schools cannot afford to remain closed systems. They must look and reach outward for learning resources. One school founder maintains that "it's the role of school to be the connector—that's how we change the lives of young people."[36] A few argue that it is simply not possible to provide young people the learning experiences they need while staying within the school itself, with forays outside of school only for specific purposes or projects, and that the kinds of learning experiences available outside of school are distinct from those available inside it. Learning must also be institutionally decentered through the involvement of a wider range of institutions and settings. That implies rethinking the meaning and locus of achievement, including authority to assess and recognize it.

CURRENT OPENINGS

Few of the ideas discussed here, my own or others', are completely new to school reform. Many have been posited and implemented on a modest scale for over a century in the progressive school experiments in the early decades of the twentieth century and the open/alternative schools that first emerged in the late 1960s and faded as a movement but continue to emerge, one by one, up to the present day (e.g., New Vista High in Boulder, Colorado, which opened in 1993). In various combinations and with various emphases, these ideas have been articulated in books, guides, and school-level experiments and initiatives. For instance the New Urban High School Project of the late 1990s developed a set of principles for high school design that is close in both detail and spirit to those I discuss here.[37]

These attributes can be found today in varied expressions and combinations in the many brand-name models and networks that thrive at the periphery of the national high school system. Some models start out as a concept, such as Early College High School and Diploma Plus, and some with an individual school that acquires a reputation and is then replicated, becoming a family of schools sharing an identity, including such well-known names as the Coalition of Essential Schools, Big Picture schools, Expeditionary Learning schools, and the newer New Tech Network schools, High Tech High schools, Envision schools, and Henry Ford Learning Institute Academies. New models continue to emerge, two noted examples being the New York City iSchool and ACE (Architecture, Construction and Engineering) Leadership High School in Albuquerque, New Mexico.

The attributes of good learning can be found, more selectively, in scores of themed high schools around the country, from STEM-themed schools (e.g., MC2 in Cleveland) to those focused on design (e.g., Miami's Design and Architecture Senior High School), various arts, environmental studies, and sustainability as well as a range of more explicitly vocational domains, from aviation and agriculture to biotechnology, health care, public safety, and so forth. In themed schools the substantive focus is in the foreground, and innovative pedagogies are in the background. For example, Options Academy/The Arts in Ohio has taken apart the traditional school day, giving students and studio instructors opportunities to organize learning in flexible groupings and temporal segments that fit particular fields and projects. It has also given students significant responsibility for managing their own learning tasks and responsibilities. The attributes of good learning can be found as well in some among a sizable number of alternative programs for dropouts and undercredited and overage youth.

It is not clear how many of the approximately 25,000 high schools in the United States seriously embrace a different vision of learning. Including some percentage of themed and vocational-technical high schools, a guess would be more than 1,000 but fewer than 2,000. It is clear that even mainstream educators in many regions of the country are working hard to rethink some, if not all, the elements of high school learning. A North Carolina high school reform commission, chaired by state superintendent June Atkinson, noted recently that "we have squeezed the last drop of educational juice from the traditional high school model. The culture and structure of every high school in the state must change if we are to prepare students for a future in today's economy."[38]

Efforts to rethink curriculum, learning tasks, and locales have included creation of differentiated pathways for young people, beginning in either the sophomore or junior year. As described in the next chapter, 10 to 15 percent of high school students take an occupational concentration (typically one or two periods each day) beginning in either the sophomore or junior year. That itself creates a modest pathway, although CTE coursework still tends to be treated as a coherent elective rather than a legitimate, defining pathway. Scores of school districts and counties around the country have vocational-technical centers that offer a defined set of occupational concentrations to students (typically juniors and seniors) from all the high schools in the district or county. For example, the Center for Advanced Professional Studies in Overland, Kansas, serves 600 youth from the Blue Valley School District, with concentrations in bioscience, business, engineering and human services. The Technical Center in Lake County, Illinois, serves 1,700 students from 22 county high schools in a wide variety of fields.

Both early college high schools (numbering about 270 nationwide) and some career and technical education programs provide opportunity to take college classes and receive dual credit and/or, for CTE, industry-recognized certification. A small number of districts have academic or vocational programs with defined course progressions that continue into postsecondary, creating what have been called high school–college hybrids. A few states are experimenting with or examining "5 Year High Schools," which create clear, articulated pathways through high school into specific postsecondary programs (usually at a community college), ideally leading to both a high school diploma and significant credit toward an associate degree.

With mastery rather that seat time becoming a more prominent idea in reform discourse, this has led in turn to the idea of individualized pathways and time frames. In Albuquerque's ACE Leadership High School students can enter at any grade level and at any age (80 percent are reportedly overage or undercredited). About one-third of students attend classes in the evening.[39] New Hampshire has abandoned the Carnegie Unit and thereby the assumption that young people are ready to graduate when they have accumulated a certain number of required and elective credits. (Under the Carnegie Unit system, a young person can accumulate enough credits to graduate even if he or she barely passes most courses.) Local districts in New Hampshire now have responsibility for defining competencies needed to graduate and how those will be measured.

Most reform discussions in the United States have resisted the idea, found in most countries, of making age sixteen a formal demarcation point, with a variety of normative postcompulsory options laid out beyond that point (see chapter 6). The predominant instinct has been the opposite: making schooling compulsory to age eighteen as a vehicle for reducing dropout and improving overall engagement and achievement. A new initiative of the National Center for Education and the Economy, nonetheless, would have young people in selected high schools in eight states take a European-style board examination at some point (typically at the end of the sophomore year) to assess mastery of some agreed-on core knowledge; this would then serve as an alternative to the high school diploma. High schools and districts involved would create different pathways for young people beyond that point, including college or community college coursework, a career and technical education concentration (perhaps leading to a technical certificate), or some kind of broader disciplinary concentration.

THEME AND VARIATION IN INNOVATIVE HIGH SCHOOL MODELS

There are many entry points to reforming high school practice, among them organizing concepts such as personalized learning and defined approaches such as early college high schools, themed schools, and name-brand models. Each serves as a skeleton for a cluster of attributes, often the same ones found elsewhere. For example, to work well the early college high school requires a different role for teachers, individualized learning plans, preparation for the college class experience, time to reflect on it, collaboration between institutions, rethinking where high school takes place, and so forth.

As prominent vehicles for reform, name-brand models are distinctive in a few ways. They are both exemplars of what public school practice might be and a repudiation of prevailing public schools, a work-around of immovable high school bureaucracies. Many of the newer models started as charters. Each has its own history and identity, mission and values, as well as its own list of core or design principles. Yet what is shared is in some ways more persuasive than what is different. Most models include some mix among a common set of attributes:

- Small school size and strong school community
- Opportunity to tailor individual learning experiences
- New teacher roles (e.g., resource, mentor, model, backstop)
- Long-term relationships between adults and youth
- Project- or problem-oriented learning activities
- An emphasis on depth in learning experiences
- Authentic and/or applied learning (including internships)
- A mastery orientation in assessment
- Opportunity to exhibit work to the larger school community. Additionally: an emphasis on complex, open-ended learning problems and questions
- Opportunity for self-directed learning experiences (and use of time)
- Design of learning projects that incorporate different disciplines
- Reflection on learning experiences through journals, work logs, and other writings
- Inclusion of such factors as work ethic, collaboration, and persistence in grades
- Substantive experts as guest teachers and mentors
- A reconceptualization of the school day
- Use of Internet technologies to extend and enrich learning
- A sensitivity to developmental tasks and issues of middle adolescence

These models appear to be competitors that borrow from each other and recognize each others' efforts. Most seek a balance between youth ownership of learning experiences and recognition that youth need to work within the norms and standards of specific disciplinary traditions as well as those of the school community. Most take "discrete, situationally occurring problem[s]" as the most "natural" unit of learning.[40] This includes actual problems in the larger community in which a school is located. Most models appear to presume that American society (and its economy) will need creative, complex thinkers with a strong social conscience who able to use technology fluently and for a variety of purposes. Director Deborah Parizek notes that her Henry Ford Learning Institute Academies strive to nurture youth with "deep and meaningful knowledge of the conditions of their world, a conscious understanding of their role in that world, a commitment to taking action to change that world."[41]

As a whole, these models are moderately democratic in their view of the kinds of knowledge and skills important for young people to acquire and of the occupations they might pursue. Dennis Littky and Elliot Warshor of Big Picture, for example, have argued in different venues that academic and applied learning are complementary parts of a whole: each is animated by the other. One study of Big Picture Learning describes a young man, inarticulate and seemingly uninterested in academics, whose out-of-school placement was with a yacht restoration school and workshop. Through that experience the young man found a voice and "an ability to write about woodworking in ways that previously had eluded him."[42]

Most models use the principle of individualization (or personalization) as a means to address heterogeneity among youth in talents, motivations, and specific aptitudes. A number recognize learning as partly a matter of identification and identity, proclaiming that they want young people to think, and even feel, like they are "scientists, urban planners, historians and activists," as the Expeditionary Learning mission statement puts it. A few models also emphasize self-knowledge, either in a deeply personal sense (e.g., Expeditionary Learning) or in terms of one's strengths and limitations as a learner (e.g., the iSchool).

The use of Internet technology for distance learning is a particularly distinctive attribute of newer models and networks. It is seen as providing a new way of extending learning resources, erasing physical distance and even national borders. One observer notes that "the activity we call learning is walking away from the institution we call school."[43] For instance, young people have communicated and developed joint projects with peers in other countries. As part of a project tied to the National September 11th Memorial and Museum, iSchool students interviewed peers in Australia and Pakistan to learn their views about terrorism and victimization.[44] Young people have held video conferences with professionals in other parts of the country who are deeply involved in a particular discipline or social issue. Students at a New Tech Network school who were reading a book about gang life for a larger gang awareness project had an opportunity to Skype with journalist Alex Kotlowitz, who has devoted his working life to this issue. A number of schools are using online course management software to create discussion groups and virtual classrooms, using online tutoring programs, posting student records and progress, and so forth. Young people can access course material and assignments from anywhere inside or outside the school building.

Many of the newer models view the design of and resources in the physical environment of the school as an important influence on learning and on the school community as a whole. Students might have available to them many kinds of learning settings within a building, in different configurations for different kinds of activities, and might have some (to considerable) freedom to move around. With more physical transparency, learning activity is visible to others and feels shared. The implicit model for some newer schools is the high technology workplace designed for project-based work in flexible teams and with informal interactions. The idea, in part, is to bring young people together who might normally not interact, yielding unexpected conversations and collaborations. An additional rationale is to contribute to young people's sense of ownership and control over their learning experiences.

Rethinking the learning day, for example, creating large blocks of time for particular learning activities or eliminating class periods altogether, is a common approach. San Diego's High Tech High has a morning block and an afternoon block. A visitor to Napa New Tech observes that "you'll hear no bells signaling the end of class periods. Students are trusted to keep track of their own time, just as they would as grownups in the outside world, and to show up where they need to at the appropriate time."[45] More flexible time arrangements go hand-in-hand with an emphasis on project- or problem-based learning. For example, because some learning is built around projects that may be days or weeks in length, young people are required to apportion time in relation to extended timelines.

Administrators and teachers pay attention both to the quality of community created inside the school and to how the school community (and learning experiences) should relate to the larger one surrounding it. In a number of models, individual teachers or teams stay with a defined group of young people for four years. Explicitly stated norms, rules, community governance, and maintenance activities are common. Community meetings are used to refine mission statements, set policies, plan, address common problems, celebrate accomplishments, and reinforce values. The Coalition for Essential Schools is known especially for its emphasis on fairness, decency, and trust within each school community, which it deems the "backbone" of its community. Its schools also emphasize the importance of smaller communities within the larger community of the school, including those created by individual teachers in their own classrooms.

The personal and collective responsibility for making the community work, along with the relative freedom of movement, individual responsibility for learning, and absorbing nature of learning tasks, contribute to a different basis for discipline and control than in the traditional high school, where young people lose the thread of learning and valuable time that cannot be recovered. But when they do decide to apply themselves, they are still inside the school community. Small size allows staff at these schools to consider, get to know, and respond to each student individually. Teachers are socialized to avoid blaming. As a tenth grader at ACE Leadership High School told a visitor, "In regular schools, you either make it or you don't. If you fit into their style, you'll succeed. If you don't you fail. ACE molds itself around us."[46]

A number of the models stress the importance of helping young people make conceptual connections between the work that occurs inside school and what happens in the outside world. That can include commissioned work, student-initiated research projects, and service learning projects in the surrounding community. Students at San Diego's High Tech High, for instance, have worked alongside local scientists to examine the question of how humans have influenced the ecology of San Diego Bay. Making connections, it can also include examination of the ethical or moral dimensions of important questions in any field and ways of defining and expressing specific norms and values. Just recently there have been efforts to make selected community-based learning experiences count as elective credits toward graduation.

Less common, the world outside of school becomes a principal site for learning. Big Picture schools are distinguished by their Learning Through Internship (LTI) program, in which students spend two days per week throughout high school in apprenticeship-like learning roles in adult work and service settings. Through years of trial and error, Big Picture has developed a detailed infrastructure to support LTIs, which includes investigating potential placements, development of learning plans, and monitoring and reflecting on learning experiences. Advisers and subject matter teachers work to see that the academic content of LTIs is organic to the experience, which is not always an easy task. The whole school organization is committed to ensuring that internships are good learning experiences, whether exploratory or in a field of committed interest.

A key assumption of Big Picture founders and staff—one that has been taken up by other models—relates to the importance of shared responsibility for young people's learning. Educators not only must look outside the school building for learning resources but must deliberately involve a range of adults and institutions in the educational process; "teachers cannot and should not bear this responsibility alone."[47] The mission statement of the Henry Ford Learning Institute in Detroit includes the idea that "public education is best accomplished when it is truly a public endeavor. This means welcoming and involving students in workplaces, retail environments, city centers and cultural institutions" and drawing in multiple partners to support young people's learning.[48] Big Picture has found that a variety of adult work settings and institutions are willing and able to provide a learning place for young people when careful preparatory work is done and when school staff play an active supporting role. For that to work, school staff have to give up a measure of authority and control. They have to trust young people as well as other adults. They have to have felt a need to continue working on, to constantly define and redefine rigor in learning, and to work hard to tie together school- and internship-based content.

Learning to Think in Particular Ways

A distinguishing feature of these models is their deliberate attention to fostering what has been called "ways of thinking." They are deliberate in their effort to encourage young people to think and solve problems using particular conceptual tools. The idea is that a curriculum does not teach critical thinking, problem solving, resourcefulness, or the ability to tackle complex tasks as discreet skills; rather, it shapes learning activities so that young people are always calling on and building such skills. For example, by providing students opportunities to revise work, they learn the principle of improving products or solutions through successive approximations. At the same time, many models have their own heuristic for capturing the thinking skills they are trying to foster. For instance, they structure learning experiences that help young people learn to think strategically, systemically, and/or ecologically—to learn to see and to make connections across various disciplines and parts of the world.

One example of this is how Henry Ford Learning Institute Academies' use of "design-based thinking," based on principles and practices from the many-faceted design field, as an organizer for learning. (The Academies also emphasizes the importance of bringing youth of color into relevant fields such as architecture and graphic, industrial, consumer, and fashion design. Fewer than 2,000 of 105,000 registered architects in the United States are African American.) Promotion of design thinking is carried out through use of design challenges as a learning frame (one major challenge each quarter); following and documenting (in design notebooks) defined steps in the design process (i.e., brainstorming, research, sketching out, developing specifications and prototypes, solving problems as a team). Director Deborah Parizek argues that "all students—even those students who struggle with, or who are not usually motivated by traditional academics—can tap into an innate capacity to be creative" tempered by a structured problem-solving process.[49]

These deliberate forms of thinking can be applied to many kinds of activities and projects in many fields, such as those that help students see how "ecological, social and economic systems are inextricably connected."[50] They are usually applied to specific problems, challenges, or projects. High Tech High, for instance, especially emphasizes project-based learning; one group of students learned about the field of conservation forensics through work with DNA bar coding. New York City's iSchool incorporates into its curriculum nine-week, interdisciplinary learning projects with a central problem, question, or project, sometimes developed with an outside partner organization or client. Examples include designing a green space in a particular setting; exploring the scientific, economic, political, and environmental dimensions of hydrofracking and presenting findings to stakeholders; and working with curators of the National September 11th Memorial and Museum to plan a youth-focused exhibit.

ISSUES IN THIS WORK

Constrained Variability

These models clearly make school somewhat less standardized, with learning extending out from individual youth rather than descending on them. There is, typically, affordance for some variability from student to student in the focus of specific learning experiences. A few models structure a curriculum that includes personally chosen majors or concentrations. In the iSchool, for instance, the "area of focus" is a selected disciplinary domain that young people pursue in both structured ways (through coursework and internship experiences) and self-directed ways (e.g., a senior project).

At the same time, none of these models creates distinctly different pathways for youth, including vocational-technical programs of study. There is only modest emphasis on introducing young people to or preparing them for the range of occupations that require technical education in a two-year college. Every model views its work primarily as preparing students for a four-year college, especially those who might not otherwise apply and enroll. Almost all measure their success by the percentage of students accepted at a four-year college. Most continue to use the Common Core State Standards, global competitiveness, twenty-first-century skills, and standardized tests as a cloak for their work, even when articulating values that contradict these dominant reform pillars. There is, at times, a schizophrenic quality to descriptions of the work they're doing in their schools. An administrator at Napa New Tech High School, for example, tells a visitor, "We have to train teachers to look at standards that states derive, where there's meaningful application of . . . knowledge. So now we start with standards and build curriculum around them. At the same time we provide a deeper learning experience that also teaches 21st century skills."[51]

Rethinking Assessment

Efforts to rethink assessment of learning have not developed as fully as have reforms in other areas. Most models seem caught in a figurative no man's land between assessment and certification approaches commensurate with the learning experiences they provide and the demands of funders, bureaucracies, and, sometimes, parents for standardized metrics. The models do try to use varied forms of evidence for determining mastery of specific knowledge and skills. These include interim and final products themselves as well as written (and sometimes video) records of work on a problem or project, with descriptions that include plans, decisions, strategies, explanations, drafts, sketches, hypotheses, revisions, and so forth. Exhibitions and capstone projects, with peers and nonschool mentors playing an evaluative role, are common. Students may build portfolios to hold samples of work across many projects. Nonetheless, qualitative and descriptive approaches to assessment are rarely accepted by those preoccupied with accountability in the forms that predominate in schooling today; nor are such principles as self- and peer assessment or the opportunity to redo work.

A number of attributes of learning in more innovative schools is fundamentally incompatible with standardized testing and also often with the abstract letter grades that communicate nothing of learning experiences. What is learned or mastered is best reflected in descriptive language and in disaggregated form. Young people may be understood to master particular material at different times in their school careers and have different "best means" of demonstrating mastery. What is learned or acquired in a particular learning project may be as much collective as individual. Important lessons learned—about self, community, society, the practice of a discipline—cannot be predefined, quantified, or understood in the linear or ordinal terms common to assessment rubrics. As an example, a group of students at ACE Leadership High School spent a trimester designing and constructing traditional clay and earth baking ovens, *hornos*, using a traditional Pueblo construction technique called "rammed earth." The project was part of a larger one on green-friendly building practices. They used math and science, wrote and read, and developed new physical skills. Right before the exhibition, their finished ovens were vandalized. As a group, they decided to rebuild them using what they had learned to improve the ovens' design and functioning. The individual and collective knowledge, skills, and personal qualities this group of youth demonstrated in this project, as well as what they learned about themselves and their cultural heritage and the lessons they took from it, are barely touched on in Common Core Standards or standardized tests.

What young people learn through school-sponsored out-of-school experiences—applied projects, internships, and preapprenticeships—is especially variable. A young woman who interned at a Ronald McDonald House reflected on how she learned about the unpredictability of life, about how to give others extra chances, about how to "accept the things I cannot change," and about how she has to be sure to live her own life while working with others whose futures are uncertain.[52] A young woman interning in the office at a business, after observing an employee named Georgie who seemed "strange" due to an obsession with cats, came to appreciate Georgie after she helped her with a problem. This young woman learned that acceptance at work has much less to do with personal idiosyncracies than does acceptance in high school: "I found joy in Georgie because I had accepted her and I had found joy in the realization that someday I can be my truest self in the work place . . . without holding back."[53] These kinds of remarkable lessons will never be found in a set of standards or on a list of twenty-first-century skills.

CONCLUSION

These attributes of good learning for high school–age youth are consistent with the straightforward qualities that young people themselves emphasize:

- Feeling that they belong to their school community
- Feeling that they are recognized and listened to
- Feeling that they can feel competent and are in (some) control of their learning
- Feeling that they have some opportunity for applied and in-depth learning experiences
- Feeling that they have opportunities for dialogue and a sense of "jointness" with teachers and other adults[54]

Young people want to be able to be themselves, to take risks and make mistakes without fear of disastrous consequences. And they want to feel genuinely prepared for the future.

The distinctive approaches to high school learning described here, from early college high schools to the many brand-name models and approaches, are, by most accounts, valued by participating youth and as well as valuable for what they are. Teachers find the work difficult but rewarding. Sponsors and proponents believe that their practices provide what young people need; they do not claim that their approach is the only one that makes sense to pursue. Nor do sponsors of innovative approaches and models claim to be the only or primary instruments for reforming our society's basic conception of high school. Most recognize that their design principles have to be incorporated into local school and community contexts with long, complex histories, and their approach to entering and working in a new setting, whether school or community, reflects that recognition.

One can worry that the proliferation of innovative practices, models, and discrete high school efforts does little more than reduce pressures on the school system. Promoting individual innovative models one by one is not going to shift the high school center of gravity in the United States. Proponents of every new approach that has spread beyond its original home, by invitation or force of will, have experienced a full range of obstacles. Rules and regulations, curriculum and testing mandates, rigid labor agreements, defensive institutional cultures, transportation, funding, scheduling, impatient administrators, crediting challenges, and the current overall reform framework have all impeded innovative work. That may be why even longstanding models that began their work inside the public schools, like the Coalition for Essential Schools and Big Picture, have come to rely on the charter movement, which by definition offers a work-around to public school bureaucracies. Most new models, such as High Tech High, started out as charters.

The attributes outlined in this chapter and embodied in hundreds of well-known, lesser-known, and anonymous schools are nonetheless becoming a distinctive presence in local high school systems. Their large base of shared attributes, if not their visibility, may create some institutional pressure to open up high school on a broader scale. As Ted and Nancy Sizer observe, "People teach, but the institutions that people build also teach."[55] The attributes discussed here pose a particular threat to those currently in power in the world of schooling: mayors and their hand-picked superintendents and accountability officers, commercial textbook and testing companies, management consultants, the U.S. Department of Education, and the small cadre of philanthropists who have heavily influenced the reform agenda. This group of stakeholders is unwittingly intensifying the conditions for the demise of its own ideas, creating an opening for alternatives.

CHAPTER FOUR

Career and Technical Education as a Base for Good Learning Experiences

The vocation acts as both magnet to attract and as glue to hold. Such organization of knowledge is vital, because it has reference to needs.

—John Dewey, *Democracy and Education*

The United States will not be able to forge a constructive learning agenda for young people until it sorts out the role of career and technical education in this agenda. This will not be easy. Stakeholders in education and educational reform view CTE with ambivalence, if not suspicion, due to its stigmatized (and by some accounts stigmatizing) history, to concern for equality of educational opportunity (i.e., the right for all youth to aspire to a college education), and to its perceived narrowness, which contrasts with the changing nature of work. CTE in recent years has been viewed, at best, as an anachronism, preparing young people "for low-skill jobs that no longer exist," and, at worst, as a subtle means of tracking youth of color.[1] It has been described as illiberal and mechanical. Even the "principled heterogeneity" for which vocational education is sometimes praised is argued to lead inevitably to hierarchy in the status of different subjects and foci.[2] For all these reasons, only 9 percent of all credits earned by high school students by the time they graduate are occupationally focused CTE credits.[3]

The American disdain for vocationally oriented learning, as with applied learning generally, is problematic. Everything we know about development, learning, and the situation of young people supports it. Young people need access to all the corners of our culture in order to discover (and develop) interests and strengths. There is widespread acknowledgment that many youth need more vital and engaging learning experiences than they currently receive. There is growing appreciation that young people need opportunity to apply knowledge, that doing so is critical to making it one's own. Many, if not most, stakeholders in young people's development believe that they need at least some exposure to the world of work, regardless of where they are heading in the postsecondary years.

Acknowledging all of these beliefs, we still do not want the aims of learning experiences during the high school years to be too explicitly vocational. We may want young people to be able "to find and act on who they are, what their talents gifts and passions may be, what they care about, and how they want to make a contribution to each other and the world."[4] But in the process we do not want to limit their options—and possible destinies—prematurely. In that light there remains a sense that vocational education is too closed and specific in character. Parents themselves tend to believe that middle adolescents are not ready to make vocational choices and therefore that vocational education is not useful to them.

Ambivalence toward CTE is apparent even with respect to the millions of young people (close to, if not, a majority) for whom the current design of high school is not effective. This group includes, but is far larger than, the one-third of each age cohort who will not complete high school. It also encompasses an additional one-third who stay in school but are mostly going through the motions, unsure what they are doing or why. Many youth in both these groups will enter the workforce after high school with few specific skills, limited personal resources or sense of direction, and little or no knowledge of the economy, the labor market, or learning requirements for specific occupations.

Elected officials, education officials, and philanthropists pay lip service to the need to rethink learning affordances for young people who are ill-served by the prevailing design and emphases of high school. Yet, their policy proposals serve mostly to intensify that design and those emphases. As a practical matter, if not a philosophical one, this makes a significant commitment to applied learning and work-based learning—two potentially powerful remedies to chronic disengagement—all but impossible. School systems have decided that they can spare neither the time nor the resources needed to make CTE work.

Local and state reluctance to commit resources to CTE is mirrored by the federal government's neglect of this critical pillar of high school education. The main source of federal CTE funding, the Carl Perkins Career and Technical Education Act, has received a steadily declining share of U.S. Department of Education funding, now less than 2 percent. (For the first time in years, current federal budget proposals, in the early winter of 2012, seek level funding for CTE in the coming fiscal year.) In key policy speeches, including one on April 19, 2011, to state directors of career and education and another on July 25, 2011, to national business leaders, Secretary of Education Arne Duncan has conveyed skepticism about the potential of CTE to strengthen learning experiences for high school youth.

There are counterweights to current policy trends. For their own reasons, business groups, notably the National Association of Manufacturers and the U.S. Chamber of Commerce, have been actively supportive of CTE. A recent report from the latter organization argues that "the time has come to use CTE as a change agent in re-shaping the American workforce."[5] A handful of influential academics and policy researchers argue for greater investment in CTE. In an implicit call for such investment, the widely cited "Pathways to Prosperity" report observes that "too many [young people] can't see a clear, transparent connection between their program of study and tangible opportunities in the labor market."[6]

The need to strengthen the vocational-technical pathway through high school is supported by data on the actual pathways young people take after high school. Young people arrive at postsecondary education in very different ways: half of each age cohort will not find its way to it at all; some three-quarters of young people do not follow a traditional route to a college degree.[7] At a minimum, the sizable group of young people who will enter the labor market after high school needs opportunities to learn about the kinds of work that might be available to them and to develop some basic competencies in one or more broad occupational areas (or clusters). Currently, the majority of youth who enter the labor market after high school have no such knowledge or competencies.

This need for strong vocational-technical programs is not just personally important to large numbers of young people. It is structurally important to the American economy. As one group of scholars notes, the capacity of U.S. institutions "to match educational alternatives with career options is woefully underdeveloped . . . not because it cannot be done but simply because it is not being done."[8] The clearest illustration of this mismatch is in the persistent inability of employers to fill openings for skilled manufacturing positions. Meanwhile, almost three-quarters of U.S. workers "are in jobs for which there is either low demand from employers, an over-supply of eligible workers, or both."[9]

During a Chicago hearing of the National Commission on Educational Excellence, which had just published the 1983 *A Nation at Risk*, a questioner asked commission members why CTE was not addressed in the report. They noted that "they had run out of time and money."[10] The report's recommendations, which emphasized the need for greater academic rigor in schooling, ironically led to both less time and money for CTE in the nation's schools, and to a decade and a half of declining enrollment. This trend was only slowed in the late 1990s by initiatives associated with the School to Work Opportunity Act of 1994, itself left to expire in 2001. In an interview with a journalist, Anthony Carnevale observed that "since 'A Nation at Risk' . . . we've set aside every pathway but one, and we've left a lot of people behind."[11]

TRIPARTITE CONTEXT FOR CAREER AND TECHNICAL EDUCATION

Defining a rationale and role for CTE requires consideration of three sets of variables: the developmental tasks of the high school years, trends in the economy and workforce, and the defining feature of the American high school. As I argued and illustrated in chapter 1, the potential value and fit of CTE is clear from a developmental perspective. Middle adolescence is a formative time in young people's vocational development. As described below, the appropriate focus of CTE is somewhat clear but in need of ongoing conceptual work, from a workforce perspective. And, as also described in previous chapters, the actual role of CTE in young people's lives is significantly constrained by the features of the American high school. Among the challenges it faces are finding space in the high school curriculum, matching young people to appropriate concentrations and pathways, assuring a substantive role for work-based learning, and building a CTE infrastructure that extends beyond the walls of high school.

Making Sense of Labor Force Needs

In the literature on labor force needs there is considerable debate about the kinds of jobs that will be available to most American workers in coming years and therefore the knowledge, skills, and dispositions that will be needed to succeed in the workforce. By some accounts middle-skilled work, like the middle class itself, has hollowed out. For instance, about a third of new jobs in the coming years will require primarily short-term, on-the-job training.[12] The majority of jobs permanently lost in recent recessions were middle-skilled. By other accounts, demand for middle-skilled workers is growing rapidly. Some 60 percent of current or projected jobs require at least a year or two of specialized postsecondary education, a dramatic increase from the past, and much of that education is technical.[13]

There are many studies and reports on where job growth will be focused (including regular updates from the U.S. Department of Labor). These reflect a bifurcated economy, with a small number of highly skilled professional and technical jobs and a large number of modestly skilled or unskilled ones. Local and state government, a significant employer in education and human services, has been steadily eliminating jobs. And some purportedly high-demand fields are actually experiencing an oversupply of workers. For example, higher education institutions are now turning out three times as many computer programmers as are needed. Even new engineering graduates, generally thought to be in short supply, are having great difficulty finding work.[14]

Manufacturing, still the heart of the American economy, offers a contradictory picture. The U.S. continues to produce a significant share of the world's manufacturing output. Both activity and output have actually grown modestly in recent years. Manufacturing also remains a critical underpinning of hundreds of local economies. It is intricately linked to other sectors of the economy and is a foundation for innovation, both in new products and technologies. Manufacturing activity also has a multiplier effect, generating many kinds of corollary economic activity and jobs.[15] Yet manufacturing jobs have sharply declined, particularly at the less skilled end of the continuum. Over the past decade alone, one in three manufacturing jobs has been lost.[16]

Manufacturing work—indeed, skilled and semi-skilled technical trades generally—increasingly bear a stigma, even though such work will constitute the majority of good jobs, and at least some (if not many) young people might be happiest in it. Parents do not want their children to pursue the trades. Policy makers and leaders in education tend to believe that "it is economically and morally irresponsible to educate the young for tasks and jobs that require skills in tool and machine use."[17] Educational structures for introducing young people to, preparing them for, and linking them to manufacturing careers have been atrophying for decades. In every city in the country, high schools have closed all but a handful of machining and metalworking programs. Apprenticeship opportunities for older youth, whether through unions or employers, remain scarce. Yet in a 2005 survey of eight hundred manufacturers by the National Association of Manufacturers, "90 percent of respondents indicated a moderate to severe shortage of qualified skilled production employees."[18] Even recent postrecession reports indicate shortages of skilled manufacturing workers ranging from half a million to a million workers.[19]

Needed Knowledge and Skills

Observers do not fully agree on the knowledge and skills most critical to current and future job opportunities. Some emphasize the substantive, discipline-specific knowledge and skills important to a range of growing (and/or evolving) occupations, including biotechnology/bioscience/

bioengineering, nursing, and new clinical and lab-based technical occupations in the health-care field (e.g., physical, occupational, respiratory and other therapists, laboratory, EKG and surgical technicians, etc.), accounting and auditing, computer-related fields (e.g., data communications), advanced manufacturing, maintenance and repair. There is clearly also some need for knowledge and skills that are both technical and broad enough to apply in different work settings. For instance, the new occupational role of process technician requires knowledge of math, materials, industrial processes, and technical terms and specifications as well as the ability to monitor computer-controlled equipment and machinery, to take and analyze samples, and to make adjustments as necessary. Yet, all of these must be broad enough to be helpful in a range of industries: oil, chemical and gas, power, water, waste management, food production, and so on.

In the trades and in traditional manufacturing fields, the jobs being created often do not look like those that have been lost. Changes in workplace technology, across many fields, have had complex effects, displacing some workers and creating new roles for those with a mix of cognitive and physical skills. Electricians may now need knowledge of mechanics for some kinds of work. Auto technicians now need systems understanding as well as electronics, hydraulics, and even industrial design. In manufacturing, computers now embody the range of physical and perceptual skills that historically guided fabrication processes, requiring of workers a range of moderately abstract, one-off skills, including programming (itself requiring a range of math knowledge and skills), metallurgy, drafting, measurement, and testing (for tolerances, etc.). As the president of a metal parts manufacturer told a reporter, "It used to be that a factory owner would say 'I need 20 guys' and pull them right off the street. Now it's 'I need 20 guys with very specialized technical skills.'"[20]

Machine operators have to develop (or redevelop) a variety of applied perceptual and representational abilities, especially for noticing trouble, finding its source, and brainstorming a solution. They also now need to be able to interpret complex printouts and charts. Workers may need to program and reprogram a CNC (computer numerical code) guided machine many times each week, and sometimes each day, returning it to a specified tolerance or adjusting it for a new job. They may have to periodically learn to master new, more advanced equipment. One study examining the demands on workers (mostly high school graduates) in medical equipment, steel making, and valve manufacturing plants found common demands across all three, notably "diagnostic, trouble-shooting and team problem solving" skills, with breadth of skills as important as depth.[21]

A central theme in the literature on labor force needs is the growing importance of knowledge and skills associated with generating, processing, and deploying knowledge itself (or at least information). Gee observes that work that is valued now "adds value," creates something new, brings "knowledge to bear on some aspect of the design or re-design of products, processes, technologies, services, environments."[22] In a complementary vein, some analysts emphasize the generic skills and dispositions needed both to find work and to continue growing in and through it. These include such basic or "essential" skills as punctuality, reliability, honesty, willingness to work hard and take initiative; attention to quality and care in working on problems and products; and evident interest and desire to learn. Increasingly they include capacity for self-direction and the ability to reason, problem solve, weigh options, use judgment, and innovate at a higher level than in the past, almost in a craftlike way. On the social side, valued qualities include the ability to accomplish tasks through work in concert with others and to use others as resources. Workers will have to be able to communicate ideas clearly, and to teach others what they know— explain their work, demonstrate a skill or procedure, and give feedback to colleagues.

It is likely that occupations will remain somewhat stable, but specific job definitions and demands much less so, and that the technologies used in specific kinds of work will be regularly updated. In that light, new workers will have to be able to adapt what they know to nonroutine problems, new situations, and new roles. They will have to find information and other resources not immediately available and be able to integrate knowledge from different sources. Not least they will have to invest in their own productivity by continuously seeking out the knowledge they need for new tasks.

SCHOOLING AND THE CONTINUING SUSPICION OF CTE

At some level, school leaders and staff are surely cognizant of the picture of a complex, demanding, changing world of work. It is reported in the media on a weekly basis. But schools' mission—curriculum and pedagogy—hardly reflect awareness of a critical need to respond to labor force needs on behalf of the young people they serve. The lack of connection between most high schools and the vocational world surrounding them is striking. Career and technical education itself is conceptualized and organized as an elective in the great majority of the nation's high schools. Principals and other staff, focused on issues internal to school life, feel compelled to keep the outside world at bay. Even counselors are ill-equipped to help young people with vocationally oriented support needs.

Yet schools are a central developmental institution, and some important developmental tasks are vocational, in the broad sense of the word. It makes sense that they should play a central role helping young people with such tasks and try to be at least somewhat responsive to the labor market and trends in work. Work will form an important part of many young people's identities, connecting them to the public world and giving them a place in it. As a practical matter, some two-thirds of young people (100 percent of nongraduates, 50 percent of graduates) will enter the labor force on leaving high school. These young people urgently need support throughout their high school years to plan and prepare for this eventuality. In a complementary vein, most of the six million employers in the United States are small and locally operated. For example, 90 percent of manufacturing companies have fewer than a hundred employees. As Dan Swinney notes, such companies "don't have the global options of larger companies. They don't have the reserves and expertise to have extensive remedial education programs for incoming employees. They literally depend on a competent public education system for survival."[23]

In large urban school systems especially, historic commitments to a strong set of vocational options have atrophied. In one recent case, a leading manufacturing firm in Chicago, frustrated by the public schools' unwillingness "to re-instate the manufacturing-related vocational pro-grams it has terminated over the years," forged its own relationships with two high schools to arrange for work-based learning experiences and re-new a pipeline into entry-level technician positions."[24] Even when techni-cal concentrations are available, choosing or being encouraged to choose one continues to be seen as more stigmatizing to youth of color than to their white peers, a sign of a lack of academic ability.[25] Rather than view-ing applied learning experiences, such as those characteristic of CTE, as a basic framework for nurturing motivation, most school authorities view such experiences as a vehicle for rekindling interest in the very standard curriculum that is so unmotivating to many youth.

High school curricula and learning standards reify a narrow band of disciplines, even as it is clear that young people are heterogeneous in strengths and interests, that knowledge itself is heterogeneous, and that our culture is made up of a wide range of roles, fields, and disciplines. Although some 60 percent of comprehensive high schools offer "specific labor market preparation in at least one program area," that is not saying very much, given that there are scores of occupational areas and hundreds of occupation types.[26] High school curricula and pedagogy sometimes acknowledge, but rarely attend deliberately, to the noncognitive skills that employers argue are important to success in work, skills that happen to be equally critical for success in college.[27] Learning remains locked in classrooms, even though most knowledge and skill in life is used outside of them.

High school educators know little about the fates of their graduates and nongraduates. High schools provide little vocational information to the sizable number of youth who will enter the labor force on leaving high school not only because their staff are ill equipped to do so but because educators view this outcome as a negative one. There is no parallel for workplaces to the well-developed networks that link high schools to col-lege admissions offices.[28] Young people are not helped to understand what a first job means, how, for example, it often serves as a first of many steps into an occupational arena.

THE ARGUMENT FOR CTE

Career and technical education provides an obvious foundation for high school to attend more directly and fully to vocational concerns (in the deep, historic sense of the word). As a bonus, its defining attributes are consistent with what the learning sciences tell us about the attributes of good learning experiences and settings, especially for middle adolescents. For instance, learning in CTE is multidimensional: there are different kinds of thinking hard, applying knowledge, being creative in approaching tasks and problems. As Rose observes, "Blended with the cognitive and technical [demands may be] craft values, ethical concerns and acsthetics."[29] Learning in CTE involves all the senses and new forms of attention—visualizing how a blueprint will look as a physical object, listening to the sounds of a machine to understand what is happening to a particular material, developing the right touch when using equipment. Learning tasks at times are characterized by the types of constraints and contingencies that are typical of adult worlds, such as the need to make inferences and decisions in the absence of full information.

A three-decade-long project to reconceptualize CTE has strengthened the field in a variety of ways that support its potential as a base for learning. This multifaceted project has broadened the ways in which CTE introduces young people to vocations and has refined and updated curricula, which derive more directly from the nature of tasks in the disciplines and fields involved. CTE has wrestled with the potential of and challenges in curriculum integration. It has brought in more teachers with industry experience, created a variety of connections to local community colleges, and forged links with employers for provision of apprenticeship-like experiences. The solidity of this project is such that CTE proponents have begun to argue that the range of new curricular and pedagogical approaches being adopted within CTE should be harnessed for broader high school reform efforts.

The curricular structure of CTE offers both depth and heterogeneity, helping young people find a home for learning and growth. It values knowledge and skill in a variety of domains, including those historically rooted in the trades. Especially when a CTE teacher knows that students will be going out to a work setting for part of their learning experience, that teacher will make sure those students are prepared. There will be no shortcuts, watered-down or oversimplified curriculum.

Participating in a CTE concentration gives young people a choice about their learning experiences in high school, and thus some control over those experiences. One observer finds evidence that young people "most suited to the technical track tend to gravitate towards that choice" and get more out of it and of schooling than they would otherwise.[30] CTE lends young people's learning coherence; in creating a distinctive pathway through high school, it creates a self-reinforcing set of experiences. One classroom-based or work-based learning experience provides resources for the next. At some point, this process helps young people begin to see (and feel) how what they are asked to learn connects to something in their futures. This has been described as introducing a measure of "vocational motive" to secondary education.[31]

Through its learning structures, CTE also gives young people opportunities to work on real tasks and problems in defined fields important to the broader culture. There is now abundant evidence that the "front-end model" of preparing young people for the demands of adulthood—abstract learning first, application much later—does not work well.[32] To challenge and revise mental structures, and especially to become part of the self, learning requires an active role for the learner and immersion in a particular social practice. CTE maps these requirements. Theory and practice are integrated. Young people have to use the concepts, principles, procedures, tools, and other physical artifacts that they are learning about to test their understanding and mastery. Especially as found in the workplace, vocational knowledge is contingent, action oriented, and heuristic.

At its best, CTE begins to move young people out of the classroom and into the world at large. It provides opportunity for young people to learn about (and more selectively experience) the range of adult roles; the kinds of technical, scientific, artistic, social, and civic tasks that adults devote themselves to; the range of roles in particular vocational arenas.

It provides opportunity for young people to learn about work itself—the personal attributes required in work settings, the enormous range in kinds of work done, the distinct pleasures and difficulties of particular occupations, how people prepare for different kinds of jobs.

Deliberate exposure to work roles and to specific occupations during the high school years broadens and sharpens a young person's awareness of the wide range of occupations (and levels within them), their conception of what might be interesting, and their willingness to try out specific occupational domains. CTE can provide young people knowledge and experience that contribute to a broadened view of both themselves and the world. Some types of CTE experience, such as in-depth internships and preapprenticeships, provide a head start for youth into competitive technical fields.

Furthermore, CTE fosters personal and institutional connections between the school and other settings. Work-based learning helps situate what is learned in the classroom. Young people can see that classroom material pertains to something concrete outside of school. This alters the experience of school itself, too, helping young people feel connected to the larger world in some measure. CTE pulls in and provides organic roles for other stakeholders in young people's development as well. For example, in Illinois the state Department of Public Health has worked with the CTE community to determine what mixture of classroom and clinical learning experiences students need to become competent nursing assistants. In effect, CTE fosters distributed responsibility for "rigor" in high school learning experiences.

WAYS OF STRUCTURING CTE

The structure of career and technical education is more complex and multifaceted than that of the academic side of high school. It reflects the necessity of reaching out to employers, industry bodies, postsecondary institutions, and other nonschool stakeholders (often without formal sanction or adequate resources to do so). Among other tasks, CTE programs have to work with local employers to find work-based learning placements, with industry bodies to select and implement industry-specific assessments, and with community colleges to establish dual enrollment and dual credit options and to create recognizable pathways for various occupational areas.

Career and technical education is offered in about 9,500 comprehensive high schools nationwide (40 percent of all comprehensive high schools), 1,000 vocational/technical high schools, and 800 regional vocational centers. CTE in comprehensive high schools is typically restricted to two or three occupational domains and is defined as an elective rather than a concentration or major. Vocational-technical high schools and regional vocational centers, which are more likely to be located in suburban and rural areas, offer a greater range of occupational specialties and higher quality occupational instruction on average due to a more focused mission, better equipment and facilities, greater depth of relevant learning experiences, and closer connections to and greater recognition among local employers. Some regional vocational centers also provide postsecondary coursework through links to technical community colleges.

According to the Bureau of Labor Statistics, there are about one hundred thousand secondary-level CTE teachers in the United States, slightly under 10 percent of the total teaching workforce. CTE teachers have distinct certification requirements that increasingly include some prior industry experience. Newer teachers are more likely to have such experience than long-tenured peers, though there are many exceptions and older teachers do sometimes have valuable industry connections. For instance, a team of researchers offers the example of one criminal justice instructor with twenty-five years' experience as a police officer whose connections help get his students "in state police cars, sheriff's department cars, [with] city police, they work at 911 dispatch [and] district court."[33] In general, CTE teachers are more likely than non-CTE peers to have taken an alternative certification route and are, correspondingly, less likely to have specific preparation in secondary education. About half of all CTE faculty are certified/licensed as secondary education teachers. CTE faculty are also older on average than non-CTE peers, and older CTE faculty are generally less likely have bachelor's degrees.

States and localities vary widely in how they organize CTE and relate it to other academic programs. In suburbs and rural areas it is common to have freestanding vocational-technical centers and sometimes separate districts. Massachusetts, for example, has twenty-six stand-alone regional vocational-technical centers, each of which constitutes its own local district, with a school committee, superintendent, board, and so forth. Larger districts in Massachusetts, as in other states, commonly have their own vocational-technical high schools within the district. According to one study, CTE concentrators in Massachusetts devote half their instructional time to CTE coursework, a significantly higher percentage than students in other states and localities. Local school districts in many states pay a certain amount (e.g., $2,500) to vocational-technical centers for each student served, usually on a part-time basis.[34]

Career academies, a distinctive organizational form within CTE that can be found in both comprehensive high schools and vocational-technical high schools, embody a specific set of curricular and pedagogical elements in a specific occupational area (or career cluster). These elements include an articulated vocational sequence, integration of academic and vocational curriculum, work-based learning, and small learning communities. The career academy is designed to foster a sense of belonging and affinity, of being "known." Career academies emphasize teachers' responsibility for students' overall development and personal challenges. It is increasingly common for career academies to be geared toward local labor markets. For example, the Houston school district runs an academy focused on petroleum exploration and production technology.

It is also becoming more common for career academies to have industry partners. For example, Cisco, Microsoft, Adobe, IBM, and others have worked with school districts around the country to develop information technology–focused academies. In Franklin, Tennessee, a consortia that includes local high schools, a foundation, the workforce board, and community college has developed a 900-hour biomedical technology program (600 hours in the classroom, 300 in internship, begun during high school and completed in postsecondary) intended to serve local hospitals and a local biotechnology firm, Biomimetics Therapeutics. The program, based at two local Tennessee Technology Centers, provides dual credits to high school students as well as job shadowing and clinical internships.

Georgia has allowed (and promoted) a charter career academy model, the Central Education Center (CEC), that originated in one county as a partnership among local businesses, a community college, and the high school district.[35] The CEC model combines elements of the early college high school and the regional vocational-technical center. It is, typically, located within a local technical community college; focuses on three to five occupational areas; provides part-time study before or after the regular school day, using some community college faculty as well as CTE teachers; grants technical certificates in the relevant occupational areas (as endorsements on the regular high school diploma); and is overseen by an advisory committee comprised heavily of local employers.

Industry partners are playing a growing role in CTE, providing guidance on curriculum, guest speakers, job shadowing, internships, apprenticeships, and postsecondary opportunities. One example of this is ArcelorMittal, a large Indiana-based steel company, which has a Steelworker for the Future Program in northwest Indiana. Students begin with high school CTE coursework in welding, electrical, mechanical, and/or manufacturing, receiving dual credit at two participating community colleges, and then move into a two-and-a-half-year postsecondary craft training program for mechanical techs and electrical techs, with a continuing pathway into jobs at ArcelorMittal. Partners are particularly crucial to work-based learning, which remains all too rare within CTE in the United States. Rhetorical interest in youth apprenticeship stands in significant disproportion to practice; probably no more than 1 or 2 percent of high school youth have an apprenticeship experience.[36]

A growing number of local CTE programs have connections to postsecondary institutions, a promising development given the erratic history of prior efforts to forge such connections. One typical example is Lakeview High School in Wisconsin, which partners (and shares some facilities) with nearby Gateway Technical College to provide dual-credit programs taken on the college campus, with graduating students then able to continue with a course of study at Gateway. A handful of states (e.g., Florida and South Carolina) are also working to develop statewide structures linking CTE to community college systems.

Practice in the CTE field relies on a variety of types of intermediaries. For example, the National Academy Foundation is an intermediary for career academies. Its membership includes five hundred academies as part of a network with common curricula in finance, engineering, hospitality, tourism, and information technology. Local businesses linked to schools through NAF act as partners for job shadowing, internships, and guest speakers. The Southern Region Education Board's Technology Centers That Work initiative provides support to stand-alone vocational-technical centers. Project Lead the Way is a well-known curriculum intermediary, with a comprehensive three-year preengineering curriculum. Many specific industries have developed curricula for use in both high schools and technical community colleges. There are also intermediaries that focus on both industry-related assessment and certification and generic work readiness or employability skills.

Local or regional CTE systems that include apprenticeships may have some kind of body that convenes stakeholders and structures the experience. A handful of youth apprenticeship initiatives are industry driven, with ties to high school vocational programs throughout a city or region. One well-known example is the longstanding (but recently terminated) Craftsmanship program in Tulsa, Oklahoma, where students participated in a three-year metalworking apprenticeship beginning either their junior or senior year, with time split between the Tulsa Tech Center, Tulsa Community College and a selected employer. The curriculum was developed by the partners and included a pathway leading to an associate degree in applied sciences. The Craftsmanship program was structured as a partnership including the public schools, the local technical training center, community colleges, the chamber of commerce, and local manufacturing council and had a number of employers as industry partners.

A similar model is MECHTECH USA, an intermediary that has forged working relationships among school systems, community colleges, unions, and a consortium of manufacturers in Connecticut, Massachusetts, and

Rhode Island with the goal of placing high school students in apprentice-ships in the machining and tooling professions. It coordinates among educational institutions to create a defined course sequence beginning in high school and continuing into community college (physics, math, technical writing, CNC, CAD, CAM, etc.) and oversees young people's careful rotation (in six-to-eight-month cycles) through the many small shops that make up this field. The apprenticeship is designed to lead to a journey worker certificate and an associate degree in mechanical engineering.

LEARNING IN CTE: CURRICULUM AND PEDAGOGY

The structure of learning in CTE, both curriculum and pedagogy, reflects assumptions that differ from those prevailing in academic high school coursework. In an immediate sense, CTE curriculum and pedagogy have always been distinct in their openness to influences from outside of schooling—from industries, occupational fields, local economies, apprenticeship programs, and other training approaches. For instance, in the Franklin, Tennessee, biotechnology program a variety of partners, including the eventual employers of graduates, shaped a rich but practical curriculum that included Biomedical Applications, Scientific Research, Laboratory Assistant Skills, Basic Pharmacy, Monitoring and Informatics courses.

In CTE learning there is a match "between the nature of competence and the process by which it is acquired, shared and extended."[37] The discipline or field, combined with the tasks at hand and the setting itself, provide ingredients for learning. These include specialized language, norms, practices, and tools of the discipline and its customs, traditions, distinct products, and performances.

Early learning stages often focus on care, precision, and safety in tool use, in which students must be certified as mastered before they can move on within a course sequence. McNeill describes a medical careers academy in which freshman are brought into the world they will be inhabiting for four years through an Introduction to Med Lab Skills Course. In the course they immediately start working with instruments and equipment, with the initial goals "centered on precision and care, on following precise directions, on learning to make accurate written notes [and on] taking pride in completeness and accuracy." This serves also as a springboard to a subsequent course in which students are introduced to the math and science involved in the particular work: "Teaching for understanding of the science content [underlying lab procedures] came only after . . . weeks and weeks of learning to observe and to write observations clearly and accurately." Initial lab courses serve as a foundation for anatomy, physiology, and other more complex material, added in layers.[38]

At its best, CTE provides a set of mutually reinforcing components: specialized classroom experiences, school-based labs or workshops, carefully staged work-based learning opportunities. As Amy Ryken puts it, "Knowledge and experience [acquired] in one component take on value and new meaning when connected to activities in other components."[39] Each experience builds on the next to multiply opportunities. For instance, a young person learns basic lab skills in his high school biotechnology class and lists them in his application for an internship, where he learns more advanced lab skills and industry procedures, both of which contribute to acceptance in a competitive community college biotech program. Young people also have multiple opportunities to acquire and deepen understanding.[40]

Curriculum

Curricular philosophy and practice in CTE have evolved considerably over the past three decades. Current thinking is reflected in the fourth iteration of the Carl Perkins Career and Technical Education Act (Perkins IV), which emphasizes a broad, phased introduction to a specific industry ("career cluster"), integration of academic and vocational coursework, provision of direct experience in an industry (work-based learning), industry-recognized certification of competencies, and creation of pathways through secondary and from secondary to postsecondary education.

State education departments, industry bodies, individual companies (especially in the information technology field), and a variety of intermediaries have been active in curriculum renewal and development.

Curriculum in such traditional fields as electrical, machining, auto maintenance and repair, agriculture, and criminal justice have been updated, and many new occupational areas have been introduced, among them engineering, medical technology, natural resources, computer programming, and Web site design. Some curriculum development work has been tied to industry skills standards and certification, some also to postsecondary curriculum in the associated fields. Reflecting substantive changes in traditional fields and the inclusion of new ones, CTE curricula now include more theory and conceptual material than they did in the past.

The introduction of the career cluster concept and the delineation of sixteen career clusters have helped create an appropriate balance between conveying the specificity of occupations and the fluidity of broad occupational fields (e.g., health science/medical technology, building/environmental design, engineering, arts, media/entertainment, public service, law/justice, etc.). The clusters, now linked to the newer concept of programs of study, have created bounded terrain for the development of coherent sequences of coursework (academic and applied) leading through high school into postsecondary study and, in turn, to industry-recognized credentials. As a map of a broad occupational field, a career cluster demonstrates to young people where specific occupations fit vertically and horizontally in career progressions and neighboring fields. It helps young people see that occupational roles are dynamic, that there is often a progression from entry-level to semi-skilled and skilled technical work.

There continues to be some disagreement over whether it is more helpful to young people to build understanding and mastery by gradually adding new skill subsets, providing small amounts of conceptual material tied to those discrete skills (tasks), or to take a "systems" approach, introducing big ideas, central concepts, and procedures and then working on smaller branches. The growing role of certification for industry has led increasingly to the former approach, because it is easier to certify competence step by step in discrete skill clusters. For example, an auto technology student learning to maintain and repair brakes and hydraulic systems may have thirty or more tasks to master using the National Automotive

Technician Educational Foundation "Hands On Competency Checklist." Understanding principles and concepts is taught as a corollary to work on operational tasks.

CTE in the United States is just beginning to incorporate the idea (common in European vocational-technical programs) that learning to practice a particular vocation involves much more than learning a discrete set of skills. Rather, it involves mastering that vocation in its entirety as a particular form of social practice. CTE is also just beginning to recognize and attend to "work process knowledge," which is defined as an "understanding of the whole work process including preparation, action, control and evaluation."[41]

Curriculum integration—infusing CTE classes with academic curricular content and academic classes with CTE content—is very slowly finding a place as a component of CTE practice. Proponents, mostly from the CTE field, argue that curriculum integration is a means of deepening vocational curricula and simultaneously motivating students to learn in fields like math, in which motivation and engagement are low. It is also a vehicle for helping learners move back and forth between abstract principle (or formula) and specific problems in specific contexts—in other words, taking what is learned on one problem or in one context and seeing its relevance to another problem or context.[42] Both the rationale for and the practice of curriculum integration remain lopsided. For example, although proponents argue that most occupational fields require math or science or good writing skills, there is little argument that most academic subjects in high school require applied or technical knowledge and skill. Even the most seemingly hands-on occupational domains, such as automotive technology, are rich with concepts, principles drawn from specific scientific fields, and cognitive demands.

The focus and depth of integration initiatives vary, from tailoring readings, class discussions, writing assignments, and learning problems to joint planning between CTE and non-CTE faculty and to full-fledged team-teaching. In a handful of schools around the country, curriculum integration has included use of a common pedagogical approach across the high school curriculum, such as design-based, project-based, or problem-based learning. Examples of curriculum integration in the literature sometimes seem forced or shallow and sometimes more organic. One study provides an example of a tailored assignment in which the teacher in an economics class asks students to use their placement experience in a hospital to discuss the positive and negative effects of specialization and division of labor on productivity in that work setting.[43] In a more substantive example, another study describes an agricultural academy in a comprehensive high school in Kentucky in which teachers used the curricula tied to the greenhouse and aquaculture center environments to reinforce complex math (e.g., logarithms), science (e.g., anatomy), and social studies. For example, a team of teachers from horticulture and government interwove material on government regulatory structures and processes, including risk assessment, cost-benefit analysis, and legislation.[44]

In a further example, Stone and colleagues describe an initiative in which CTE teachers from six occupational areas were paired with math teachers with the goal of identifying math concepts embedded in CTE curricula (e.g., number relations, numerical estimation, probability, algebraic functions, geometric formulas, etc.) and then developing lessons that CTE teachers could incorporate that would provide explicit practice in these concepts. The premise in this initiative was, in part, that use of "authentic situations serves to anchor the symbolic and abstract math in situations that are familiar and real to students." CTE teachers were encouraged to "take a moment to show their students the mathematical formula behind a problem so that when students saw that formula in other situations, including on standardized tests, they would remember the problems they had solved in the applied context." In an effort to simulate real world conditions, the teacher pairs worked together to create varied problem sets using the same mathematical principle. Students would also be given similar problems, in more abstract form, in their traditional math classes. (Students proved able to transfer knowledge and strategy from one applied problem to another but were less able to transfer from applied to abstract problems.)[45]

In general, the goal of curriculum integration remains more promise than actuality. It has proven difficult to implement curriculum integration in self-contained CTE settings such as regional vocational-technical centers. Where schools have made a serious, institutionwide commitment to it, the results have been very positive.[46] To work well, curriculum integration requires a clear schoolwide understanding of rationale and strategy, investment among academic faculty, and affordances for school staff, both time and mandate. In the math example, teacher teams developed curriculum maps to align math and CTE content. Math teachers provided long-term support to the CTE teachers, to strengthen knowledge and self-confidence and to help adapt math problems to widely varying math abilities in any CTE cohort. CTE teachers came away from the experience not just with deeper math knowledge but with a deeper understanding of their own curriculum and pedagogy. Math teachers came to understand CTE much better—for example, that the kinds of math application differ among occupations—and to appreciate CTE's strengths as a learning context.

A common theme among academic faculty in one multisite study of curriculum integration was initial skepticism, disdain for a perceived lack of rigor in CTE courses, and worry that curriculum integration would eat into already inadequate learning (and test preparation) time. With exposure to substantive occupational fields, academic faculty grew curious, more interested, and eventually appreciative of the dynamism and vitality that applied learning problems give to curricular material.[47]

Pedagogy

Learning and teaching in CTE are distinctive in purpose and method. They are partly about building theoretical and practical knowledge of the field at hand and partly about socialization into that field. Learning and practice are viewed in an integrated way. Concepts and factual information are often applied immediately, whether in the classroom or in a lab, workshop, kitchen, or other application setting. A common pattern of moving from the classroom to the lab or workshop, sometimes on the same day, makes students more attentive to the classroom lecture. One review finds, not surprisingly, that vocational classes are three times more likely (64 percent versus 21 percent) to ask students "to apply academic skills to tasks that might be found in a job or career."[48]

The distinct set of learning and vocational tasks, and often a physically distinct location, creates a strong learning community among CTE concentrators. Teachers encourage young people to work together, and it is common to see three or four youth gathered around a table or lab bench or automobile working together on a set of tasks. The common "work" appears to bind CTE students together and bridge social or other distinctions among youth. An African American medical academy student in California observed that "it is the work. I mean you can go and ask somebody else if you don't know the work, because people in the academy are into the health field and they are not too much concerned with all the racial issues that are going on in the school and world."[49]

In parallel to a distinctive learning framework, CTE has been found to use a variety of powerful instructional approaches, including modeling and demonstration, just-in-time teaching and feedback, assessment tied to everyday practice, problem-based learning, and team learning.[50] Mistakes are often corrected immediately—by an instructor, a peer, or the learner herself—rather than left as mistakes. Instruction seeks a balance between individual creativity and constraints, whether physical or task related. For example, "an auto instructor showed students several ways of repairing piston rings. At the same time, he stressed that an engine imposes its own limits: while there may be several different approaches, in the end the engine has to run correctly."[51]

CTE teachers tend to be aware that mastery in an occupational domain will require many kinds of abilities—visualization, spatial, manual, procedural, and manipulative skill; understanding of technical symbol systems (in diagrams or blueprints); and so forth. As such, vocational pedagogy is characterized by textual diversity: "conventional textbooks, instruction manuals, technical reference books of many kinds, invoices, spreadsheets, lab, police and media reports, rate guides, software documentation, blueprints, wiring diagrams and maps."[52]

Learning Outside of School

CTE is distinctive in its affordances for learning outside the walls of school. Approaches vary from locale to locale. Internships tend to be concentrated in the summer and/or during part of the senior year. Apprenticeships (or preapprenticeships) usually require a two-year commitment. Apprentices might work fifteen hours per week during the school year and full-time in the summer, or have a block schedule. In some apprenticeship programs young people are paid, in others they're not. Programs typically include some type of certification of competencies acquired. They may include complementary coursework, with both work hours and coursework credited toward high school graduation and postsecondary concentration in the same field at a community college. There might also be some crediting toward the hours required by union- or industry-sponsored apprenticeship programs.

Whether in intensive internships or apprenticeships, the workplace provides both a distinctive site for learning and a distinct kind of learning situation. This is where young people come to understand work as social practice and to build work process knowledge. A workplace is typically specific in terms of content and procedure and multidimensional in terms of the kinds of demands made on the young person. Workplaces introduce young people to "heuristics, work styles, and other situated understandings about materials, tools and techniques" in a field.[53] Work processes and tools themselves provide important feedback—measurements, readings, or physical feedback to the hand or eye. Process and products are "public" in important ways: learners' work on problems and tasks is observable by others in the work setting; feedback to/from others is easy to provide/receive.

Learning to manage oneself in a work setting, to be responsible, read situations, use feedback, know when to seek assistance can only be learned through direct experience. A work setting may present the young person with instructions that are not helpful enough, choices and directions that appear to conflict with each other. Young people begin to see what it will take to be successful at work. A biotechnology apprentice at a Bayer research and development lab who was invited to sit in on selected meetings reported that "sometimes the meetings were boring, but I got to see how people organize, bring notes to talk about their ideas and see other people's opinions."[54]

Apprenticeship is in many respects the strongest model of work-based learning, due to its duration, its structure (which provides for deepening involvement over time in core activities of the enterprise), and the responsibility on each side of the apprenticeship contract. In Stephen Hamilton's memorable phrase, the young person's role is "constructively ambiguous": part learner, part worker.[55] He joins in the work of the host enterprise, and adults in that enterprise simultaneously join the young person in his own personal "work." Both adult and youth are active. They share responsibility for the tasks to be accomplished and the products to be created, although each has a different role. The adult mentor is responsible for sharing his or her disciplinary knowledge and skills with youth. Youth are responsible for working hard to begin to become proficient at something specific and for contributing to the community they have joined.

All forms of work-based learning provide young people additional teachers and mentors. It is not uncommon for a small employer or unit of a larger one to informally "adopt" a young intern or apprentice as part of their work family. Work-site mentors recognize the young person as a learner and are more likely to explain the logic of the setting, why tasks are done the way they are, why people relate to others as they do, why certain tasks are or are not important. They are more likely to teach the small things critical to socialization within particular work settings, such as "the cultural significance of tools and tool maintenance . . . the rudiments of asking questions, seeking assistance, projecting a professional image."[56] Young people sometimes have opportunity to reflect on the nature of work itself with mentors, learning, for example, about being supervised, about when to ask for assistance and when to muddle through on one's own.

PARTICIPATION IN CTE: PATTERNS AND EFFECTS

A long-term decline in vocational course enrollment has slowed and, by some estimates, even been reversed. Some 15 percent of all coursework taken by high school students is categorized as CTE coursework, and two-thirds of that (or 10 percent of all high school coursework) is considered to have an occupational focus. The remainder is nonoccupational computer-related courses and some family and consumer sciences courses. The majority of students who take CTE courses use them as electives to round out their studies or as a means to experiment lightly with a particular occupational area.

The percentage of high school students considered "vocational concentrators," those completing a program of study in a specific occupational area, varies depending on definition, inclusion rules, and data source. (A prototypical concentrator takes CTE for one period a day during the sophomore year and two periods a day in the junior and senior years.) Rates reported for CTE concentration range from 10 to 20 percent, with most at the lower end of that range.[57] About 50 percent of CTE concentrators, somewhere between 5 and 10 percent of all high school students, are "dual concentrators," meaning that they are both concentrating in a vocational area and completing a "rigorous" academic course of study.[58] The most common occupational concentration is business support and management, followed in order of frequency by communication and design; agriculture and natural resources; manufacturing, repair, and transportation; consumer and culinary services; computer and information sciences; health sciences; business finance; engineering; construction and architecture.

It is difficult to determine young people's vocational intentions from their CTE course-taking patterns. Students who take courses in some areas—notably agriculture and natural resources, health fields, construction and architecture, and manufacturing—are more likely to be CTE concentrators than students who take coursework in others areas, such as business or information technology. Motivation to concentrate in CTE itself varies, from strong interest in a field, to lack of interest in high school coursework, to a perceived need to secure a job after graduating. Young people in large urban districts also fall into CTE concentrations by virtue of the high school application process. Applying to be a CTE concentrator (especially in a career academy) is sometimes the only route to acceptance at a particular high school. Once accepted to a high school, students sometimes select a CTE concentration simply to escape the negative atmosphere of the larger school.

All told, about a quarter of CTE concentrators continue focusing on that field either in college or through training and/or work.[59] As implied above, there are a number of reasons for this; but an important one is the lack of clear pathways beyond high school. A high school CTE concentration, even with some clinical experience, provides only the beginning steps into most occupations. It is best understood as a foundation and entryway to further study and/or training in that field, not a self-contained experience. Yet concentrators (and their teachers) often lack easily visible and manageable connections to next steps in local or regional colleges or formal apprenticeship systems. Two- and four-year-colleges prefer to start from scratch with students, even those who have had high school CTE coursework in one of a college's specialty areas. Many parts of the country have no unions, let alone union-sponsored apprenticeships.

CAPTURING THE EFFECTS OF PARTICIPATING IN CTE

Career and technical education programs across the country have become aware of the importance of capturing and certifying experience, knowledge, and skill acquired by young people in ways that address a policy context that is skeptical of it, in terms useful to potential employers, in a form that is portable, and in terms that allow for postsecondary credits in technical college programs. Employers uniformly report distrust of high school records due to grade inflation and because such records tell them little directly about the knowledge, skills, and dispositions they are looking for. Current standardized testing regimes "are designed with prediction [of college success], not skill and knowledge certification, as their primary goal."[60] Yet, in coming years close to half the workforce will need "some form of occupational certification, registration or licensure to perform their jobs."[61]

Stakeholders in schooling have not undertaken (or even considered) the same kind of national effort to elaborate an assessment approach for CTE as is under way for core subjects. Such an effort would require very different thinking, as well as different participants. Capturing what is learned in and through CTE, and the kinds of personal development attributable to it, are complicated. Collectively, the knowledge, skills, and dispositions acquired are heterogeneous. Within a discipline, knowledge and skill may be straightforward and easily measurable; indeed, they may be readily seen in practice. Alternatively, capturing knowledge and skill may require innovative approaches to assessment, such as creation of problem scenarios, unusual client requests, programming tasks, and so forth. Young people are acquiring field-specific knowledge, skills, heuristics, and judgment, such as visualizing, recognizing, and diagnosing problems with a machine, procedure, calculation, result, etc. The practical reasoning involved includes mental processes that may be less explicit but are still important to capture, as when deciding when to use and when to ignore rules of thumb or when solving a persistent problem by reverse engineering.

To differing degrees, young people are also acquiring a general ability to apply knowledge and work through problems, knowledge of the work world and of particular kinds of work settings. They are developing self-management and self-presentation skills, new modes of thought, social abilities, commitments, and self-knowledge. Those youth who have had a sustained work-based learning experience are acquiring work process knowledge, which encompasses operational skill and understanding, situational awareness, control of techniques, equipment and other workplace resources, and understanding and mastery of the workplace itself.[62]

Measurement challenges derive both from the multifaceted nature of what is learned and acquired and the embedded nature of it. To an extent, practical knowledge becomes embodied or incorporated into actions. Martin Fischer notes, for example, that "experience of the proper functioning of a machine's clutch" may be difficult to verbalize, since it is a compilation of sensory impressions.[63] Growth of expertise in a discipline or occupation is nonlinear; it has branches and sometimes many dimensions. In many fields, competence reflects a mixture of knowledge of principle, content knowledge, and practice or performance under work-like conditions. In other words, vocational competence is conditional. It is also relational, involving the relationship among an individual's abilities, a particular task, and a particular setting.[64]

EMERGENT ASSESSMENT APPROACHES

Although much of the work of capturing the benefits of participation in CTE remains to be done, states and local school districts have begun to take this work seriously. They have begun incorporating industry-specific standards and certification-of-competence assessments into their CTE programs. In some cases this has meant working toward program as well as student certification. Those who design and sponsor credentialing systems for specific trades or industries are themselves gradually coming to understand high school CTE as relevant to their work. Many of the industry bodies that have developed national skills standards and credentialing systems have begun to adapt this work to high school CTE. (In 1998 the U.S. Department of Labor empowered a National Skills Standards Board to develop standards in the sixteen career cluster domains. The Bush administration terminated this effort in 2002.)

Knowledge and skill standards may be broad, as in advanced manufacturing, or relatively specific, as in nano- and microtechnology. Information technology companies such as Cisco, Microsoft, and Adobe include assessment protocols and certifications tied to their high school curricula. For example, after completing a two-year course sequence in networking, students can take the Cisco Certified Networking Associate exam. The National Institute of Metal-Working Skills has begun to be more active in the high school arena, as have health-care occupations, such as nursing through Certified Nursing Assistant credentialing. Many occupational fields, like criminal justice, accounting, and agriculture, work through such testing intermediaries as the National Occupational Competency Testing Institute.

Most assessments use paper-and-pencil or computer-based formats, with basic concepts, vocabulary, and specific problems, tasks, and scenarios to be recognized and addressed. From employers' perspectives, written assessments can screen job applicants in or out but do not ensure that students can apply theory, principles, and procedural knowledge to actual practice. Some assessment systems therefore include a performance-based component that draws on a sample of actual work tasks and uses volunteers from industry serving as juries. Many assessment frameworks are leveled and/or allow for step-by-step certification of knowledge/skill clusters within a broader occupation. Classroom teachers may also have a role in certifying skills mastered using a checklist type of format.

Efforts to capture the growth that occurs in work-based learning, using mentors and others in workplace settings to certify experience and competencies acquired, are few and far between. Wisconsin's Youth Apprenticeship Program provides an exception, relying fully on workplace mentors to assess and certify young people's growth using checklists developed by industry representatives working with educators. In a related vein, few, if any, assessment schemes capture deepening expertise in particular occupational domains (within the limited timeframe for growth afforded by even the most substantive work-based learning experiences)—that is, the progression from procedural skills to strategic thinking, the creative use of a technology, the solving of problems in innovative ways, and developing the ability to cope with unexpected events and contingencies.

General Skills

Starting with SCANS (Secretary's Commission on Achieving Necessary Skills) in the early 1990s, there have been numerous efforts to define generic workplace (or work readiness or employability) skills. In parallel, there have been a growing number of work readiness measures using a range of assessment procedures: responding to questions or simulated scenarios on a computer screen and, less commonly, performance assessment using work tasks or scenarios or rating by a knowledgeable adult. The most popular measure currently in use, WorkKeys, has been adapted for and linked with the National Career Readiness Certificate, which is issued by a number of state workforce agencies.

Generic skills frameworks typically begin with both basic and technical literacy and numeracy, such as reading for information (manuals, instructions, etc.); interpreting graphs, charts, and simple gauges; using mathematical formulas; and so forth. They may also ask the test-taker to rate herself on a range of social and behavioral variables thought to be attractive to employers: whether she likes working with others, maintains composure in stressful situations, enjoys solving difficult problems, has a positive outlook, thinks and plans carefully, generally likes other people, and so forth.

There are a few central criticisms of generic work readiness as a concept as well as a variety of concerns about the approaches used to measure it. One asks whether, beyond a handful of basic requirements, there is such a thing as generic skills outside of specific contexts or learning/practice situations. It is clearly helpful to discern who can read for information or understand graphs and charts and who self-reports that they enjoy working with others. But many seemingly generic skills like critical thinking and problem solving take different forms in different fields and are developed gradually with experience.[65] Communication skills are at least partly setting specific, as are such social skills as the ability to read a situation. Important personal attributes or traits like extroversion/introversion, conscientiousness, and openness may or may not be measurable, but do they carry different valence in different kinds of work settings.

Most generic work readiness skills relate only modestly to job retention and progression. In general, it is difficult to measure and even more to predict who will come to be a valued employee, who will have greater or lesser capacity to cope with the opportunities, or what the ambiguities of practice might be in a particular field.[66] The process of growing into a job, or not doing so, involves scores of unpredictable variables, some of which reside in the workplace itself. Capability and motivation interact in complex ways. Young people may bring life experiences that seem complicating but may prove invaluable. Employers, who distrust high school transcripts, also tend to distrust paper-and-pencil measures of employability skills and look instead for experiences such as apprenticeships that signal the acquisition of specific, substantive skills relevant to their workplace. Tests may be efficient and inexpensive, and take only a few hours to complete, but they are no substitute for what is learned by watching an apprentice at work over many months.

LITERATURE ON THE BENEFITS OF CTE PARTICIPATION

Given the emergent state of formal competency assessment in the CTE field, there is still a variety of kinds of evidence about how participation benefits young people. That evidence is mixed with respect to schooling-focused policy variables, more uniformly positive with respect to a range of domains that are not usually considered in policy analyses of schooling. Almost all the effects of CTE participation are magnified when young people have sustained work-based learning experiences. Such experiences, in the form of in-depth internships and apprenticeships, have a range of distinctive effects on technical knowledge and skills, knowledge of specific occupations, understanding of work, problem-solving abilities, and self-knowledge and identity.[67]

Evidence of benefits for academic progress from taking a CTE concentration is largely positive; though evidence of benefits for achievement as measured by grades and test scores is more equivocal. For some youth, taking a vocational concentration increases the likelihood of completing "a rigorous academic core."[68] The demands of CTE courses appear to "prime" young people for related math and science courses.[69] Studies have found that CTE concentrators, especially boys, are more likely than similarly situated peers to persist and graduate from high school.[70] Taking a vocational concentration leads some youth to reevaluate how they are approaching high school. They may come to think more closely about what it might take to pursue particular disciplines or careers and how much they still have to learn. For the most vulnerable youth, completing a CTE concentration provides stronger, more enduring personal and labor market benefits than second-chance job training programs.[71]

CTE concentrators tend to develop more specific postsecondary plans than their peers in general education. As former program director and CTE scholar Amy Ryken notes, "By participating in these experiences students come to understand that they actually have educational and career decisions to make."[72] CTE concentrators are more likely than their peers to choose a technical or two-year postsecondary pathway, although not always in the same field as studied in high school. They are more likely to follow through on any plans made and to persist with postsecondary studies.[73] Responding to, and gradually internalizing, the demands of work-based learning especially primes young people to get a lot out of both further studies and early work experiences.

Within a developmental frame, participating in a vocational concentration, especially when it includes work-based learning, adds structure to a young person's experience of middle adolescence. It provides some young people a kind of home base for learning and growth, and it seems to organize and focus them. Concentrators convey a sense that they know where they are and where they stand in the learning process. They acquire a sense of ownership and responsibility for their learning and concrete reasons to learn specific material in the classroom. A biotechnology concentrator tells Ryken, "If I were to have fallen behind in my math class, then I may have messed up with the math part of my biotech class."[74] That student is worried that lack of progress in classroom work would impede work-based learning opportunities. For some youth, a CTE concentration begins to alter their sense of who they are. A young woman taking the first steps toward nursing noted how "you tend to establish a whole new identity at the careers center."[75]

The Distinctive Value of Work-Based Learning

Workplace learning experiences are particularly rich cognitively, affectively, interpersonally, and, often, physically. As described earlier, almost every demand and dynamic is new. Young people begin to think differently, more strategically and contingently. They learn to reason more flexibly and to make inferences "even in the absence of full information."[76] They learn to use past experience as a guide, to muddle through and persist, to step back and take another look, to change their angle of attack. They learn to work with care. As a biotechnology apprentice puts it, "GLPs [good laboratory practices] are long and boring, but they are essential in making sure the rack studies go smoothly."[77] Young people have the opportunity to—and they have to learn how to—work through a problem or practice a skill until they get it right. For instance, reflecting on his students' biotechnology apprenticeships, a high school teacher observes that they "do things over and over again. It forces them to reach a standard, more so than I can do in the classroom."[78]

Young people get to learn about and sometimes try out different roles in a particular kind of work setting, gaining a deeper sense of which roles might suit them. Adults in the workplace might share their own professional experiences, giving young people a more specific sense of what it is like to work in that field. Youth who have more expansive work-based learning experiences begin to acquire the particular identity that accompanies a trade or profession, including interpersonal styles and ways of acting and looking. As one develops knowledge and skill in a discipline, one can pose questions and act on them more fully, which in turn brings them more fully into that discipline.

An occupational identity, however partial and temporary, provides an anchor for broader identity work. Apprenticeships especially help in this regard. Being an apprentice, and being recognized as one, counters some of the stigma associated with the vocational-technical route through school. Youth of color, in particular, may still worry about discrimination, but as they get involved in a field and are challenged and accepted by adult professionals based on their work itself, this tempers inhibitions related to such worry. Reflecting on his workplace experience, a young Latino enrolled in a medical academy program commented, "I'm sure I'll find racism and financial difficulty, but race is no excuse."[79]

Work-based learning provides an array of both broad and very particular "meta lessons" about work, workplaces, and vocations. Young people learn that tasks and problems in work settings are rarely as neatly defined as those in the classroom. There is—there has to be—more unpredictability in the "correct" outcome of work on a learning/producing problem than is usually found in school. Describing his experience in an auto repair internship, one young man notes that although he had read about how to do a brake job, "step by step," the manual did not "show you what to do if the bolt's rung off or . . . rusted up . . . it makes the repair a whole lot more difficult. And you have to learn through somebody else's experience."[80]

Young people develop a deepened understanding of what work is and what it means, its rhythms, its distinct pleasures and difficulties. They might learn that there are different kinds of days at work—good and bad, faster and slower, rougher and smoother. They might learn about teamwork; for example, a young person interning as an operating room assistant, observing surgeons, nurses, and anesthesiologists, sees in a visceral way what it means for people with different roles to organize themselves around a common goal.[81] Young people learn that almost any field is deeper than it seems from the outside, and a field that may have seemed mundane has many elements that make it interesting to consider.

Work-based learning has been found to increase young people's social capital, in particular sources of support and connection to postsecondary options and continuing work opportunities. Local employers appreciate young people who demonstrate their commitment to a trade by undertaking a sustained work-based learning activity. Internship and apprenticeship sponsors come to know individual young people and make them part of that work family. In the Wisconsin Youth Apprenticeship Program two-thirds of participants continued to work at their host enterprises, either full-time or during summers or part-time as they pursued postsecondary study.

CTE experiences in general give young people a more accurate temporal map, including steps and timeframe for working toward particular occupational goals. Conversations with mentors help young people better understand the pathway to postsecondary study or work in a particular field or discipline. Mentors can help young people align ambitions and, when appropriate, to better understand, think through, and plan for the mix of formal and nonformal learning and work experiences they will need to prepare for specific occupations.[82] As young people come to understand the work that one needs to do to join a discipline or accomplish a particular goal, they can compare that to what they have been doing and plan to do in their educational lives. Applied tasks that draw on academic skills help young people understand more clearly why and how academic knowledge is useful, that such knowledge is not just an arbitrary imposition of adults on young people.

Especially those experiences that include work-based learning provide the young person a basis for more detailed and accurate basis for self-appraisal and judgment of personal capabilities. Such experiences help young people see and feel that postsecondary choices have to fit who they are and, conversely, that one does not have to conform to expectations that do not feel right. They provide expanded but also more accurate and grounded reference points for aspirations. They ground thinking about the future that may be fanciful or impulsive or simplistic: either college or a dead-end job—neither of which may appeal to a young person. As a whole, CTE experiences give young people a more generous and concrete sense of possibilities while also helping them develop a sense of personal limits, to understand that one cannot be or do everything in the world. The result for at least some participating youth is a sense of personal competence, a grounded sense of integrity.[83] What they experience and acquire through CTE provides a solid piece to an otherwise fluid identity development process. A young person knowing that she has committed to and worked at something, coped with difficult tasks and both failed and succeeded at them changes the way she approaches subsequent tasks, considers options, and relates to others who have committed themselves to a particular pursuit.

CHALLENGES FACING CAREER AND TECHNICAL EDUCATION

We cannot continue to remain trapped between a resistance to vocationalism, based on its history in our schools, and our recognition of its developmental and social importance. The vocational is, obviously, about occupations and work. It is often technical in nature. But it is also about a home for learning and growth and for exploring identity. Proponents of CTE have been much clearer about the former than the latter. CTE needs to continue to articulate how it understands young people and their learning needs. Proponents must map the distinct strengths of CTE, such as applied learning and heterogeneous content, onto the developmental needs and tasks of young people and the larger need for cultural renewal.

CTE (more, ironically, than academic studies in high school) has to be flexible, nimble, cooperative, and patently useful to youth, their parents, and their employers.

Americans appear ambivalent at best about both the role and appropriateness of technical training and the idea that young people are making career choices by participating in CTE. The value of applied, vocationally oriented learning experiences for young people who are unsure about vocational interests especially has to be clarified. What options, if any, are foreclosed when a young person chooses a CTE concentration? Why would very specific, in-depth learning experiences in an occupational area be as useful to young people as general academic learning?

There is, in fact, evidence, that such experiences provide useful a foundation for broader understandings of many kinds. Participating in CTE helps young people see that the adult world is full of variety and texture; it illustrates the richness of culture and possible of ways of contributing. Yet the CTE community itself is hedging its commitment to depth, one reason for the shift to a "new vocationalism," which posits that CTE should be oriented more toward career exploration, basic understanding of broad occupational areas, and development of generic, foundational work skills than toward development of very specific occupational skills.

The principle, and value, of heterogeneity is just as important as that of specificity and depth. Like academic curricula, CTE embodies important cultural material and offers a source of identity for some young people. More than academic curricula, however, it recognizes and values heterogeneity in both young people and in cultural endeavor. When we bring work-related material into schooling, we are fostering democracy in a very particular kind of way by reminding young people of the heterogeneity of the local and national community and of our common endeavor, and the possibility of contributing to society in different ways. A variety of voices, from different points on the ideological spectrum, note the importance of such heterogeneity. These observers argue for the need to value a diverse set of pathways and end points. If we diversify high school education at its core, we decrease the risk of some youth being pushed to the periphery, or pushed out altogether.[84] Rethinking the core has all kinds of implications for pedagogy, standardization and breadth of curriculum, time use, and so forth. It also implies that CTE cannot be separated out, treated as a distinct part of the curriculum. CTE classes cannot be a separate part of young people's learning day, unrelated to every other class or subject in school.

Although CTE is gradually becoming a positive, rather than a default, choice for young people, the historic tendency among educational teachers and administrators to view it as a means of reengaging already disengaged students has yet to change. (A good example is how under state law in California half the students in career academies, called Partnership Academies, must be "at risk" due to underachievement, poor school attendance, disinterest in school, or family economic hardship.) If CTE is going to provide serious, substantive pathways for more than a handful of young people it cannot be a sideshow, isolated from the larger currents of schooling. It has to be normative, an important component in a coherent system that ties curriculum together inside school and ties young people's learning experiences together across settings. The whole teaching faculty, throughout a high school, will have to understand goals and roles differently, and there has to be a clear reason for such change.

Some proponents argue that, for both theoretical and practical reasons, the best approach to strengthening the role of CTE is to fully integrate it into all high school learning, in effect making CTE disappear as a distinct option. A career focus would be present, but in the background. Theodore Lewis, worrying that heterogeneity inevitably leads to hierarchy, argues forcefully for a "unitary curriculum" for all young people.[85] Other scholars argue for CTE's distinct identity and importance as both a type of learning experience and a foundation for strengthening the economy. They view CTE's distinct identity as a strength to be built on. Still others emphasize CTE's unfinished project of reinventing itself. In fact, changes in CTE have not yet found their way to the majority of large urban school districts. Reasons for this include the difficulty of altering entrenched practices in large bureaucracies and the fact that urban districts tend to have a very full reform agenda combining many kinds of curricular and school redesign initiatives. School reform stakeholder groups in urban districts also are especially likely to have ambivalent or negative views of CTE due to perceptions of its historic role in perpetuating class- and race-based sorting of young people.

ENSURING SPACE FOR CTE IN THE HIGH SCHOOL CURRICULUM

The purpose, structure, and place of CTE in high school education remains poorly understood, even among stakeholders supportive of it. As noted earlier, the core curriculum of American high schools remains unchanged. The principle change that has occurred—an increase in the number of academic courses required for graduation—has left CTE staff and others who support CTE feeling boxed in. Katherine Oliver, a senior education official from Maryland, notes that a lack of uptake for CTE in her state is due to "pressures being placed on students to take more academic courses."[86] James Stone, director of the National Research Center for Career and Technical Education, observes that the school day is "a zero sum game," with applied learning often losing badly.

Young people need a lot of learning time in career and technical education, far more than most are now spending in it. Erica Swinney of Austin Polytechnical High School in Chicago, which focuses on advanced manufacturing, observes that the more time young people spend in the program the more they see the personal and tangible value of it. Interest grows with experience and skill. Young people also begin to see the logic of the program elements and competencies.[87] The varied benefits for CTE participation do not accrue in a linear way but instead appear to be somewhat backloaded, multiplying with both length and depth of involvement.

One modest approach to addressing the time problem would be to give core academic, as opposed to elective, credit to students taking CTE courses and having work-based learning experiences with content comparable to that in related academic courses. For example, students taking Medical Anatomy and Physiology could receive credit for meeting high school science requirements. To make this approach viable, CTE and academic teachers have to tend to the task of elaborating and deepening vocational knowledge. Though learning in CTE is potentially rich and complex, it requires "special pedagogical conditions" to make it so, conditions that are often difficult to achieve in either school or the workplace.[88]

Curriculum Integration

Curriculum integration is supposed to be an important vehicle for strengthening both the academic and the vocational curriculum. However, it has tended to be a one-way process focused on the value of bringing academic content into CTE curricula rather than on "the actual or potential cognitive content of vocational education and the work from which it draws."[89] In that light, curriculum integration has been pursued more actively, if still ambivalently, by the CTE community than by academic departments within high schools. A national curriculum integration work group notes that "the field of CTE is attempting not just to integrate curriculum but also to re-connect educational traditions that have historically been legislated and funded to operate separately."[90]

A different kind of curriculum integration, between school and work-based learning, is maybe even more difficult to achieve than between academic and vocational learning. Young people typically report little connection between the two. Work sites do not ask or expect young people to bring what they are learning at school to their tasks at work; and school-based staff often know little about work processes and work tasks in various industries. What young people learn in work-based learning experiences does not seem to transfer to school tasks. For example, the math that students learn to use in the workplace often "does not appear to transfer to paper and pencil tests," in part because the principles remain implicit, in part because no one helps young people see any correspondence.[91] More generally, the world of work remains an untapped source of curricular material in many disciplines, including English, history, and economics.

Integrating Theoretical and Practical Knowledge

It has proven challenging to develop CTE curricula that integrate theoretical and practical material, although there are good examples of effective integration. One example is Project Lead the Way's preengineering curriculum, which is full of math and physics, some chemistry, and (especially in the textbooks) history, economics, and other subjects and has a rich and interesting vocabulary. In general, vocational knowledge tends to be treated in curriculum as primarily procedural, operational (e.g., naming, learning the purposes and uses of specific tools, differentiating between techniques, diagnosing problems, trouble-shooting, etc.). Instructors' questions are more likely to focus on procedures, rules of thumb, and conventions than on underlying concepts and basic assumptions.[92] Daily learning experiences are still too dominated by task lists. The practical thrust of much CTE is inevitable. For example, one study of a biotechnology initiative pointed out how much basic procedure has to be introduced and mastered in the high school lab to ready young people for work in the field: "pipetting/micropipette, streaking, asceptic technique, making media, pout plates, DNA extraction."[93]

MATCHING YOUNG PEOPLE TO A PATHWAY

As I've noted throughout this chapter, the labor market has become more complex and fluid, with traditional occupations changing and scores of new ones appearing. The most appropriate starting points and pathways into both old and new occupations are less clear. Some argue that structures like career academies, which lock young people into a defined course sequence in one occupational area, are ill matched both to developmental needs and labor market characteristics. And postsecondary education itself is in some flux, with traditional technical programs disappearing or changing form and many new programs emerging. Altogether, the process of matching young people to a constructive high school pathway, which was never straightforward, is now even less so.

Ideally, young people need a staged introduction to specific fields about which they are curious or in which they think they have interest. That would include direct exposure (through film and site visits) to a set of related occupations, to a sense of curricular content and demands, and to the opportunity to talk with older youth concentrating in that field. Preparation aside, different occupations require very different personal qualities and capacities. Current paper-and-pencil tests like those supplied to schools by ACT provide only the most general start to what is a very complex process that has to include close observation by teachers and a sequence of workplace activities.

The Association for Career and Technical Education has fretted in reports and public comments about lack of resources for the school-based counseling needed to help young people better understand options and the steps from one experience to the next. Young people increasingly have access to visual representations, such as those provided through career clusters diagrams that show how sets of jobs are linked and the educational paths leading to a job cluster. But many young people, and their parents, will not fully understand how to use such resources for planning and choosing a course of study. Middle school teachers and counselors, many of whom have outdated and inaccurate understandings of CTE in their own districts, especially have to be encouraged and supported to develop a deeper understanding of CTE.

Conceptually, there is debate about when and how young people should be expected to commit to an occupational concentration. A young person might well enjoy becoming a machinist or dental hygienist or graphic artist, but it is not fully clear how learning experiences in high school would best lead to that outcome. Much more needs to be understood about developmental and experiential readiness to make important choices about high school pathways. For instance, as noted earlier, young people's reasons for choosing particular occupational areas are often vague, seemingly not thought through. Many youth may simply not feel ready and able to make good choices. One young woman asks, "Is it possible for me to find a profession that will keep me happy for a lifetime? Is it possible for anyone? . . . I am seventeen years old, and the thought of having to come up with a plan for the rest of my life . . . is terrifying."[94]

It seems clear that young people "who have definite career objectives tend to develop a more intricately motivated approach towards vocational learning," both at school and in the workplace.[95] Yet it is not clear how many youth have such objectives; the data are contradictory. For example, while one recent national survey found that a majority of high school juniors and seniors said they had tentatively picked out a career, another survey found that young people in the United States increasingly lack any sense of direction.[96] Some youth "are aware that they are uncertain about their plans and that they are not engaged in clarifying them; instead they live on a day-to-day basis and hope that 'clarity will happen.'"[97] The more general problem is that young people only come to understand gradually "that they have educational and career decisions to make."[98]

Pathways into CTE, such as the career academy, may require a commitment by the middle of eighth grade, when young people are applying for entry to specific high schools. Some young people reportedly feel "driven" into CTE, and others into concentrations that do not fit them well.[99] There is, nonetheless, evidence that uncertainty about vocational aspirations is also due to a lack of knowledge about postsecondary options and pathways and a limited understanding of occupations.[100] And for some young people, delaying the experience of more practical, applied (i.e., more engaging) learning until eleventh or even twelfth grade actually comes too late, for they are already disengaged from school and its agendas.

PROVIDING A SUBSTANTIVE ROLE FOR WORK-BASED LEARNING

The bulk of learning in CTE in the United States still takes place inside of school. The great majority of CTE concentrators take brief job shadowing forays into workplaces, and a handful will have summer internships. Such hit-or-miss experiences are neither deep enough nor sustained enough to give young people a strong sense of the work world and particular occupations. One group of scholars observes that "continuing on our current course, by placing almost all our bets on classroom-based pedagogy, is likely to produce little more than the marginal gains we've seen over the past two decades."[101] As a practical matter, many occupations require a significant number of clinical or apprenticeship hours, either formally for certification and licensure or less formally as a signal of solid industry experience.

Work-based learning through apprenticeship-like experiences has to become a central component of CTE. As a cultural and a learning setting, the workplace is uniquely valuable. There is abundant international evidence that, when CTE includes significant work-based learning experiences, work and school outcomes for young people are much better. The purposefulness and grounded nature of apprenticeship experiences are internalized by young people and solidify their developing selves.

A fair number of school-based CTE programs provide opportunities to learn using the tools of a profession on simulated versions of the problems of that profession. A smaller number of programs "do a fair job of replicating the physical environment found in work settings . . . shop floors, laboratories and examination rooms."[102] But most public education systems lack the resources to replicate expensive tools, equipment, and operations found in abundance throughout workplaces. Students in manufacturing concentrations, for instance, are only just beginning to have access to CNC machines. Across almost all disciplines and occupations, it has proven difficult to translate critical elements and conditions of practice to the high school classroom.

Knowledge and experience found in the workplace are distinctive. Knowledge is less abstract, rule-bound, and fixed and more generative, action oriented, and heuristic. School-based labs or workshops or kitchens simply cannot replicate the conditions of the work setting: contingencies, varied personalities, contradictory requests, time pressures, and the like. No school-based kitchen, for instance, can replicate the speed, pressures, tension, and barely controlled chaos of a restaurant kitchen. Workplace tasks and problems are often "just-in-time," requiring an assessment of what one is equipped for and, alternatively, where one needs additional resources. As a youth electrical apprentice noted, practice in school is like "pretending to be doing something."[103]

Accessing the richness of work-based learning is not simply a matter of placing a young person. There is, critically, the task of creating a time and place to reflect on and make sense of the experience. It is often unclear who is responsible for supporting that reflection. Both school-based teachers and workplace mentors have to do more than teach young people how to use tools, machines, or instruments; they have to help young people see the kinds of questions they can answer and problems they can address with these artifacts of a discipline. Echoing this need, some of the youth in one biotechnology apprenticeship program (those in production rather than research settings) noted wishing for more explanation for some of the procedures they were carrying out. Yet, a mentor in one of the companies involved tells Amy Ryken, "We want to prep students to be biotech process employees . . . They need to be able to react to the process we have established. They don't always have to know why."[104]

To balance the emphasis on know-how in most workplace learning experiences, school-based instructors (and, to the extent they can, feasible workplace mentors) have to attend to conceptual frameworks, especially the structure and "system of knowledge" in a field.[105] Taking advantage of workplaces as learning environments requires deliberate effort to organize and make explicit the knowledge and experience in them. Concepts and principles that are embedded and tacit, or primarily physical, may have to be rendered in symbolic form to be useful and transferable. School-based vocational educators have to be both mandated and supported to take some responsibility for the quality of work-based learning. That would include workplace audits by CTE teachers, before young people were placed, to identify what is potentially available for learning.

The typical work-based learning experience also has to be of greater duration. Mastery in any field is a gradual process that requires experience, practice, and repeated opportunities to grapple with a variety of problems. Locating—and gaining access to—workplace knowledge has become more difficult in some contexts. (Such knowledge may be located as much in the organization as a whole as it is in more experienced workers who can pass it on in a discrete way—the traditional "master.") Young people need an extended time period at a work site to allow for gradually deepening skill and understanding—of specific tasks, the organization of tasks, the setting, and the "know how" that accrues only gradually through experience. That is why apprenticeships are three years or more. Short internship experiences can provide exposure to the nature of work in a field, but rarely do they allow for a deep applied learning experience.

A significant national effort is needed to promote the idea of work-based learning for high school–age youth. The idea remains poorly understood by most employers. Neither private firms nor public employers are "set up to absorb 16–18 year olds in any substantial numbers, even as trainees." Moreover, "most employers would be skeptical that kids at that age could make a productive contribution."[106] The growing emphasis on efficiency and productivity in the workplace is making workplace learning even more difficult to arrange and support. It is reducing resources available to invest in teaching and learning. Making apprenticeship a more effective component of CTE will require its formal recognition as a culturally valued learning institution for high school–age youth. Until it is recognized as such, it will not be taken seriously either by schools or employers.

As with CTE in general, the worry that work-based learning is too specific is misplaced. The core of most occupations—concepts, principles, formulas, tasks structures, operations, problems—is stable. The possibility that a particular job, technology, or set of work tasks will not be there in four or five years is not an argument against work-based learning. Experience with particular technologies or machines affords kinds of understanding that provide a foundation to work from in the future. Specificity is not an enemy of understanding, insight, or perspective. And workplaces pose a range of challenges that create all kinds of learning opportunities. The demands of workplaces make real and give substance to the concept of twenty-first-century skills, which otherwise is little more than a long list words.

BUILDING A CTE INFRASTRUCTURE THAT EXTENDS BEYOND THE SCHOOL

CTE requires a perspective on and approach to educating young people that extends beyond both the walls of school and the timeframe of schooling. As described above, important vocational learning settings are located throughout communities. Pathways begun during the high school years continue into the postsecondary years. Real world assessment and certification of knowledge and skills require real world partners. Local high school CTE systems have to fit local and regional job markets and vocational-technical programs in community college systems. In spite of these realities—none of which is new—the United States lacks any over-all vision of how different sectors must work together to provide young people useful learning and work experiences as well as clearly articulated pathways into different occupations

One can argue that the task starts with local CTE systems themselves. For instance, their planners, curriculum developers, and school staff have to study and respond to emergent occupational fields within industries and across the economy. High school CTE staff are in a unique posi-tion, and have a unique responsibility, to be familiar with good nonschool learning settings, to see young people through to the next steps, to man-age appropriate forms of assessment, and to see that young people are exposed to all the stages in preparing for an occupation. But they certainly cannot and should not be expected to accomplish these tasks alone. At a minimum, CTE funding formulas need to change to allow for broader roles and tasks. For example, CTE teachers need time and resources to take a more central role in locating, arranging, and supervising work-based learning experiences and in collaborating with workplace mentors to ensure a strong learning experience.

Almost every occupation offers an array of continuing education, fur-ther training, and related activities for professionals. CTE teachers must be actively supported to participate in these and to share what they are learning with colleagues. CTE faculty who have not been out in industry for some time (or at all) need the opportunity to spend time in workplaces through externships or similar vehicles. For example, the community col-lege system in Sacramento, California, has worked with local employers to develop a forty-hour summer externship program for CTE teachers. In addition to learning about work roles in different industries and acquir-ing ideas to revise curriculum, participants in externships develop new relationships outside of school, which in turn change their perspective and focus. Externships are also motivating and energizing for teachers for renewing their commitment to their work.

Meeting the complex responsibilities to make CTE work well goes far beyond more appropriate support for CTE teachers. It requires a cross-system approach developed by local school systems in concert with representatives of employers, community colleges, unions, and the workforce development sector. It requires attention to issues of impetus, ownership, resources, mutual understanding, and recognition among sectors. For instance, in identifying young people for apprenticeships, high school staff have to be willing to consider—and give up some control over and credit for—their strongest students as well as those who are not thriving in their academic coursework. Local unions may have to be willing to open up new pathways into formal, registered apprenticeship. Employers may have to work with state labor regulators to secure waivers from specific sections of child labor laws.

Currently, the impetus for building relationships usually falls to CTE itself, and sometimes to individual teachers. Unlike their academic department peers, CTE faculty have no choice but to work across institutional boundaries. Yet such tasks as defining programs and needed competencies, and ensuring the availability of learning resources and experiences to implement them, cannot fall just to local CTE staff. Working relationships between schools and other institutions cannot be mandated or legislated by fiat; they have to develop slowly and organically. They do, though, require structural vehicles like the CTE Liaison Hubs in California and the Learning Exchanges in Illinois, created to provide a locus for secondary and postsecondary education, industry, state, and local officials to meet, plan, develop strategies for aligning efforts, stimulate internship opportunities, etc. Less directly, such vehicles help link CTE to the labor market through the relationships developed and through the need to jointly plan learning and certification.

IMPLICATIONS OF A CHANGING (GLOBAL) ECONOMY

Career and technology education programs, like the schools as institutions, have to work much more directly to consider the implications of a changing economic world for curriculum and pedagogy. They have to ask philosophical questions as well as practical ones, such as what their responsibilities are toward young people in the context of a new international economic system, with its global wage arbitrage, growth of at-will contracts, and freelance work, among other features. High schools have to respond in some fashion to the prevalent notion that competitive advantage for the United States resides in high-skill, high-value-added manufacturing, the creative use of information technologies, and strength in STEM fields.

This "high road" vision for the United States may or may not be realistic; many doubt it based on available evidence from the labor market. As described earlier, demand for skilled and semi-skilled technical work in the coming years will be strong but narrow. Additionally, historic routes of progression within specific industries no longer function. In many manufacturing settings, for instance, work is either unskilled or highly skilled, and there is no path between the two. That explains in part manufacturers' reluctance to hire high school graduates. Without further technical education, which employers typically cannot offer, these young people will not be able to move into skilled production positions. Even in STEM fields the picture is complex. In analyzing the reason that more young people are not entering or staying in the STEM fields, Jeremy Roschelle and colleagues report "diminishing career opportunities and worsening work conditions for U.S. engineers and scientists because of increasing off-shoring and the presence of professional immigrant workers."[107]

Regardless of which trends one chooses to emphasize, high schools in the United States have to wrestle more directly with the implications of shifting labor market patterns for their curriculum, pedagogy, and distribution of resources. They especially may want to reexamine their current unreflective bias toward STEM fields. At a practical level, high schools will have to work hard to grow work-based learning opportunities in an environment that does not appear conducive to them. Globalization-related pressures on employers, especially the pressure to reduce labor costs, have made it more difficult to invest in work-based learning for young people, a scarce phenomenon to start with. This trend is problematic in part because many fewer workplaces are structured as communities of practice where new workers have opportunity to work alongside and learn from experienced workers.[108]

Those who work in CTE will have to figure out how and where they begin to socialize young people to the new rules—especially the new contradictions—of work in a global economy. For example, while young people have to strive to develop a range of high order cognitive and social skills to compete for jobs on a global stage, they will have to be willing to accept less remuneration for those skills. As described earlier, workers will have to share knowledge with others (i.e., their personal intellectual capital) and work with others to support a common agenda while knowing that they are competing with those others for their place in the firm, their society, and the global economy. They will have to be loyal, investing in a firm or a position while being aware that the firm may not be loyal to them in return. They will have to demonstrate integrity even when the firm does not do so. They will have to "respond positively to change" even when such change is not beneficial to their own work.[109]

Space needs to be created in CTE curricula for young people to study the social meaning and political economy of work, including labor history and unionism, the labor market, social insurance, work-family issues, globalization, and the social impact of prevailing economic practices. One scholar, for instance, illustrates how the vocational curriculum can incorporate both study of the environmental consequences of economic practices and learning activities focused on preventing or ameliorating environmental damage. He observes that in this and similar ways, "vocationalism can place education in a real life context that is meaningful, collective and transformative."[110] A handful of high schools have used the study of work and occupations as a thematic emphasis, either on its own or in complement to career academies. These schools have found that exploring the many dimensions of work provides a strong thematic organizer compelling to young people and to faculty.

Young people must be introduced to the contradictions of work in today's world, as subtle or abstruse as these may seem. Take, for instance, an employer's request that workers to give up the simple demand for a measure of job stability so that the firm can be nimble and flexible enough to compete with low-cost competitors around the globe. The same request, with the same rationale, has been heard from every generation of employers for over a century.[111] Take the seemingly straightforward emphasis that workers contribute to the company's shared knowledge base. From that perspective, the historic, if implicit, acknowledgment of a largely adversarial relationship between capital (represented by management) and labor is no longer accepted, because every worker is now a partner and self-manager. Every worker is expected to help his employer cope with uncertainty, even at the expense of his job. Responsibility for motivation, investment, desire to work hard and contribute used to be shared between employers and employees. These are now viewed almost completely as a worker's responsibility. Young people must, in other words, be exposed to the potential for exploitation of workers, using the very traits that are argued to be critical to being competitive in a global economy.

CHAPTER FIVE

Looking Beyond School

A Role for Nonschool Learning Experiences

The culture's symbolic tool kit actualizes the learner's very capacities.
—Jerome Bruner, *The Culture of Education*

The range of endeavors within a culture sets the boundaries for growth and providesthe means for it. Yet just one endeavor, schooling, occupies such a large place in learning and socialization in the United States that it crowds out other settings and types of experiences. Its central role, or at least the importance of the credentials it confers, may even be growing. Schooling, though, is a weak giant. With the exception of a handful of innovative models and opportunities afforded through career and technical education, schooling provides few openings for young people's full and direct involvement in "the mature activities of their communities."[1] It is in this way that nonschool learning experiences provide what schools do not. Nonschool learning settings provide new places, roles, and purposes for learning and new understandings of learning itself. Less directly, they offer numerous lessons about good learning during the high school years. They illustrate the enormous variety of what there is to learn and learn about and why every sector of society has a role, as well as a stake, in supporting young people's development.

Nonschool learning embodies the full richness and diversity of cultural endeavor. It is found in a wide range of institutions in a wide range of domains, creating small, distinctive communities within the larger society. In my research I've studied youth learning through the visual, performing, and literary arts; handcrafts, media, and journalism; design fields; a range of basic and applied sciences; community development; library and museum science; environmental stewardship; entrepreneurship; culinary arts; and sustainable agriculture. And there are many more domains in which youth have found learning opportunities.

As implied by the breadth of fields, nonschool learning experiences are rooted in, and therefore have to be sought out in, an enormous variety of settings—studios, workshops, laboratories, hospitals and clinics, government offices, libraries, museums, libraries, theaters, orchestras, bakeries, restaurants, urban gardens and organic farms, prairies and forests, waterways, urban neighborhoods and the streets. The diversity of such settings makes concrete the notion that the world itself is a site for learning.

An Example: Albany Park Theater Project

Chicago's Albany Park Theater Project, founded by David Feiner and Laura Wiley, is a youth theater company that focuses on devising original theater based on real life stories. Ensemble members "serve as both ethnographers and artists."[2] The creative process starts with a specific stimulus—a social issue or problem, the life story of a particular individual or family from the Albany Park community or of an ensemble member. Youth go out to the community to talk to people about their experiences and life stories. Tape-recorded interviews are then transcribed and ensemble members take turns reading the transcript out loud, in part to hear the words of the story in different voices, in part to identify possible staging strategies, movement and music ideas, scenes, episodes, turning points that might serve as scaffolding, etc. Different youth notice different aspects of the stories as they are read back, creating what Feiner calls "a kind of collective intelligence." Youth may also do background research to situate the material "in a cultural, historical and political context."

The emergent clusters of material are workshopped, both as theater training exercises and to find versions of a scene that work best:

> Say there's sixteen kids there that day; we might divide them into four groups and say, "You've got a half hour. Go away and come up with a way of staging this scene and then come back." And we look at four groups' versions of staging of that scene, we videotape them and then we discuss what elements look best. We might complicate that activity by saying, "Okay, today you can't use any text; today is all physical but no words, today is all sound, it's got to be music."

During these early play development phases, a script takes shape, under adult guidance, along with choreography, sets, and a score, and a unique casting process begins. That process, intended to allow ensemble members to find their most effective role, involves a kind of negotiation among individuals' interest in a specific role, other ensemble members' thoughts about who would be best suited and adult staff perspective. Once roles are set, rehearsals take place over a two-to-three-month period, with adults in directorial roles, sometimes alongside a youth director. The whole production cycle may take six months, with defining experiences and types of learning evolving with the stages of the process. The actual performance experience is deepened by having ensemble members follow up with the audience, taking questions about the production process and the play itself.

Feiner cites a number of keys to Albany Park Theater Program's work. One is a balance in responsibility, initiative, and decision making between youth and adults. Youth are full owners of the works created and are understood as less experienced collaborators. Adults make the work manageable, "knowing how much of the larger process, how big or small a chunk, to break off every day." The theater-specific process—making interpretations, choices, changes—is viewed in part as a way of encouraging youth to be more active generally in their lives, to take responsibility "for the factors that shape their well-being that they perceive to be out of their control." That might include working through competing demands in their lives or beginning to take more responsibility for important relationships with family, peers, fellow ensemble members, school staff.

Another key is the openness of artistic and creative decisions all along the way: "There isn't someone in the room who knows the right answer from the beginning, including the adults . . . there are [still] better choices and better answers than others, but there is also ambiguity." There is always a mix of experienced and new ensemble members, so there are always models available, whether for exercises that might not seem to make sense or ways of working together when critiquing a scene. Feiner also describes the importance of conversation and reflection to the direct process of making theater: "We talk about the kind of community we want to be, the kind of people we want to be and also the way we're making art." He describes the program as "a world [in miniature] where what you choose matters . . . where what you choose affects you and affects other people." The whole process calls on and nurtures a variety of kinds of qualities; ensemble members "learn to work together to solve complex problems that don't have a right answer . . . and they learn to do that in a way where they don't see the ultimate fruition of their work for a very long time."

ADDRESSING DEVELOPMENTAL IMPERATIVES

Regardless of field or discipline, learning settings like the Albany Park Theater Project share certain essential features. Sponsors and providers are not focused primarily on youth development as such. Rather, they strive to provide developmentally compelling entry points into the adult world and a channel for young people's idealism, energy, and unfocused aspirations. As one young man in a product design apprenticeship notes, before participating he had "determination but no direction."[3] Such settings both help actualize new capacities and provide rich ingredients for identity work. They build a scaffolding for maturing and help young people acquire a clearer sense of "what really is at stake in becoming an adult."[4] Nonschool learning experiences foster in young people a sense that they belong in the world of adult endeavor and have a right to be present in it (and, conversely, they provide an opportunity for adults to take responsibility for welcoming young people into that world).

Through good nonschool learning the young person has the opportunity to work in a sustained and gradually deepening way in a specific discipline, field of work or service, under the tutelage of and alongside an adult skilled in that discipline, and in some settings alongside more and less experienced peers. He not only begins to master the distinct knowledge, skills, practices, and habits but perhaps also begins to acquire the social identity of one who works in that discipline or field. Nonschool learning settings may or may not be professional settings, but, at their best, their task demands, mentoring, and feedback work together to help the young person learn to think and act like a professional in a particular domain. Young people may be viewed as service-learners, interns, preapprentices, apprentices, or workers; they may be paid or unpaid, but they are always engaged in both learning and actual practice in a field. An intern at the American Museum of Natural History writes in her journal, "What surprised me most today was that my mentor talked to me like I was one of his equals, not like how a teacher would talk to a kid in school. I found it interesting that my mentor trusted me to take a very important job which was to collect notes on the exhibit before it closed."[5]

Good nonschool learning experiences build background knowledge in the discipline at hand and provide young people a sense of the richness of particular sociocultural practices. At the same time, young people are introduced to the variety and texture of the adult world: kinds of occupations and work, including creative and cultural activity; types of communities; parts of the world, such as farms, prairies, disinvested neighborhoods; and core social and political problems and ways of making a difference in addressing those problems. Nonschool learning experiences are sometimes more expressive in nature, sometimes more practical and instrumental. Young people learn that such questions as "How can I express this particular idea, emotion, or life experience visually on canvas?" and "How can we selectively rid a wetland prairie of invasive nonnative plant species without hurting native ones?" are equally important to our culture. In this way, nonschool learning broadens vocational and social imagination and deepens the foundation of experience that young people bring to later adolescence.

Nonschool learning experiences often have a hybrid structure that allows for both experimenting and committing, learning and contributing simultaneously. Roles are real—young people are viewed and treated as budding artists, scientists, chefs, and woodworkers—but also have a "what if" quality. Young people can both practice and begin to inhabit an endeavor, pretend to be and really be something. Even when more explicitly vocational, such experiences still have a developmental orientation. They draw on young people's need to belong, adding a focus and substantive dimension to this impulse. They are concerned with forging identity, fostering a sense of vocation, an orientation toward the work world and broader adult world, and a sense of possibilities. Worklike qualities may be combined with opportunity for self- and social exploration.

Because nonschool learning is a diverse enterprise, encompassing a wide range of disciplines, fields, situations, and settings, it is able to account for diverse interests and strengths among youth. It plays a different role for youth who are at different places within a particular field and in their own overall development. While often demanding, its demands are graded, tied to young people's deepening engagement and growing skill in a field or discipline. The stakes rise gradually. While it encompasses the social imperative to prepare young people for further learning, work, and civic life, it is structured to do so incrementally or cumulatively. It can accommodate the possibility that, for some young people, a particular learning experience provides a place to be engaged but without the life consequences of high-stakes settings.

A CLOSER LOOK AT THE CHARACTERISTICS OF NONSCHOOL LEARNING

As implied throughout the book, good nonschool learning experiences for young people have certain common qualities that are embedded and organized within distinct communities of practice. Behind such communities is the idea, first expressed in 1916 by John Dewey in *Democracy and Education*, that it is the social setting itself which is educative, the things and people in that setting and the learner's participation. In recent decades a small army of scholars has studied and explained why this is so.[6]

Communities of practice, or "social practices," represent a distinct material and social world within the larger culture with very particular ways of "doing and knowing."[7] Their particularity includes specialized knowledge, ways of thinking, and types of tasks as well as distinct language, norms, practices and tools, customs and traditions, distinctive conceptions of excellence, distinct products and performances. The "works" of the community solidify pride in effort and create a sense of both progress and continuity.[8] A skilled adult mentor, combined with the traditions of the discipline, the tasks at hand, the products to be created, and the setting provide ingredients for learning. There are good reasons for doing things a certain way, in a certain order. The curriculum as such tends to be embedded in principles, practices, operational procedures, techniques, and heuristics. Assessment and feedback are interwoven with learning and practice.

In some communities of practice, learning and work are both individual and collective. Less experienced learners can work alongside more experienced peers as well as skilled adult mentors in real roles, watching, listening, and emulating. They can see all the steps in creating a product before they are ready and/or able to accomplish these steps independently. Adult mentors and, in some settings, more experienced peers serve as exemplars, modeling the practice, general behavior, and affective commitment of a person with that particular identity. An adult mentor from Chicago's Free Street notes that "there's always a diversity of skill levels in the ensembles . . . We're always leaning toward the most experienced practitioners and everyone else is sort of slip streaming with them." He added that newer participants "gain permission to take creative risks by seeing the more experienced practitioners."[9]

Alice, an Oregon high school student, spends the summer in the lab of Zanna Chase, an oceanographer at Oregon State University, through the Apprenticeship in Science and Engineering program. Alice has her own work, analyzing sediments for different chemical compositions, and Chase encourages her to observe and learn about undergraduate and graduate student research going on throughout the lab. On occasion, Alice will help out on another project. For example, she helps a graduate student prepare solutions for a field study measuring copper concentrations in sea water. Chase gives her readings relevant to her own and other work under way in the lab and has her join weekly lab meetings where staff and students review work and discuss problems. Chase wants "to have her leave and be excited by science . . . So I tried to stay aware of this—my lab as a context for her, to make sure she was exposed to a variety of projects and parts of the work, to invite her to seminars and thesis hearings . . . to see there is a large field out there."[10]

Young people learn by immersion and through direct experience, through trial and error, practice and repetition. The Free Street mentor notes that "they figure it out by doing it. You absolutely have to have the experience of doing it to get it. And we provide space for that."[11] Learning is structured to provide gradually more responsible roles, gradually heightened challenges, more independent decision making (e.g., requiring the learner to play an executive role). Increased participation leads to a deepening identification with the field at hand. Learning and belonging become more closely linked.

A community of practice provides opportunities for young people to learn and produce within a framework of distributed responsibility and joint effort; for young people to link their own ideas and works to those of others, in turn requiring young people to consider others' ideas and perspectives. Participants may play different roles, gaining a sense of what it takes to maintain this type of community. They may have to step outside of themselves, accomplish tasks with others, be responsible to others, and place their self in the service of a collective goal. Feiner says that his young theater artists learn to work in a way that "makes room for several different peoples' ideas . . . they learn to look at other peoples' ideas, suggestions, solutions to problems . . . they learn how to operate in a terrain where we can assess one another's choices and one another's actions." A Marwen Arts Art at Work teaching artist describes this as "chipping in, pitching in, asking what the project needs to move ahead? If you're cutting tile one hour, you're helping choose colors the next, then helping some-body cut glass in the next hour."[12]

An Example: ACME Animation

ACME Animation, founded by Dave Master, uses online mentoring and video conferencing to bring young people into the animation field. Ani-mation, a hundred-year-old discipline with a set of deeply rooted prin-ciples and techniques, has adapted itself to the digital era while maintain-ing much of what defined it in the past. It retains its craftlike qualities, including the perceived value of learning directly from experienced prac-titioners and the importance of being able to observe experts at work. Mentor James Lopez, for instance, uploads his own sketches and "draws" the principles he is trying to convey to young people, noting that there is no substitute for "seeing" the animation process while he is explaining it.

Animation is a surprisingly demanding discipline, taking hundreds of hours to master at a basic level. It incorporates knowledge and skills from drawing, design, composition, filmmaking, and computer-generated graphics and imagery. Young people must learn elements of storytelling, such as plot construction and character development, and how to con-vey such distinctive concepts as pose-to-pose, exaggeration, and squash and stretch. As an industry professional on one video conference tells a group of students, "What you do in animation is you set people up for what they're about to see and then you give them what you set them up for." ACME Animation works with both individual youth and with high schools and colleges around the country. Youth begin at an auditioner level, proceeding on to intern and apprentice. They do required exercises (e.g., animating a dropping leaf or bouncing ball, the latter of which Mas-ter says incorporates 80 percent of the physical principles a student could ever have to learn). Young people post their own work and build a port-folio, receiving feedback from peers at their own or more advanced levels and from professional animators who volunteer their time to the program. The video conferences include periodic master classes by animation pro-fessionals as well as public presentation and critiques of selected students' work. Having a real audience for one's work-in-progress is simultaneously intimidating and motivating. One student observes that "at first you're afraid. You're on camera. Everybody sees your artwork, so you're basically standing there naked. But get used to it. You're not afraid to get in front of people and talk about this work that means so much to you."[13]

In a pay it forward approach, young people earn the right to receive individualized professional feedback by providing detailed critiques (i.e., concrete suggestions, visual attachments) to peers at their level or lower. Work-in-progress is posted in specific galleries, making it open to feedback from the larger online community. One of the adults who supervises the program notes that "you're not just getting it [feedback] from above but trying to teach it to someone else as well. You have to really think very carefully about what you've learned." The Web site is structured so that everyone can see the professional comments received by everyone else, exposing the whole community to the "highest technical standards, the language of the guild, and the art of mentoring." They also get a taste of the hierarchy and work culture of the animation studio.[14]

REAL TASKS WITH REAL CONSEQUENCES . . .

In good nonschool learning settings, the tasks and problems reflect those encountered in actual work in a discipline and often real-world constraints. Knowledge is sought and skills are developed because they are needed in the moment, or they're needed to carry out a particular social role. For instance, a young person practicing journalism comes to see that "a reporter may write a certain way because she views her job as serving the important societal function of being a community watchdog."[15] Young people are required to create, construct, and produce within constraints of time, resources, production schedules, and deadlines. At Oakland's Youth Radio, youth are responsible for producing a weekly radio show that airs at a defined time and night of the week. In reflecting on Youth Radio as a nonschool learning setting, adult mentors observe that rather than understanding it as a low-stakes setting, it is more accurate to describe it as intense; deadlines are real, products will be heard by real public audiences.[16]

Young people have to adapt to the social purposes of a cultural activity, the requirements of commissions or the constraints of physical settings. Youth working on public art projects (murals and sculptures) in Chicago's Marwen Arts/Art at Work have to learn to adapt their own creative ideas to the varied rationales for doing public art, from engaging peoples' imaginations to strengthening a sense of community, humanizing, or beautifying a site or symbolizing its history. They have to take into account the physical and functional nature of a site, local zoning ordinances, community preferences and sensitivities, and the ways potential purposes and qualifiers relate to a client's goals.

Work on tasks is, typically, genuinely useful, not make-work. In the Nature Conservancy's summer residencies for urban youth, tasks have ranged from restoring native shellfish populations and bays and estuaries to surveying the behavior and population of endangered bird species. Young people's efforts lead to tangible products or performances that are often genuinely needed by someone—a business, a community, a particular population. Youth write and produce documentaries, prepare marketing plans, build wooden boats, grow vegetables and sell them in a farmer's market, study the causes of public health problems, collect data on social issues, restore prairies, clean up rivers, create sculptures. Young people become integral parts of the functioning of restaurant kitchens, science labs, medical clinics, and dance companies.

Each setting has its own way of motivating young people and giving them a stake in the work. For some it's the particular problems being addressed. For others it's an opportunity to show one's work to an audience. Some settings use commission-based work to give young people an adult-like stake, whether the associated income goes to them or to the sponsoring organization. For instance, young people's productive contributions ensure that sponsoring organizations such as Boston's Artists for Humanity have a measure of freedom to shape the overall work to meet youths' needs and aspirations.

An Example: Sweat Equity Education

Sweat Equity Education (originally Sweat Equity Enterprises) offers a design apprenticeship intended to expose young people to the creative end of the development process for consumer products.[17] The apprentices participate in a design workshop for three afternoons a week for at least a year, and sometimes more, and receive a stipend. After completing the program they receive an industry-accepted-and-approved credential, signaling readiness for entry-level work in fashion or select product design positions.

Young people work in teams to complete commissions from specific companies for such diverse products as sneakers, watches, skateboards, outerwear, and game controllers. They learn and go through a product design process that includes market research and open brainstorming, concept development and critiques, hand drawings, computer mock-ups (using Photoshop and Illustrator), fabrication of prototypes, group critiques, and refinements. Designs are sent to factories run by the respective companies, where samples are fabricated and shipped back to the design teams for further critique and refinement and then shipped back for fabrication of a final prototype. Products created by youth apprentices have ended up in retail settings and/or been adapted by company.

When they join the workshop, young people receive workbooks that describe and illustrate the product design process and provide examples of professional-quality output. For instance, the workbook includes professional technical drawings so participating youth can see what they have to aim for. For each project, young people establish what they need to know to do informed design work. Background research for the shoe project, for instance, included foot anatomy and shoe components. Young people learn how designers use visual and other resources for inspiration (i.e., they do not design out of thin air). For the outerwear project they conducted research on garments worn around the world as inspiration—Samurai warrior coats, blankets worn by indigenous people of the Andes, etc. Youth both figuratively and literally take products apart to understand how they are engineered. Design professionals join the process at many points to provide technical information, critique, and affirmation and to remind the apprentices that this is a professional activity with a real product at stake.

The multistage and multifaceted experience in Sweat Equity Education is intended to work at a number of levels. Young people learn, out of necessity, to pay attention to time, resources, feedback, instructions, and the goals of the project at hand (as a constraint on imagination). They learn about traditional design elements—form, function, materials—and manufacturing. They face the challenges of translating ideas or images in their heads into a physical form on paper and into the computer and of understanding that they are using their creativity and knowledge of peer culture but not designing for themselves but, rather, for a particular market segment. They get a visceral sense of the detail and complexity of professional design process and come to understand the meaning of industry standards. They learn to "push through," as one youth puts it. They develop as well a different understanding of, and a more disciplined perspective on, their own sense of creativity. They come to value research and to enjoy work with others. As one young participant notes, "Working with other people actually makes things easier; you inspire them, they inspire you."

. . . AND OPPORTUNITY TO CONTRIBUTE TO THE LARGER CULTURE

Good learning experiences provide young people the opportunity and the conceptual and technical tools to engage the larger culture: to serve and contribute to, enrich, alter, and sometimes contest that culture. They learn firsthand about and help address the problems and tensions attendant to our common life. For example, in their environmental remediation work on the Bronx River, under the auspices of Rocking the Boat, a traditional wooden boat–building program with an on-water component, young people learn about how the river came to be polluted and how to turn frustration with that knowledge to productive ends. At times young people may have an opportunity to join debate about ideas and practice in the field in which they are learning and working, the opportunity and responsibility to wrestle with the ethical issues attached to a particular endeavor. In Oregon's Apprenticeship in Science and Engineering program, for instance, apprentices working for a plant geneticist grapple firsthand with the ethical issues involved in genetically modifying organisms. Their mentor discusses with the young apprentices the differences in purpose, motive, and expectations between human genetics and medicine, animal genetics, and agricultural and forestry genetics.[18]

Young people can also learn through their actions that they are not powerless to address problems that affect them and their peers personally. For instance, in a number of cities youth have organized to raise attention to and advocate for change in school discipline policies that they have experienced firsthand as being destructive to learning. In Wichitaw, Kansas, a group of young people who were part of Hope Street Youth Development focused on the problem of disproportionately high rates of school suspension among youth of color. They worked with school staff to raise awareness of this as a problem of structural racism and to help the latter reframe their understanding of youth behavior and find more effective and just school policies. A staff member of Students4Justice in Denver told an interviewer that "youth are experts in racism," although they do not always know what to do with that expertise.[19] Similarly, in Chicago a youth organization called Voices of Youth in Chicago Education has joined with other advocacy organizations to seek an end to the standard two-week suspension policy, which reportedly led to the loss of 300,000 days of instruction one recent school year.[20]

The arts, social documentary, print journalism, and other media have provided young people a distinctive set of tools to tackle cultural material that might be controversial and to address injustices that they, their families, their communities, or others experience. Youthful ensemble members in the Albany Park Theater Project learn that theater can be a powerful vehicle for exposing the roots and consequences of injustice. In gathering background material for molding an idea into a play, ensemble members have interviewed undocumented day laborers, survivors of the Cambodian genocide, and survivors of sexual abuse.

Young documentary filmmakers at New York City's Education Video Center have focused on such topics as the challenges facing undocumented youth, the corrupting influence of credit cards, racial stereotyping in popular culture, police violence, and the connection between school and work. Founder Steve Goodman argues that a particularly valuable social role for young people is as critical producers and consumers of mass media—its assumptions, what it focuses on and ignores, the ways public issues are handled, and so on.[21] Young people can play a critical role in part by using the power of media itself to draw attention to what is not said or attended to, such as by using the documentary form to give voice to those who have little or none. Young people might also use the power of media to illustrate approaches to addressing problems that do not fit with dominant policy approaches or accepted wisdom. Engagement in these ways teaches young people to act with conscience and empathy, what Goodman calls "moral agency."

Civic engagement provides another means for critical participation. Young people have generally not been "seen as being integral to civil society," and yet civic engagement is often a good fit with young people's concerns, passions, and questions.[22] There are a number of venues for civic engagement, including community development and grassroots organizing, community service, urban planning, public health, conservation work, and environmental activism. There are also many kinds of tasks: documenting conditions, remediating sites, gathering data, brainstorming and designing solutions to a problem, making physical models, presenting ideas in public forums or to officials. Young people may find themselves in roles that require balancing passion with compromise, negotiation, and evidence-based argument.

In all these kinds of activities, learning is linked intimately to engagement with civic, social, economic, scientific, or other problems. This kind of engagement turns young people's attention outward. As a young European working on a campaign to raise public awareness about young people's rights and support needs observes, "Now self-awareness is not about me and my social circle, it's about youth and the needs of youth in

Europe, it is finding the aims that are worth fighting for in the world in which we are living."[23]

An Example: Y-PLAN

Y-PLAN, based in Berkeley, California, involves youth in local urban planning and community development initiatives.[24] Graduate students in urban planning mentor youth through a ten-to-twelve-week planning process focused on a particular project, such as designing a community garden, redesigning a historic train station, improving a semi-abandoned park space. Working in teams, the young people take photos, do community mapping, conduct interviews and surveys, and learn to use design software and make physical models. They develop plans and have to defend them before community groups, public officials, and other stakeholders. Professional designers, architects, and engineers are brought in to provide feedback, help with ideas, discuss their own work, and lead trips to the field so that young people can see how those professionals look at built spaces.

The lessons these young participants learn are social, political, civic, occupational, and historical. In interviews with neighborhood residents for a project on redevelopment of an abandoned park, youth learn about the social and political processes that had undermined the neighborhood as a whole. In the process, the suddenly broadened community of "teachers" has also learned a great deal. "City officials have learned to ask questions that are more realistic to the kinds of knowledge students might have."[25] And adults in general have learned that while youth lack formal knowledge of design principles, they do have knowledge of their communities and of how people use space and often an intuitive sense of what will work.

One important limitation of models of civic engagement like Y-PLAN is their transient nature. Most are centered around internship experiences and discreet projects or initiatives and are therefore difficult to sustain.[26] For some youth the occupational dimension is valuable. Most young people are unaware of professional roles related to planning, design, community development, environmental activism, etc. For the majority of participating youth, civic engagement is more about adding a perspective on the world and a dimension of self that might endure into adulthood. It serves also as a new and relatively powerful social role, like work in some ways, but distinctly suited to adolescence.

DEVELOPMENTALLY APPROPRIATE AGENCY

The rooted quality of communities of practice connects young people strongly to a particular part of the larger cultural world, creating the conditions for investment and work toward mastery. In a complementary way, young people are more likely to invest in a learning activity when they have opportunities to make that experience their own. Especially in adolescence, it is crucial that young people have opportunity to be agents within valued domains of social practice and in the world more generally. Growth of agency occurs in part through the very experience of striving for mastery, as young people struggle with challenges, constraints and complexity, trial and error. It occurs especially when and as young people have an opportunity for reasoned ownership of their learning experience.

Young people need opportunities to create meaning that is shared rather than imposed—to offer ideas, to question, to make their own connections, to use their own strategies for solving problems. They need opportunities to practice transforming things, connecting things in unexpected ways, inventing new images, creating new artifacts, and surprising themselves and others with what they can do. When meaning making is shared, young people are reassured that the world is not a finished product. The things of value in the adult world, whether artistic, scientific, social, civic, technological, or political, are their things too and are open to further development. Boston's Artists for Humanity provides a good example of these principles. Although it is not a youth-led organization, youth are taken seriously and their artistic vision and intentions are respected, in commissioned work as well as personal projects. Teaching artists let young people know directly and indirectly that, as the graphics teaching artist puts it, "this is their studio, their workplace."[27]

What makes agency/ownership developmentally appropriate is not just freedom and voice; it is also the constraints that ground those qualities of learning. Young people are treated as capable and responsible but are not put into positions for which they are ill-prepared. They have some autonomy, but only where and when autonomy makes sense. They are tied to reality, even as they test it, by the customs and standards of the discipline or field at hand.

- In describing young musicians' experiences in Venezuela's El Sistema, one observer notes that "craft grows within the enabling constraints of deep traditions and demands of instrument and music."[28]

- A touchstone for the documentary work at the Education Video Center is the longstanding journalistic principle of getting the story right, regardless of what one wants or wishes to have found.

- Adult producers at Oakland's Youth Radio maintain that "we are not in the business of soliciting stories we agree with. The ones that challenge our own personal politics are among the most important we can produce."[29]

- An adult mentor with Chicago's Free Street Theater notes that "we make our expectations very clear and there's wide area in there to explore . . . Our experience is that if a lot of people feel safe inside; and then they can really blossom and explore." He adds that young people seem to "feel freed by understanding exactly what is expected. It's freedom within boundaries."[30]

- The teaching artist for the Student Production Workshop at New York's Roundabout Theater says that adults have to strike a balance between affording youth a sense of ownership of the work and helping nurture a sense of integrity derived from joining a tradition and internalizing its standards: "We try to make the line between the adult being more active and less active as organic as possible."[31]

- A painting teaching artist in Artists for Humanity thinks that "it's good to set up a structure with basic expectations and rules, a level of respect for community norms, but to be open to the learning that is naturally occurring throughout the process."[32]

These are examples of what one writer describes as "enabling constraints," "a balance of sufficient organization [and] sufficient openness . . . not what must be done but what might be done."[33] Young people's own lived experience is treated as legitimate, as an ingredient to bring to the work at hand and as a basis for interpreting and evaluating the world around them. At the same time, their emergent personal history is interwoven with, and is thus enriched and altered by, the history of the setting and discipline.

The best settings accept youth in the deepest sense and at the same time provide them space for growth and transformation of self. Adult mentors respect young people's individuality and self-definition. Young people are taken for who they are, "no labels, predispositions," as one of the adult staff with Chicago's Joffrey Ballet puts it.[34] The social categories often imposed on youth are put aside. Young people are not overage or undercredentialed students; they're not dropouts or disconnected youth. The founder of a youth-operated television network in Chicago, CTVN, notes that "we're open . . . we don't say 'you can't read, get out, you're in a gang, get out.'"[35] At the same time, young people's selves are understood as developing rather than as fixed. Adults are not overly solicitous of what young people think they want and who they say they are at any particular moment in time.

EMPHASIZES STANDARDS YET STRUCTURED TO SUPPORT GROWTH . . .

The professional standards of a specific community of practice are a critical touchstone for learning and work within that community. These are adult standards in an importance sense of the word. But young people are not adults, and they are usually novices in a particular sphere of activity. They may be just experimenting with it. And in cognitive and affective terms, they are growing rapidly. For these reasons, a balanced emphasis on process and product and a participatory structure that allows for gradually deepening involvement are particularly valuable in learning settings for youth. Attention to products is critical not least because they signal where a young person is in his or her growth in a field and provide an emblem of that growth.

The specific field or discipline provides teachers and learners a self-evident set of criteria for evaluating work. A plant geneticist serving as a mentor with the Apprenticeship in Science and Engineering program emphasizes to youth, "If you screw up the experiment, well then you've got to do it again . . . There's a lot of personal responsibility as a scientist; you're in this because, for now at least, this is your identity, you want to know the answer."[36] Yet this mentor's lab, like good learning settings in general, is also characterized by "a culture of iteration." Mistakes are understood to be part of—indeed, integral to—the learning and producing process. The decisions, choices, and strategies leading to a solution and the lessons derived from work on a problem are often as important as whether the solution is precisely right or wrong.

Task demands, expectations of mastery, and depth of understanding increase gradually. It is accepted that young people will take varied amounts of time to acquire mastery. Adult mentors do not expect young people to demonstrate professional standards until they are deemed ready to do so. In St. Paul's Urban Boat-Builders program, youth start out by making tools or items relevant to the eventual boat-building process, such as wooden mallets, bevel gauges, or canoe paddles. Each participant has to meet both a functional and aesthetic standard before she can move on.[37] Similarly, in preparing for work on a commissioned sculpture, new apprentices in St. Louis ArtWorks spend weeks learning and practicing 3-D design and making models. These design exercises serve as grist for later full-scale production.[38]

Growth of knowledge and skill are recognized publicly, both by the specific community of practice and sometimes the larger community. Young peoples' work on Education Video Center documentaries is affirmed by public showings, and the staff work hard to find venues for finished work. The YO-TV documentary on the International Criminal

Court was shown at a Human Rights Watch Film Festival, and the documentary on Katrina was screened at the Tribeca Film Festival. Center founder Steve Goodman says that youth "don't get the whole picture until they've been through the whole process . . . Once they've done the work, shown it to an audience and see what the impact is, they begin to realize what they've been a part of . . . that they've made something that goes out into the world and contributes."[39]

Young people are afforded opportunity and conceptual structure to describe and reflect on what they doing and how they are growing, on themselves as learners, makers, and team members. And they gradually acquire greater responsibility for doing so. They have to account for their experience to, in effect, make their learning explicit. For instance, painting and drawing apprentices in Chicago's After School Matters will present almost-finished work to peers, describing what they were attempting to achieve, what they struggled with, how they addressed problems, and how successful they judge the final product will be. In providing feedback, an instructor and peers will help an apprentice "name" and describe his experience and place his progress in the larger framework of the field.[40]

Learning in the Applied Arts Studio

Ceramicist Constant Albertson and photographer Miriam Davidson argue that the applied arts studio combines many attributes critical "to encouraging students to give themselves over" to learning experiences.[41] The learning materials and tasks are practical, demanding, and compelling. The reasons for tasks are obvious. In part due to their own learning experiences, teaching artists are aware of the importance of balancing freedom and structure. Applied arts studios typically function as a learning and work community, with participants sharing tools, equipment, and space as well as knowledge. There is a sense of mutual reliance, with some activities being collective, such as firing the kiln, and an equally strong sense of mutual regulation, since "messing up" can affect others' progress, such as in the preparation of ingredients for making a glaze or processing film.

Albertson and Davidson observe that in both fields "there are concrete, functional markers that must be reached in order to have success.

Learners can quickly see the consequences of their decisions and actions. [And] there are clear consequences if the technical processes involved . . . are not properly sequenced or well carried out. Cause and effect are clear and absolute; no concept is good enough to survive poor execution." Yet, even with well-established standards, procedures, and criteria for quality of products, there is plentiful room for individualizing both process and product. Tools can be used in creative ways; a young person can experiment with exposures, with chemical fixers, or with a new firing technique for the kiln. Taking risks goes with the territory, and the learner knows that he or she has "permission to fail."[42]

. . . AND DESIGNED TO NURTURE DIFFERENT KINDS OF GROWTH

Good nonschool learning experiences, though particular, draw on and engage many parts of the self—the intellectual and the practical, the logical and the perceptual, the affective and the the moral, and often the physical. They are marked by cognitive and emotional involvement and the stretching of capacities. David Feiner describes young theater artists "using their voices, their bodies in ways they're not used to doing elsewhere, expressing themselves in ways they're not used to elsewhere, beginning to become emotionally vulnerable."[43] In discussing the reasons that El Sistema, a youth orchestra model originating in Venezuela, is so compelling, an observer notes "the balance of personal emotional connection and focus on technique."[44]

The more young people attend to a discipline, the deeper their sense of it and the more interesting it becomes. Interest and experience, combined with the material itself, create a gravitational pull. When a young person does background research for an environmental remediation effort, when he or she learns how to record carefully the procedure just used in a laboratory, learning acquires a different valence. Young people begin to see the consequences of their commitment in the quality of products or performances. In El Sistema, young people's direct experience of the growth of music quality, as a consequence of intense work put in over an extended period of time, renews and reinforces their commitment. Over time good learning experiences demand more of the self and provide young people opportunities to use more of themselves. The founder of CTVN, the youth-led TV station in Chicago, observes that "it's creative and exciting when you come up with an idea, but then it's like 'the real world'; to fashion it into something is hard work."[45]

As with career and technical education, the complex qualities of non-school learning experiences foster many kinds of growth, both domain-specific and general, and a variety of meta-lessons. As young people are working toward proficiency in a domain, they are steadily acquiring new tools and building a conceptual structure for that domain. They begin to acquire the kind of intuition and judgment that is the first step toward mastery. They become more resourceful in addressing problems and begin to acquire "adaptive expertise," the ability to hold on to lightly or let go of ideas, to test alternatives by putting them out for examination and testing, to be less rule-bound. One young man, learning the traditional practice of dry stonewalling, describes it as "mileage in the brain."[46]

Good nonschool learning experiences teach young people to work with deliberateness and care. They learn the pace and rhythms of working in a particular kind of setting or on a particular kind of problem. In the oceanography lab described earlier, Alice, the apprentice, had to adapt a procedure that had been published in another study, using reagents to leech off silica. To do so she conducted a repetitive series of mini-experiments, leeching samples for varying lengths of time, a painstaking process that took a whole day. Another ASE apprentice, working as part of a plant ecology team restoring wetland prairies, learned to find pleasure in the careful, detailed work of marking off sample plots and returning to them to measure and record the reemergence of plant types over time. She learns that the quality of the data produced will be critical in convincing state and federal authorities of the need to invest in such restoration work.

Young people build persistence and patience. They develop a grounded sense of competence, personal qualities and limits, and they learn about what it takes and means to get good at something. They also come to recognize that a range of thoughts and feelings are part of any learning experience, that these can facilitate and motivate and can also impede learning, and that they can manage their thoughts and feelings as they pursue their goals. New feelings are recognized, examined, and gradually integrated into the self. Almost all of these realized capacities, knowledge, skills, and dispositions are the kinds that young people will need to bring to postsecondary learning and work.

THE PREPARATORY AND VOCATIONAL ROLE OF NONSCHOOL LEARNING EXPERIENCES

Good learning experiences provide opportunity for young people to relate what they are doing inside of a particular experience—tasks they are working on, roles they are playing, knowledge and skills they are building, people they are meeting, experience they are acquiring—to what they are doing or might do outside of it. Such experiences provide background knowledge for planning and decision making and expanded, but also more accurate and grounded, reference points for aspirations and for a more finite and at the same time more generous and concrete sense of the future. A mentor in one local setting notes that putting young people "out in the world" impels them "to deal with the way they think about themselves and their future and their work and the people around them and their own skills."[47] Of a young participant in an ecology project, a staff person notes (simply) that "it was important for him to realize that there were things other people did in which he could take part."[48]

Conversations with mentors can help young people better understand the pathway to postsecondary study or work in a particular field or discipline. Mentors also serve as a source of new social connections, referral, and information not always publicly available. They may know the college programs in their field particularly well and have relationships with potential employers. For instance, a few of the instructors at RiverzEdge Arts in Woonsocket, Rhode Island, have graduated from the Rhode Island School of Design and provide invaluable connections for participants interested in pursuing fine or applied arts studies.

Like career and technical education, nonschool learning experiences can deepen understanding of what work is and what it means, its rhythms, pleasures, and difficulties. They can also help young people see that vocations (and vocational cultures) are different from each other. Adults might share their own professional experiences, giving young people a more specific sense of what it is like to work in a particular field. An architect who mentors youth through Marwen Arts' Art at Work program involves his young apprentices in some of his own daily activities in part because he wants them to observe how he thinks and works on tasks.[49] An apprentice to a plant geneticist learns over the course of a summer that a good part of doing science "is in all the hundreds of gory details, from how you pipette properly to how you make up the chemistry of a control for a particular experiment," which gives the young man a much deeper sense of the day-in/day-out work of science.[50]

A young person might be able to observe the range of roles in a particular kind of work setting. One young science apprentice observes that "since I've been working in the soil bio-physics lab, I've noticed that everyone is working on a different project."[51] An oceanographer who mentored a young woman in her lab for Oregon's Apprenticeship in Science and Engineering program notes that she "tried to stay aware of my lab as a context for her [learning], to make sure she was exposed to a variety of projects and parts of the work, to invite her to seminars . . . to see that there is a large field out there."[52]

Particular experiences may introduce young people to newer (or, occasionally, older and revived) ideas, occupational fields, social problems, and ways of using disciplinary knowledge and skill that have not yet found their way into career and technical education curricula. For instance, graduates of Rocking the Boat's on-water program have gone on to study and work in a variety of disciplines associated with such work, such as field biology and sustainability studies.

Indeed, creative and cultural work in such fields as performance arts, design, broadcasting and film, music, game development, and Web site development are becoming a viable part of the economy. Young people have been drawn to these fields and often created new ways of working in them. At the same time, young people who find a home in this sector typically need help understanding how one might make a career in it, especially since many adult practitioners cobble together a living from many sources.

NEW ADULT ROLES: EXEMPLAR AND BRIDGE

One of the most important features of nonschool learning is the opportunity it affords young people to learn from, work with, and be supported by adults not normally part of their daily world. As described earlier, adult mentors' deep knowledge of the field at hand, sense of intentionality, and direction provide strong organizers for young people's experience. Joint activity between a young person and an adult mentor—working on a task or activity together—provides a particularly rich context for growth. The intersubjectivity, the sense of a shared reality, between young person and mentor can make a learning experience memorable.

> In Oakland's Youth Radio, youth work alongside adult producers and sound engineers, some of whom are program graduates. Issues of adult authority tend to become subsumed by the work at hand. In discussing the adult instructors' role, Vivian Chávez and Elisabeth Soep note that while youth and adults "may not see eye-to-eye in what they want for a story," they are focused not on each other but on the task, "what they want their work together to accomplish." They describe the model as a "pedagogy of collegiality." Within this framework youth and adults are seen to learn from each other and be mutually dependent on each other. Each contributes something unique to the work—young people a fresh perspective and sensitivity to issues and emerging currents in culture, adults professionalism, life and technical experience, and a measure of wisdom.[53]

Adults provide young people concrete opportunities to practice learning new kinds of relationships with a degree of reciprocity but with different roles. They provide models of how one responds to the technical and interpersonal challenges found in everyday life. As a young man learning printmaking prepares to print, he covers the rag paper with blankets but forgets to first lay newsprint to absorb excess paint. "Robert [the instructor], without alarm or irritation, remind[s] him about the steps in the process and the reasons for those steps."[54] In describing what is important about the adult mentor in the El Sistema orchestra system, Eric Booth notes that it is "not just the way she teaches, but the way she thinks, listens, responds, notices, formulates questions, reflects, dresses, plays [an instrument]."[55]

Adults frame the work at hand and help young people use a learning setting as a resource. They create some constraints while attending to where in the learning process within a discipline it is appropriate for the learner to have freedom to be more creative. A novice muralist in Marwen's Art at Work program, for instance, will work alongside the teaching artist for many weeks before being given her own section of mural to work on. In effect, adults help ensure that learning takes place "within but at the outer limits of the learner's resources."[56] Adults observe young people at work—what motivates them, how they approach tasks, where they get stuck—and "fill in gaps." As they are working with or demonstrating to a young person, they may make their own thought processes, decisions, and understanding of choices visible. The young person begins to see what the mentor sees.

Adults may have to work to foster a young person's interest in the domain, discipline, or field at hand. Or they may have to help young people see that there are good reasons for learning particular content or following specific procedures. This is why we are so particular about steps in the dark room or laboratory or at the drafting table. Adults may have to push young people's thinking while at the same time accepting their attempts to think; or they may have to encourage them to muddle through, to step back and take another look, to change an angle of attack. They may have to help young people put learning and mastery struggles in context so that those struggles are not overgeneralized or overinterpreted. More subtly, adults may have to help young people learn to trust the skills they are developing, especially when they are working in ways and in roles that are outside of how they see themselves.

CONCLUSION

The many kinds of very particular, yet also very rich, learning experiences described in this chapter "feed our moral imagination, giving us new ideas about what is worth striving for." Each type of social practice both "forms its own social world and affords perspective on the world as a whole."[57] At the same time, nonschool learning experiences have a tendency to provoke thoughts about the larger world surrounding a particular practice. One woman, reflecting back on time spent in a print shop during her senior year of high school, observed that as she "got the hang of turning hot lead into type, and type into the words that brought a newspaper to that small Kentucky community, my mind sprang to life, turning over issues of identity and politics, ethics and responsibility that school had never awakened."[58]

Nonschool learning is often very grounded; indeed, sometimes it has a sense of what might be called materiality. Yet it also addresses the less tangible dimensions of the adult world in a way particularly helpful to young people. Good nonschool learning experiences provide some of the complexity young people need for identity work and some of the solidity they need as they manage the tension between individuality and social demands. Such experiences help reassure young people that "it is alright to be, to be oneself, and to become what other people trust one will become" and yet, simultaneously, that "there is no map when it comes to matters of maturing."[59]

CHAPTER SIX

How Other Countries Structure Learning in and out of School

At college you learn about theory, however at work you notice the exceptions: practical work is quite different from what you learn at college.

—A youth apprentice from the Netherlands, quoted in Corri Van de Stage, "The Work-Based Learning Route in the Netherlands and in England"

Other countries struggle, as the United States does, with fitting together learning arrangements, young people's developmental capacities and preoccupations, and labor market needs. As in the United States, deliberate efforts to foster equal opportunity and social inclusion have sometimes had the opposite effect. Young people are unsure about (and sometimes unaware of) good options. Movement toward adulthood is more extended and precarious than in the past, due to changing economies, high youth unemployment rates, and generally more fluid labor markets. And the question of "how to prevent a whole group of youth and young adults from ending up on a social scrap heap" has become more pressing.[1]

Yet, other countries also offer starkly different approaches to defining and addressing the support needs of young people. In general, European debate about who youth are and what they need is more deliberate and normative than the equivalent American debate. Youth in Europe are seen to be entitled to their own age-specific social goals and institutional

163

supports. If, in the United States, schooling is the "great equalizer," in many other countries work is thought to play this role. That is in part due to a philosophical and legal emphasis on work as a right and expression of citizenship and to a belief that workplaces are important learning settings for young people. In many countries, secondary education is characterized by a clearly defined set of choices with clearly defined pathways into different kinds of work. All choices are respected and confer a distinctive kind of prestige.

Until recently, discussions about youth in most countries were framed in social terms, as issues of social inclusion and social citizenship, even when they concerned labor market preparation and integration. Youth policy focused on what affordances were needed to help young people find a place in society and experience a sense of belonging.[2] That has changed as economic circumstances have become more perilous and the costs of social democratic values have been questioned for the first time. Market-oriented language emphasizing the need to prepare young people for global competition has become more prominent in policy discourse. This shift has been accompanied by an intensifying debate about how best to characterize young people's experiences as they move through middle into late adolescence, how best to define and where to locate responsibility for young people's well-being.

In the current climate, particularly in the European Union, pathways toward adulthood have become less transparent. Movement through middle and late adolescence is less predictable, the benefits of education less direct. Transitions may take years to work through and do not end definitively. What in the past were normative pathways are now riskier. For instance, more young people cannot find work in the disciplines in which they are trained, whether through university, technical institution, or apprenticeship. Close to half of young people who have found work of any kind are on temporary contracts.[3] Guy Standing posits a new class of people, the "precariat," disproportionately young and residing at the margins of the labor force, "living bits and pieces lives, in and out of short-term jobs, without a narrative of vocational development."[4]

Young people are either choosing or feeling compelled to manage their own "learning biography" and to create individual paths, new forms of loyalty, and sources of identity, in some cases deemphasizing occupation, work, and schooling. They are putting their energy into creativity in music and other expressive arts, online communities and interest groups, civic organizing, specific causes (e.g., animal rights, gender rights, even internship rights), entrepreneurial efforts in social media and other fields. Youth have created new forms of work (which sometimes involve a kind of play), new kinds of work "settings" and infrastructure. They have discovered for themselves the power of learning through experimentation and collaboration, freely sharing ideas and techniques. These are new cultural activities in which mastery is defined informally.

Such creativity is, nonetheless, counterbalanced by evidence of growing psychological distress among youth and a sense of anger at a range of institutions that represent adult society, especially political and financial institutions.[5] This anger derives from a sense among youth in some countries that efforts to solve structural problems are being made at their expense.

On top of generally worsening social and economic conditions for young people, societal structures producing and reproducing inequality are as powerful as ever. Regardless of external conditions, young people retain some agency. Their choices do not always follow the logic that adults and adult institutions assume they should.[6] Yet individuals do not free themselves from social structure by avoiding or repudiating it. Outcomes cannot be construed as "simply personal choices."[7] Social class, race, gender, and family background are still influential in shaping those choices and opportunities. Systematic differences persist in young people's knowledge of academic and vocational options and their access to learning and other social resources.

Consciously or not, young people still orient themselves to the world through "deeply embedded dispositions" formed by class, race, family, and community of origin.[8] A recent study in Finland, a country with a supposedly open, nondifferentiated upper secondary system, found clear social class and occupationally based differences in parents' views of their children's abilities and their thoughts about what their children should do and might be able to strive for. These differences in turn influenced young people's own thinking and choices.[9] A study of Danish youths' decision making around postcompulsory education found working-class youths' reasoning and decision making more shaped by personal and familial necessity than that of their more advantaged peers. The former group of youth had spent their lives "close to necessity" and did not have the luxury "to engage the world in reflexive, abstract terms."[10]

Shifting policy frameworks in a growing number of countries are exacerbating the effects of new and persistent social strains on youth. Education and workforce development policy has been reoriented to emphasize choice, individual agency, and personalization. Government responsibilities are being pushed down to the local level. Policy makers urge young people themselves to take responsibility for creating their educational careers and for dealing with obstacles to social and economic participation.

Many observers have been critical of the shift in policy emphasis. One notes that youth now have too much responsibility "to decide and to act in a self-directed way."[11] Young people may be actively adapting to changes in the structure of opportunity and the increasingly protracted process of moving into stable work or studies, but they cannot simply be viewed and treated as "entrepreneurs of themselves." At a societal level, policy frameworks that emphasize individual choice and responsibility intensify the effects of both advantage and disadvantage. The new policy emphasis on choice tries "to create markets where markets cannot operate," wasting both fiscal and human resources. It is fostering a variety of new managerial bureaucracies, on top of existing ones, and leading to "a free-for-all, which favors, as one would expect, the well-connected and the well-to-do."[12] Not least the shift toward individual responsibility implies that government has no role in reforming the social and economic world toward which young people are moving.

Learning Structures and Opportunities

Discussion about young people's needs and the effects of social structure has parallels in debates about appropriate learning affordances. Most industrialized countries invest heavily in learning during the secondary years, far more in relative terms than does the United States.[13] More of that investment also goes to support learning outside of school, through youth-oriented organizations and for work-based learning. Belief in the value of applied learning experiences has led to a broad view of what is considered productive activity during the sixteen-to-nineteen age period. Vocationally oriented, and especially work-based, learning is seen as developmentally valuable for young people, and the workplace is a powerful venue for individual growth.

Access to learning opportunities, while viewed as a right of citizenship, is nonetheless a contested social and policy issue. Many countries have a history of rigid and rigidly separated learning pathways through adolescence that, though putatively meritocratic, closely mirror social class and parents' occupations. Recent critiques of countries in which vocational education pathways are thought to be valued as highly as academic pathways find a variety of kinds of subtle discrimination.[14] For instance, although vocational-technical learning is respected in most countries discussed here, it tends to serve disproportionately working-class youth. (More advantaged youth will participate where there is some permeability between vocational education training [VET] and higher education—that is, where pathways between the two are both open and recognized by the higher education system.[15]) Within VET there continues to be differences in access to work-based learning opportunities based on family background (e.g., parents' occupations and educational attainment) and ethnic origin. Immigrant youth and those from ethnic, religious, and racial minority groups are especially likely to be directed into less prestigious apprenticeships.

These kinds of subtle discrimination are viewed as compromising social democratic ideals. To address them, some countries, such as Finland, have recommitted themselves to a universal educational experience for all youth through age eighteen. Others have focused on strengthening work-based learning opportunities for disenfranchised youth, especially immigrant and migrant youth. Apprenticeship itself is sometimes used to address problems of social exclusion (and social anger), as has been the case in France and Great Britain, where expanded apprenticeship programs were included in governments' response to rioting in immigrant communities. More tentatively, a handful of countries have sought to redefine educational equity in the new "knowledge economy" to include equitable access to new forms of intellectual capital.

The economic situation throughout Europe has complicated efforts to equalize learning opportunity. With unemployment rates for eighteen- to twenty-five-year-olds extraordinarily high in many countries, it has become more difficult to meet commitments to provide work-related learning opportunities for sixteen- to eighteen-year-olds. It has also become more difficult to conceptualize vocational learning in generous yet deep terms in bifurcated economies in which the middle is hollowing out and in which craft-based occupational traditions are atrophying.

A Distinctive Youth Work Role

Youth work, often called the third sector to distinguish it from education and workforce development, is a distinctive type of developmental support and plays an important role in many countries. It is the one sector that emphasizes the developmental needs and rights of youth and the importance of civic development, providing counterbalance to the instrumental preoccupations of other sectors. Although youth workers tend to focus directly on serving disenfranchised youth, they view their societal role in broader terms. Morena Cuconato and colleagues observe that different institutions, from the "soft sector" of youth work to the "hard sector" of vocational preparation, complement each other, creating a continuum of youth development supports.[16] Each type is critical at different moments in and phases of a young person's life. Supports provided by the youth work sector also ensure that the abstract goal of social integration acquires concrete meaning in the lives of individual youth.

Youth workers have played an important role in facilitating access to new kinds of experiences for young people in fields they may not know about or seek out for themselves. Of one young person linked to an ecology project in Denmark, a youth worker observed that "it was important for him to realize that there were things other people did in which he could take part."[17] Youth workers have contributed also to broader efforts to address what one recent study in New Zealand identified as "truncated" labor market literacy. Youth in this study had little apparent understanding of how educational experiences contribute to vocation, beyond leading to particular qualifications. They lacked vocabulary or concepts for discussing vocational questions. They viewed the adult world as a "kaleidoscope" of occupations, fields, and ill-defined opportunities and had no idea of how to sort them out.[18]

As economic pressures have begun to unravel the social fabric in many countries, the youth work sector has been especially attentive to manifestations of this process in young people, including feelings of blocked development and opportunity, anger, alienation, and a felt need to begin to build alternative social forms. Youth workers have seen an important role for themselves in helping youth cope with the contradiction of youth policies that emphasize social integration through vocational education and training in countries that cannot promise youth a place in the economy. They can explain contradictions and help young people who are frustrated in their search for work or an apprenticeship and who are increasingly angry at the failure of adults to address societal problems. The youth work sector has helped education and labor force institutions make sense of a lack of uptake or high default rates in training schemes. It has also been a partner in efforts to design transition programs that are more developmentally and cultural sensitive.

Youth work has assigned itself a distinctive role in fostering a sense of social solidarity among youth and in supporting young peoples' civic development, and youth workers have played a critical role in training and providing backstops to youth-led political and civic organizations. Youth work centers and organizations have provided a platform for young people to join in community development efforts, service projects, political debate, arts, and environmental work. Youth workers were among the first to recognize the social value of young people's creative contributions, especially with digital technologies and social media, as an untapped economic resource. In response, the youth work sector has pushed for new kinds of apprenticeship and means for validating nonformal learning experiences in creative fields.

As learning has come to replace youth development in much of the discourse on adolescent needs, the youth work sector has tried to promote a broad conception of learning, one that is less schoolcentric. This conception emphasizes the need to democratize learning as well as to balance labor market concerns with social and civic ones. Youth work initiatives in Europe also have been accompanied by a number of efforts to capture and validate (i.e., give young people credit for) nonformal learning experiences. The most recent is called Youthpass, a system for documenting participation in a specific nonformal learning activity, including description of the experiences involved and knowledge and skills acquired. Proponents note that although Youthpass is not an alternative approach to certifying occupational qualifications, it does communicate to potential employers something of the learning and life experience of a young person.

STRUCTURING LOWER SECONDARY EDUCATION

Lower secondary education, which typically serves young people aged fourteen and fifteen, has struggled for a clear identity in many countries. A central tension has been whether to view it as a distinctive level of schooling, with its own purposes and content, or as an extended transition between primary and upper secondary, with a focus on preparing for choices to be made about the latter. There has also been some tension around curriculum, whether it should be common for all or leveled, broad or specialized. Although various national cultures find expression in varied education choices, many countries in the Eurozone and Asian-Pacific region begin attending to heterogeneity among youth by the middle school years through curricular differentiation, with an intensified focus on pathways by the lower secondary years. Countries vary widely in whether and when they deliberately place youth on different learning tracks. Some countries (e.g., Germany, Austria, Hungary) begin sorting children as early as age 9 or 10; others (e.g., Switzerland, the Netherlands, Italy) by age 12, 13, or

14; others (e.g., Australia, Sweden, Denmark, Norway) at age 16; and still others (e.g., United Kingdom, Finland, Canada) never do so at all.

Until recently there was surprisingly little debate about the effects of early, late, or no sorting on the assumption that national policies fit national cultures and would therefore be difficult to alter. Criticism of sorting has grown recently due to both changing internal social dynamics in some countries and to findings from cross-national studies using PISA (Program for International Student Assessment) and other data. For instance, research in the Netherlands finds that early selection processes tend to reproduce social class and immigration status.[19] Reflecting on the early differentiation of children in Austria, one research team notes that it leads to "a loss of knowledge potential that can never be made up for later on."[20] Research that compared PISA scores from countries with various sorting policies found that early sorting increased later inequality in achievement.[21]

Those disposed toward deliberate early sorting point out that it occurs regardless of whether it occurs deliberately and transparently or as a de facto practice. In the United States, for instance, children are already informally tracked and grouped by first grade and, sometimes, even by kindergarten. In contrast to those countries with defined differentiation points, in the United States "decisions about differentiation are diffused over the whole K–12 curricular span," and such decisions are often opaque to young people and their families.[22]

Countries with differentiated upper secondary systems typically begin tracking children in middle school (lower secondary). Most have layered approaches, with prevocational curricula for career exploration and opportunities to move from one track to another at specific points in time. The Netherlands, for example, begins differentiating young people at age twelve. Parents are advised as to whether an academic or vocational route will be more appropriate based on school performance and test scores. Some 65 percent of young people participate in "preparatory" vocational, or prevocational, education, which provides further opportunity for assessment and decision making.

In Switzerland, differentiation among learning pathways and planning for postcompulsory options also begins by age twelve or thirteen. Young people are placed in one of three types of first-level secondary schools (basic, intermediate, or advanced). They typically have the same core teacher during all three years of first-level secondary schooling, giving that teacher a strong sense of a young person's learning profile, strengths, and limitations. During the (equivalent of) the ninth grade year, young people are introduced to the range of apprenticeship options and visit work places, doing as much as a week of job-shadowing in specific firms. Postcompulsory placement decisions are made when young people are fourteen or fifteen.

Germany actually begins formally sorting children into one of three clearly defined tracks (academic, mixed academic-practical, vocational) as early as fourth grade, although there is some openness for a few years after that. Placement is based on grades and teacher and counselor recommendations, although parents have some input. During the last year of lower secondary school, German youth have opportunities to explore options within their track. They may do brief internships in particular industries in order to help with choice of an apprenticeship. Recently there has been criticism of the early sorting of children in Germany, "legitimated by the tenacious ideology of 'innate talent' [and the] classification of children as having either practical talents or theoretical abilities."[23] Yet there continues to be strong societal support for this practice based on a shared perception that it serves the majority of youth well.

Other countries that differentiate youth in upper secondary provide a common curriculum until that point. For instance, Italian children have a common educational program through age fourteen, at which point they take state exams and are counseled or selected into different types of *liceos* or *institutos*—classical, scientific, linguistic, artistic, technical/vocational. Finnish youth have a common curriculum until age sixteen but are required to receive two hours of guidance and counseling per week to help them prepare for various postsecondary options.[24] In England, lower secondary schooling offers a common curriculum but is also characterized by continuous experimentation, with many models attempting to create elements that would engage or reengage young people discouraged by schooling. For instance, further education colleges (equivalent to American community colleges) have been recruited to offer options that draw on their distinct resources to introduce fourteen–to-sixteen-year-olds to occupational fields and collegelike learning. One initiative, Increased Flexibility for 14 to 16 Year Olds, created voluntary local partnerships through which youth could take vocational coursework at a further education college complemented by workplace experiences. The idea was to expose young people to a specific occupational field that they might be curious about while at the same time creating more engaging learning experiences. Youth participating in this initiative reported liking the practical focus, being able to concentrate on one field for weeks at a time, being responsible for their own learning, being able to pace themselves on tasks, being free physically to move around, and, especially, being treated like adults. Youth appreciated that mentors and tutors did not use authority in an arbitrary manner and that they held their own craft or trade, as well as others, in esteem. They reported appreciating physical demonstration as a teaching and corrective approach, the opportunity to meet and work with new people, and the general experience of "learning in a different environment at this stage in their school career."[25]

POSTCOMPULSORY LEARNING: AGE SIXTEEN AS A DEMARCATION POINT

It is common in Europe and some Asian-Pacific countries to treat age sixteen, the end of ninth or tenth grade, as a demarcation point, after which learning options and arrangements for young people become more negotiated, if not individualized. The varied national approaches to structuring learning, training, and work experience from age sixteen to nineteen or twenty are described as *postcompulsory learning* or *transition regimes*. Policy frameworks may be universal in emphasis, focused on all youth, as in Finland and Denmark; compensatory, focusing primarily on disenfranchised youth, as in the United Kingdom and France; or include elements of both, as in the Netherlands and Australia. Countries differ in their emphasis on a common upper secondary curriculum for all youth. Upper secondary learning is not typically defined by grade levels. Pathways and timeframes may be more flexible or less so. In some instances, young people are considered to have left school, in other instances to be continuing with it. For example, youth who undertake apprenticeships are typically considered primarily trainees and employees rather than students and may even be paid for taking required coursework at vocational colleges.

Most countries have at least a few defined postcompulsory routes, notably academic studies, focused on preparation for university; vocational education, with or without concentration in an occupational area (and with or without apprenticeship as a prominent element); or further general study equivalent to a community college. The last typically includes both general and vocational coursework and provides some opening to university studies. Young people who do not secure a place in a university may matriculate in a vocational or technical college. A handful of countries have technical institutes that provide a preprofessional course of study for selective professions such as medicine, law, education, or business.

Data are not easily comparable, and percentages vary from country to country, but overall about 20–25 percent of each youth cohort take an academic route, 40–60 percent a defined vocational route, and the remainder mixed routes or none at all. Variation among countries is related to the selectivity of academic secondary systems, the size and strength of youth apprenticeship systems, and differences in how academic and vocational learning are understood to relate to each other, as, for example, distinctive or mutually enriching. Variation derives also from differences in where countries locate responsibility for learning, especially for securing work-based learning places. For example, in countries in which private firms have a strong sense of civic responsibility and/or responsibility for youth, there is more opportunity for apprenticeship.

Defining Rights and Responsibilities

Although young people are not required to continue schooling beyond age sixteen, in most countries they have certain rights (or guarantees) to learning and/or training experiences in exchange for some kind of obligation (moral or contractual) to try their best when taking up offers. In Norway, for instance, a legal framework called Youth Right guarantees young people who have completed lower secondary education the right to three years of upper secondary in one of three programs of their choice (there are twelve programs in total). The three years of continuing support must be used within a five-year period. Students who decide to switch can transfer some credits from one program of study to another. But making the combination of rights and obligation work together within a non-compulsory framework has proven difficult in many countries. Questions of the responsibility of different institutions to offer and then subsidize learning/training experiences, how and whether to enforce young people's active participation, and how to direct young people's efforts have contributed to lack of societal clarity about this age period.

Most European countries view the task of helping young people through the postcompulsory period as one that has to be shared among the school system, higher education, workforce agencies, employers, and the social welfare institutions. In the Netherlands, for instance, government works closely with the private sector to create a variety of work and worklike experiences and to define qualifications in different sectors. There has also been a regionwide movement to push responsibility for organizing learning experiences down to local regions or municipalities, on the grounds that local authorities know local resources best. Swedish laws, for instance, make municipalities responsible for ensuring a place for all people who have completed lower secondary schooling. In Wales, local partnerships called Community Consortia for Education and Training have been able to organize cohorts of learners by specific interests and to help local school leaders learn about new or growing occupational niches, such as in applied arts, design, and tourism.[26]

Many countries have developed separate systems for youth who are unemployed and not in education or training, primarily "protected" or sheltered training/work experiences. The idea, which has been subject to criticism for being inauthentic, is to bring youth "back to the main road" of the VET and/or further education system.[27] Alternative pathways may include various kinds of contracts and mutual agreements that have proven difficult to enforce. France, for instance, has developed a Contrat d'Insertion dans la Vie Sociale (Integration-into-Society Contract), for young people aged sixteen to twenty-five who are neither in school nor work. The contract commits the state to support a one-year (renewable) individualized plan of vocational coursework and workplace learning, with youth paid a percentage of minimum wage for participating and employers guaranteed certain tax breaks. Youth (and/or their legal guardians) agree to follow through on opportunities provided. Vocational programs for disenfranchised youth typically pay a wage or stipend, which may be dependent on active participation in some approved program of training or study.

NORTHERN AND CENTRAL EUROPE: VARIATIONS ON A THEME IN VOCATIONAL EDUCATION AND TRAINING

Vocational education and training, the international equivalent of CTE, plays an integral part in upper secondary education in most northern and some central European countries. VET is based on a complex understanding of vocation as a social role and identity, one that signifies a particular place in the larger culture. It is understood as a way to bring young people into adulthood, as a socialization as well as a learning experience. Nonetheless, approaches to VET vary, including the relative importance of school- and work-based learning (and of theory and practice); the roles of the business sector, unions, and other stakeholders; and the prestige of VET in the larger educational context. In general, apprenticeship plays an important role in non-U.S. VET systems, often a defining one. There are notable exceptions, including France, Sweden, and the United Kingdom. France, for instance, continues to support a school-based approach to VET, with strong technical tracks (Sections de Technicien Superior) in upper secondary school. Sweden also emphasizes mostly school-based VET, in part because industry has taken a hands-off approach to young people's learning and preparation. (Though an upper secondary school reform initiative just recently under way does emphasize apprenticeship.) Britain deemphasizes VET altogether.

The majority of countries with well-developed VET systems have national standards for certification and entry into specific fields. These are usually tied to qualifications frameworks, which are intended to certify types and levels of competence (and experience) in a specific field, organize learning experiences, and create vocational equivalences to academic credentials. Countries have varying numbers of qualification types, from 80 or 90 to as many as 350. There may be a few levels of qualification achieved through a combination of examination and years in apprenticeship. Most countries now participate to some degree in the European Qualifications Framework, intended to create a transportable credential.

Countries vary in whether they understand vocational training as something apart from formal education, occurring after it in a sequential manner, or as something to be integrated with education, occurring simultaneously. The extent to which young people who enroll in VET continue studying traditional academic subjects (e.g., history, economics, languages) also varies. School-based and workplace experiences are sequenced in a variety of ways: part of each week in school and part in the workplace over two to four years; interspersed blocks of time (e.g., three to six months each) in school- and work-based learning; two years of school-based VET followed by some number of years of work-based experience; etc.

In Switzerland young people in the VET system spend part of each week in school and part at a work site. In Denmark and the Netherlands young people spend alternating blocks of time (e.g., three to six months) in school and the workplace. Norway follows the "two-plus-two" model, with students taking two years of school-based coursework, covering a range of academic as well as technical subjects, followed by two years of apprenticeship. Young people enrolled in vocational/technical upper secondary schools might have the option of taking exams that lead to technical or general university studies. In some countries, Switzerland being one example, a young person can continue studying for a professional or technical baccalaureate after completing an apprenticeship. Conversely, in a few countries young people on university pathways may be required to spend a day a week in an apprenticeship experience, as is the case in the Netherlands, or have it as one option, as in the United Kingdom.

Reasons for variety in models include the search to find the best approaches to keeping young people engaged in learning; employers' need to have a predictable workforce, one present every day; and the desire to keep college pathways open for youth. There are also differences among countries in beliefs about the role of vocational education in preparing young people for adulthood, including (but not only) work life. Some national cultures, like that of Germany, hold that vocational knowledge in general and work-based learning in particular are powerful organizers for personal development. That leads to a training approach based on the idea that the "whole occupation" has to be acquired; the theoretical and practical, technical, and social form a whole that cannot be broken into discrete modules. A handful of countries, Norway for one, view vocational education as a vehicle for nurturing a fully developed, "integrated" human being, with the development of social, civic, and ethical awareness as important as preparation for work.[28]

Dual System Models

Countries in which private firms play an important role in vocational education and training, in cooperation with trade unions and educational institutions, are said to have a "dual system." These countries, including Germany, Austria, Denmark, and Switzerland, combine strong youth apprenticeship systems with part-time vocational schooling. Large numbers of firms participate, as do sizable percentages of youth. In Germany, one in four firms offers apprenticeships, with 70 percent of medium-size firms and 87 percent of large-size firms doing so. In Austria, some 40,000 companies provide apprenticeships to some 130,000 young people, representing about 40 percent of youth in each age cohort.[29]

The dual system model derives from a distinct view of the role and responsibility of the private firm and a sense of partnership among stakeholders, including trade unions. Self-interest is one motivating factor. For example, firms can get to know young people well (and secure some relatively inexpensive labor) before they hire them into a labor system with extensive worker protections and guarantees. Other motives are just as important. Private firms view themselves as responsible not just to shareholders but to their employees and communities. Employers believe strongly in the importance of investing in young people.[30] Taking on (and paying the salaries of) apprentices and participating more generally in VET is viewed by companies as an expression of this broader responsibility.

In dual system countries, government typically plays a structuring role through legal statutes spelling out roles and responsibilities of stakeholders and the imposition of taxes designated to subsidize vocational training. Governments also stimulate the creation of industry-specific advisory bodies and intermediaries with representation of employers, chambers of commerce, trade unions, educational institutions, and student organizations. These bodies assume some responsibility for apprenticeship- and classroom-based curriculum development, assessment, and sometimes placement and a portion of training. Among countries using the dual system model, Germany is notable for its complex web of social partners and advisory bodies operating at the national, regional, industry sector, and company levels.[31] Partners include employers' federations, chambers of commerce, chambers of craft, trade unions, vocational colleges, firm-based training centers, and local worker councils. Germany has a long-standing craft code, and many firms belong to one of ninety-four crafts. These have retained the historic guild system of master craftsmanship with controls over the right to "trade" and to train others.[32]

A Prominent Role for Youth Apprenticeship

In many countries apprenticeship for two, three, or four years is a prominent learning experience, a well-defined route to employment, and a valued social role and identity. Apprenticeship gives definition and grounding to the period after compulsory schooling ends. Because it is an extended as well as an extensive experience, apprenticeship provides "protracted socialization into work processes, social learning, deep technical learning, proximity to work, and a sense of identification with a specific employer."[33] It is viewed in some countries as a vehicle for reconciling the different interests of labor and capital, as a way of creating common ground. What apprenticeship does not and cannot do is ameliorate broader youth labor market problems. These problems have in fact put enormous pressure on important foundations of the institution, including implied employment guarantees at the firm providing apprenticeship, support from trade unions, and societal views of apprenticeship as an important pathway for young people.

As with VET in general, government typically plays a statutory role in apprenticeship systems, defining legal responsibilities and general training requirements, and it may subsidize parts of young people's training experiences, with employers expected to pay some or all of the wages of apprentices. Apprentices typically are protected by labor laws (and in some cases union contracts) and are paid a defined percentage of journeyman-level or skilled work wages, perhaps a third or so. They also may receive an education/training allowance or stipend.

Although apprenticeship traditionally has been located in workplaces, private firms have begun to shift responsibility to their own or industry-specific training centers for parts of the apprenticeship experience. Small, specialized firms may not be able to provide the range of training experiences necessary in a field, so they too rely on outside sites for some parts of the apprenticeship experience. Mandatory coursework in vocational schools or colleges typically includes theory tied to an occupational field, labor law, and history and perhaps also languages, business, math, and employability skills. In addition to more traditional apprenticeship in manufacturing trades, there are many newer options, for instance in the caring, human service, and health professions, in emergent fields like information technology, biotechnology, telecommunications, and the creative and cultural sector. Skills qualification authorities have worked to design qualification structures that acknowledge the distinct nature of work and the more fluid definition of roles and expertise in newer sectors.

Germany: Growing Tensions for a Paradigmatic Model

Germany's widely studied youth apprenticeship system is usually viewed as a model for a full-fledged commitment to youth apprenticeship, in spite of growing difficulties in finding enough placements for youth. About half of all youth in Germany combine work and schooling through a three-year apprenticeship leading to a qualification in one of 350 occupations.[34]

That requires about 600,000 new places each year.[35] An additional 15 percent of each youth cohort take a VET concentration in some newer field, such as health professions, and 25 percent pursue university studies.

Youth apprentices in Germany are considered employees for the three days a week that they are at the work site. The sponsoring company pays them for those three days while the government funds young peoples' attendance at part-time vocational schools. Vocational schools, run by each state, are closely tied to industry and unions, and youth apprentices are in vocational school two days a week for the first year or two and a day and a half after that. The vocational curriculum includes workers' roles and rights, labor law, and history.

Many observers have commented on the importance of cultural sanction to the historic success of Germany's youth apprenticeship system. The German culture values, with both "recognition and status, a wide array of occupations not requiring university training."[36] The concept of occupation is also understood broadly, as both a set of knowledge and skills and a social identity. Young people who choose the apprenticeship route do not view themselves as learning failures or second-class learners; rather, they have a positive identity as learners and workers. All the stakeholders—employers, trade unions, education authorities, and government as a whole—are fully committed to youth apprenticeship.

Even as it is lauded as a model, the German apprenticeship system is experiencing new criticism and a number of strains. Differentiation among apprenticeship types has become an issue, with observers noting that youth from lower track secondary schools are more likely to be pushed or pulled into craft and blue-collar occupations. Meanwhile, young peoples' own interest in certain traditional apprenticeships, especially those classified as handiwork (e.g., auto mechanics), is declining.[37] The gap between the number of young people seeking apprenticeships and the number of available places is growing, "forcing an increasingly large share of youth into pseudo-training" experiences.[38] At the same time, a growing number of young people are considered not ready for apprenticeships, and youth with weak educational backgrounds have to wait two or more years for a slot. Fewer apprentices—now less than 50 percent—are being hired by their firms; and some 30–40 percent of young people now change fields after having been through part or all of an apprenticeship.[39] The rigidity of Germany's pathways is also leaving a significant number of young people without clear options at the end of tenth grade. In one recent year, in Berlin, 13,500 of 44,000 young people finishing tenth grade were "off track" with no obvious next steps.[40]

Other dual system countries have experienced similar tensions in their apprenticeship systems, especially gaps between demand and places. That has led sponsors to become more selective with respect to educational and social background (and such factors as fluency with the native language). In Austria, for instance, which now lacks apprenticeship places for close to a third of applicants, immigrant and migrant youth have had an especially difficult time securing an apprenticeship. Their proportional share of apprenticeship placements is only half of what it should be. There is evidence that Austrian "companies still reject the applications of young men and women due to their ethnic origin."[41] For their part, employers claim that a growing proportion of all youth who seek apprenticeships lack basic academic and self-presentation skills and evidence of a work ethic.

AUSTRALIA, UNITED KINGDOM, AND CANADA—THE OUTLIERS

Australia has recently reembraced its longstanding goal of strengthening its vocational education system. There have been mostly symbolic moves in this direction for a number of years. For instance, youth in some states and regions of Australia are required to make career choices in the middle of high school. Career and technical education and training experiences for high school–age youth have been linked into the national vocational qualification system. VET authorities have reinvigorated the career academy structure, with industry-specific high schools in such domains as minerals and energy, aviation, wines and tourism, creative arts, health sciences, and STEM fields.[42]

VET participation rates among Australian high school students remain modest. Some 10 percent of high school–age youth undertake school-based apprenticeships and traineeships, the latter based partly in workplaces and partly in schools in trade training centers. The largest percentage of these apprenticeships are in service professions, followed by business and information technology. An additional modest percentage of youth begin formal trade apprenticeships at age seventeen or eighteen through trades councils. There are also a variety of preapprenticeship programs for disenfranchised youth, intended to both prepare them for and link them to formal apprenticeship opportunities. In the 2013 school year, school authorities, in coordination with other workforce stakeholders, are starting a new program, trade cadetships, that will have two stages: foundation and preapprenticeship. The latter will provide some immersion in a specific trade, with the goal of directing youth into formal apprenticeships and addressing skilled labor shortages in some fields.

Efforts to rethink secondary education in Australia have included a number of stakeholders with different interests, leading to strain and some conflict over goals and sources of authority. Participants in the process include local and regional school authorities, national school curriculum authorities, higher education accreditation bodies, national vocational qualifications bodies, and workforce bodies. Individual secondary schools themselves have struggled to accept new roles and responsibilities, to support learning and working in a range of occupational areas, and to view themselves as responsible for learning experiences outside the walls of school.[43] Industry has asked for and received a significant role in shaping the emergent upper secondary VET system, including vocational curricula. The growing role and influence of industry has heightened philosophical tensions over the purpose of education and training. As Alison Taylor notes, the reform process has been driven by a perceived need for economic restructuring, "underpinned with a supporting discourse of equity."[44] The tension between social and economic goals has been a persistent presence in each new scheme presented for youth and for the economy.

The United Kingdom has struggled for more than four decades to find learning structures that might overcome a history of schooling defined by extreme social stratification, competition, and selection. Policy makers have been criticized for constantly changing course, for creating and abandoning new frameworks and initiatives. Currently, there are two policy emphases at the secondary level. The first involves support for creation of new types of secondary schools. These have included two models with a nonvocational focus—academies, which confer increased control on a local school community, and free schools, which are similar to American charter schools—and two models with a moderate vocational focus: university technical colleges, which are sponsored by a university, and studio schools, which are just getting under way.

The studio school is the most distinctive of this group of models, incorporating many of the innovative elements described in chapter 3, including project-based learning, with practical projects (including commissions) occupying 80 percent of the curriculum; personalized learning, with each student having a personal coach; longer school days, to give young people a sense of the work day; and small school size, about three hundred students. Each studio school has an occupational theme, such as creative arts and media, health care, tourism, or engineering. Each school also has local business and/or nonprofit partners that provide work-based learning opportunities, four hours a week for 14- and 15-year-olds and two days a week for 16-to-19-year-olds.

The second current policy emphasis focuses squarely on VET. Vocational routes in the UK have long been and continue to be viewed as second-class options. Recent governments have been accused of conveying mixed signals when it comes to belief in vocational-technical studies, emphasizing their importance as an option while focusing policy and resources on increasing rates of participation in higher education. They have been accused also of trying to reframe vocational learning "in ways that superficially may appear to adhere to the rhetoric of rights and inclusion, but which in practice [continue to] disenfranchise" some categories of youth.[45]

Some criticism has been directed at education and workforce authorities' overemphasis on qualification frameworks as a conceptual basis for vocational education and an accompanying underemphasis on the importance of defining and ensuring good learning and working experiences. One researcher reports that "one third of all 16–19 year olds in England are following vocational courses leading to qualifications that are more or less valueless in the labor market."[46] Such courses often lead also to a dead-end in opportunity for learning progression; that is, they do not provide a pathway to some kinds of further education. The current approach to vocational education may be a modest departure in that it asks industry to take a more central role in vocational curriculum and learning experiences, a request that has not yet been taken up. It calls as well for fourteen employer-led Sector Skills Councils that, in turn, are supposed to create Diploma Development Partnerships consisting of employers, higher education institutions, schools, and other stakeholders to define knowledge and skills for sector-specific diplomas.[47]

Education reformers in the UK also view expansion of apprenticeship for sixteen-to-eighteen–year-olds (and a broadened view of the concept of apprenticeship itself) as a key to a more equitable education system for older youth. Different levels of apprenticeship have been created to allow for broader participation and different levels of commitment. Apprenticeships have been shortened, with a growing portion just a year in length. Apprenticeships have also been opened up to nontraditional fields such as customer service, food preparation (McDonald's is a major sponsor), retail management, hospitality, child care, hairdressing, and the creative and cultural sector, which includes such diverse occupations as advertising, crafts and cultural heritage work, literary and performing arts, video and video games, arts management and curatorship. One example of a new type of apprenticeship is the Conservation Technician, an entry-level role in libraries and museums for which a consortium of twenty institutions has worked to define skills sets and job descriptions. Agencies responsible for workforce development have joined with those representing the cultural sector to develop a blueprint for better defining and broadening the array of entry-level work in creative and cultural fields and bringing young people into them. Funds have been raised for Creative Apprenticeships in community arts management, cultural and heritage venue operations, live events and promotion, music business, and technical theater.

The expansion of apprenticeship fields has provided new avenues for growth for young people previously without access to this sort of learning.

One study of the first-year apprenticeship experience of young women (sixteen and seventeen years old) preparing to be child care workers found growth not only in their knowledge and skills but in their ability to recognize "the developmental role of the nursery nurse" and to keep "their own feelings under control in the face of crisis and provocation" and to develop a "suitable disposition for child care work." These young women were beginning to grow into a specific adult identity. Moreover, participating youth told researchers that "the patience and self-control they had learned in the nursery was now part of their persona at college and at home."[48]

Many of the new apprenticeships nonetheless provide a diluted work and learning experience, which has been criticized as a vehicle for inducing "low-achieving youth into semi-skilled sectors."[49] Shorter apprenticeships make especially little sense for occupations in which it does take time to acquire important knowledge and skills, since it is in years two and three that apprentices provide a return (in productivity) for a firm's investment in training them. Yet the majority of youth seeking an apprenticeship experience have chosen or been directed into the less demanding of the nontraditional fields listed above. Many of the newer apprenticeships also come with little or no guarantee of a relevant job and thus are viewed as holding places for hard-to-employ youth. Robert MacDonald views them as the continuation of a history of "disguising" youth unemployment by "warehousing young people in training schemes."[50]

In some respects, the United Kingdom has been experiencing the opposite problem of countries with strong historic apprenticeship systems. While these countries have begun to ask themselves whether they need to broaden historically deep and specific apprenticeship experiences, the UK is struggling with the question of what a modern apprenticeship should be about given the changing nature of work. Employers and unions have been reluctant partners, limiting the number of apprenticeship slots.[51] Employers—90 percent of whom do not currently sponsor apprenticeships—have been wary of the potential expense. Those that do provide apprenticeships prefer older apprentices. Also, government authorities have struggled to define the role of further education colleges (equivalent to American community colleges). More fundamentally, the UK's history of ambivalence toward and reversals in VET illustrate the limits of efforts to open up learning without attending to fundamental problems of social stratification and exclusion.

The structure of and emphases within secondary education in Canada closely resemble those in the United States, with moderately greater efforts to promote youth apprenticeship.[52] Only a modest percentage— 10 percent—of credits taken by high school youth are vocational in nature; college-going has become a central goal, and vocational education continues to be viewed as the option for less academically talented young people. The academic-vocational divide is internalized by young people, who tend to see themselves as either hands-on or book learners. Transition planning and supports are intermittent and modest in scope, leaving many youth unprepared for either postsecondary learning or the labor market. The relationship between sectors, especially between schools and employers, but also between the community college system and employers, is weak.

At the same time, stakeholders in both secondary education and workforce development in Canada have been more inclined than their U.S. peers to try to improve supports for young people. There has, for instance, been some modest effort to broaden responsibility for vocational education beyond the school system. Employers in the Quebec province must either provide some affordances for work-based learning or pay into a fund that supports such learning for young people.[53]

A number of provinces (notably Alberta, British Columbia, and Ontario) have well-defined or emergent preapprenticeship programs for high school–age youth. A one- or two-year preapprenticeship experience during high school might lead to entry into a formal union apprenticeship program or further study at a technical community college or serve as a self-contained experience. Programs typically include school-based coursework designed to complement work site activities, occupation-specific classroom time at a regional training center, and paid work placement, all of which provide credits toward graduation.[54] Students might take an applied math, science, or English course designed to complement vocational activities, generic vocational coursework (e.g., healthy and safety, work practices and procedures, worker education agreements), and coursework specific to the trade involved (e.g., for automotive repair, courses in power trains, steering, brakes, electrical, etc.). Some apprenticeships also include "integration days," time away from the field to reflect on and integrate workplace experiences.

An Example: Alberta's Registered Apprenticeship Program

For their participation in Alberta's Registered Apprenticeship Program (RAP), young people receive both high school course credits and formal trade-specific apprenticeship credit of up to one year. For each 125 apprenticeship hours, students receive credit for one high school elective, up to eight courses' worth, which constitute all available elective credits. RAP is structured to have some attributes of a true apprenticeship in that young people are paid for their work time and viewed by stakeholders—schools, employers, trade unions—as both high school students and registered apprentices (under the purview of the provincial Apprenticeship and Industry Training Board). There are forty-nine trades in the program. In 9-to-5 trades young people tend to work in blocks, perhaps spending six months at school and then six weeks at work. Young people can continue in the apprenticeship after graduating from high school.[55]

A researcher who has studied RAP observes that even though youth apprenticeship in the Canadian context is more closely tied to the world of work than other vocationally oriented school approaches, it is nonetheless constrained by the lack of larger cultural sanction for the choice of work over academics during the high school years.[56] Young people reportedly bear a good deal of responsibility for making the experience work. For instance, they have to search out employers willing to take an apprentice, and they have to arrange their schedules. RAP apprenticeship experiences remain unconnected to a sanctioned pathway through high school, thus, its designation as an *elective* in high school curricula. Because RAP is viewed as an individual choice, it is not embedded in a larger picture that helps young people see what various pathways are from high school to further options and choices. Young people bear responsibility for integrating applied and academic learning, and they usually choose to keep the two separate. As one young woman notes, "Going to work and going to school are two different things."[57] Apprentices also report feeling caught between two worlds, feeling neither like students nor like workers.

As in the United States and the United Kingdom, youth apprenticeship in Canada tends to be treated as a response to a problem, a fall-back option, a discreet experience, rather than an important pathway toward adulthood. It is neither systematized nor institutionally rooted. This limits its impact as a learning institution for young people and a pathway recognized by them and their families.[58] One report on Ontario's youth apprenticeship program notes that, even in a supportive educational and business climate, as exists in Ontario, recruiting youth apprentices "is made more difficult by the social stigma that surrounds the skilled trades."[59]

Canada's youth apprenticeship system relies on voluntary (as opposed to statutory) collaboration among schools, technical colleges, training organizations, and employers. Such collaboration requires ongoing negotiation of all the elements of apprenticeship. For example, one study found differences among partners in how narrowly or broadly apprenticeships should be cast, the right balance of theory and practice, and whether or not learning and working experiences should be organized around the assumption that young people would proceed into formal union apprenticeships. Partners typically have to negotiate how students are selected and which students should receive priority for an apprenticeship. Employers might prefer the strongest applicants, and schools might want a more diverse mix.[60] Not least, partners differ in their views of what apprenticeship experiences are for. Employers want to make sure young people develop the skills needed in their particular enterprise, while other partners focus more on knowledge and skills needed for life.

SHIFTING FOUNDATIONS FOR POSTCOMPULSORY LEARNING

Other countries' more differentiated, and generally more vocationally oriented, approaches to learning during the high school years, along with a philosophical link between learning opportunities and citizenship rights, provide a compelling example for the United States. Yet lessons that until recently seemed clear have been muddied by severe financial and economic strains, especially in the Eurozone. Tensions have emerged between social democratic traditions and governments' belief that youth policies have to prioritize economic competitiveness. An emphasis on individual initiative has weakened the political and, increasingly, social commitment to vulnerable youth. Speaking of the sizable numbers of young people with ill-defined prospects, a German youth worker asks, "Where in society do our kids have the opportunity to reflect upon the demands they have to face when they have left school?"[61]

In much of Europe, vocational education and training continues to play an important role in both meeting the needs of youth and reconciling social and economic tensions. Many policy goals are pinned on it, ranging from addressing skills shortages and preparing youth for a knowledge economy to helping the education system itself respond to technological change, promoting competitiveness, and reducing social exclusion and inequality.[62] Work-based learning in particular continues to be seen to provide not only invaluable vocational preparation but also a strong identity for young people, and in the process it teaches them about themselves, about the process of working on challenging tasks, about the work world. VET is seen also to smooth out an increasingly rough-and-tumble transition process for young people.

Labor markets are evolving much faster than education systems. The latter cannot adjust rapidly enough to help each cohort of young people prepare for changing opportunities in the work world: "The education system can propose, but the labor market disposes, and its judgments often over-ride the good intentions built into policy."[63] Those involved in vocational training have tried to adapt by revising vocational curricula, creating more modularized training opportunities, broadening apprenticeship frameworks, and looking to industries to update their own training programs. Most VET frameworks are accompanied by a rhetorical emphasis on the need for lifelong learning. Some observers nonetheless view the idea with suspicion, arguing that it is really about letting young people fend for themselves.

As in the United States, work throughout the industrialized world is changing in ways that complicate decisions about personal investment in education and training. For many young people transition experiences are now defined by uncertainty, for some by blocked opportunity, unemployment, and dislocation. In interviews with a diverse sample of Australian youth, Anita Harris and colleagues found "a strong sense of anxiety about futures that could not be predicted or controlled."[64] Young people are finding a gap between received wisdom and personal experience. Cultural advice about the value of education, planning, and commitment and the costs and benefits of particular choices has proven unreliable. Unpaid internships (and even unpaid apprenticeships) have become more common. Securing and completing a traditional apprenticeship is less likely now to lead to stable employment. Changing employer commitment and changing expectations among youth, combined with changing youth populations, have led to difficulty for some youth in finding an apprenticeship slot and among employers in finding youth to fill slots.

No country reviewed here has been able to resolve a central conundrum: Regardless of how education is structured, the structures themselves end up reinforcing inequality and discrimination. Where VET is used primarily as a vehicle for fostering social inclusion, it has sometimes exacerbated perceived group differences. The common policy of ending compulsory schooling at age sixteen, in concert with a strong VET system, is intended to create the flexibility to meet individual needs. Yet there is some evidence that it heightens risks for the most disenfranchised youth, especially those from immigrant communities. For a variety of reasons, these youth are less likely to find a postsixteen path. A study in Austria concluded that the selective nature of the school system, with youth on defined pathways as early as age ten, "combined with the short duration of schooling, add to young people's disadvantages instead of reducing them."[65] In the United States, by contrast, the normative expectation—and in some states the legal requirement—of staying in school until age age tends to keep at least some of the most disenfranchised youth on an educational path. (Many others, of course, continue to be legally enrolled but are mostly checked out, mentally and, in some cases, physically.)

APPRENTICESHIP IS CHANGING

A variety of pressures are impinging on apprenticeship as an institution, and some are questioning its future role in secondary education. Apprenticeship has historically been located in between high- and low-qualification occupations, a shrinking space in most economies.[66] Traditional craftlike apprenticeship opportunities are declining. As noted earlier, even firms with a history of strong support for apprenticeship are coming to view it as a commitment they can no longer afford given intense pressure to reduce costs. A still small but growing number of firms are outsourcing their own apprentices to specialized training organizations, diluting and disembedding the experience.

The traditional youth apprenticeship format has been criticized for being too specialized and too inflexible, locking young people into a very particular learning/working experience for three or four years. One controversial response has been to broaden the concept of apprenticeship, in effect to make it more like an internship. A second in many countries has been to extend apprenticeship into the rapidly growing service sector, including caregiving, allied health care, and retail work. Another response has been to broaden the occupational focus of traditional apprenticeships and reduce the number of apprenticeship types (e.g., from three hundred or more to fewer than a hundred). Still another has been to reduce the length of apprenticeships. But all these proposed or emergent changes neutralize the historic strengths of apprenticeships, including depth of learning, extensive socialization into the work world, and opportunity to develop stable social identities within society.

The role of apprenticeship in a knowledge economy also remains poorly thought through, because the knowledge, skills, and dispositions needed for creating, monetizing, and marketing symbolic goods and services are hard to pin down. Educators argue that the intellectual capital (cognitive skills and knowledge) needed for new types of economic productivity are not easily acquired through traditional work-based learning. For these reasons, the perceived need to direct youth into postsecondary institutions, especially universities, is growing even in countries that historically valued technical and manufacturing occupations and noncollege routes. Young people themselves are more likely now to choose an apprenticeship pathway if it does not foreclose the option of attending university at a later date.

Many youth nonetheless continue to view apprenticeship as the key to a good job. One young man in Britain interviewed for a story on youth unemployment told the reporter that he "sees apprenticeship as his only hope. He recently completed an information technology training course at a local academy. But that training led nowhere, so now he is resting his hopes on securing an apprenticeship at the British military contractor BAE Systems that promises—if he can secure one of the few positions—to provide him training as an electrical engineer."[67]

The foundations of learning clearly are shifting in many countries. The vulnerable position and poor prospects for youth have led to all kinds of semi-authentic transition schemes. For instance, in one of its classic euphemisms, the European Union has an initiative called Youth on the Move, intended to help young people look across national borders for work and work-based learning opportunities. Young people have had little difficulty seeing through such schemes. In fact, their promulgation appears to contribute to frustration and anger. In interviews with a diverse sample of 280 youth from a number of countries, Manuela du Bois-Reymond found that what young people most wanted was honesty: "It would help if they [teachers and counselors] admitted and discussed with their students that there is no security and stability any longer" in the adult world.[68]

CHAPTER SEVEN

Orchestrating and Validating
a Diverse World of Learning Settings

The process of learning and identity construction appears to be located in between academic institutions, work life experiences, individual life strategies and socio-political contexts.

—pjb Associates, "Students as 'Journeymen' Between Communities of Higher Education and Work"

It is amazing to see that the more you learn, the more experience you acquire, the more sources of development you find.

—A youth worker reflecting on her own experiences with nonformal learning, in Zara Lavchyan, "Spiral Learning"

In the foregoing chapters I have focused on the importance of deep, sustained learning experience in specific settings. I have argued that young people gain important knowledge and experience and begin to grow up within particular settings. Discrete experiences in some favored domain act as spurs and anchors and initial paths toward adulthood. In this chapter I shift focus, and to some degree my argument. I argue that discrete learning experiences, no matter how rich and interesting, must add up developmentally, intellectually, and vocationally. This implies a different, less obvious role for adults and adult institutions, one that entails perspective, awareness, and a more outward orientation.

Individual institutions will have to accommodate the idea that critical knowledge and experience are distributed across many kinds of settings and the parallel idea that the process of growing up occurs across experiences and settings. They will have to learn to balance their attention between the immediate needs of each learning experience and the coherence of experiences across settings and over time. Institutions will have to make room for individually appropriate pathways. They will have to encourage and support young people to cross self-imposed social, physical, and intellectual boundaries and then stick with them through unproductive as well as productive periods. For all these tasks adult institutions will have to work together to create an infrastructure able to accommodate individual learning processes viewed in less linear, more organic terms, with nodes, branches, exchanges, and pathways. Relationships, roles, and opportunities that extend across institutions will have to be fleshed out and made clear to young people and their families. Some learning settings will have to be made more visible and accessible and be supported more deliberately by state and local government.

American society needs stakeholders in young people's development, not in particular systems or institutions. A variety of institutions, with different missions and concerns, must feel jointly and deeply responsible for young people without feeling that they own them or that they have the right to define what they need. Wisconsin's statewide youth apprenticeship program works so well because employers view it partly through a civic lens and their participation in the program as a civic responsibility. They worry about their own future workforce, but not solely about it. Employers often become personally invested in their apprentices, worrying about how they are doing in school, the quality of their school-based coursework, and their plans for the future. They take pride in apprentices' growth in school and their passage to postsecondary learning.[1]

INTERINSTITUTIONAL TASKS

To create the scaffolding for a distributed yet coherent as a set of learning experiences, work will be necessary at many levels, normative, conceptual, and practical. Stakeholders in young people's learning will have to tackle broad cultural assumptions and develop specific interinstitutional mechanisms. To create a foundation for greater coherence, diverse institutions and sectors will have to work to develop at least some shared vision of good learning, its personal and social purposes, means, and resources. As described in the previous chapter, other countries provide ideas for a broadened set of purposes, for instance addressing social inclusion and social citizenship, the valuing of all kinds of work and diverse cultural contributions, and the need for careful socialization into specific occupations.

Making young people's learning experience more coherent as a whole will require mutual learning and mutual recognition across a broad spectrum of sectors that historically have acted on their own, focusing on their own internal logic. These include schools, community-based organizations, juvenile justice, cultural institutions, civic organizations, single-cause organizations, public and private employers, higher education, state workforce development agencies, trade unions and their training arms, among others. Individual institutions will have to acknowledge different roles while not defining their own role too narrowly. During the course of the high school years, individual institutions' responsibilities will shift and change.

Perhaps using specific substantive projects as a platform, institutions will have to debate the value of different kinds of knowledge and work together to consider and act on the implications of a broader conceptualization of learning—what kinds of learning experiences are valued, what counts as learning, where it is understood to take place, what kinds of adults can and should be involved. A business providing an internship to a young person might try to learn about other venues in his life and how its expertise could serve those venues, using that young person as a link. A community-based organization could ask itself how a young person in its youth program might learn about and contribute to its early childhood programs or its food pantry, recruiting a local community college to mentor that young person in a relevant discipline. The starting and ending points are almost limitless.

Deliberate efforts will be needed to build trust—from institution to institution, sector to sector. For instance, employers typically will not seek out youth on their own, but they might be willing to carve out a place for youth if they could trust referrals and help shape a planning and preparatory experience.[2] In some contexts a history of mutual skepticism and misreading will have to be addressed head on. For instance, parts of the education community have questioned the motives and appropriateness of the business community as a partner in education. The business community has been viewed as disparaging of the work of public school educators and has been known to question the interests and motives of educators. Educators view the corporate world as partly or largely responsible for the difficult living conditions facing many children and their families. In a recent study of efforts to bridge the world of schools and employers in Chicago, a researcher was told by one participant that "when companies and schools try to bridge the world of work with the classroom neither side could envision what the other side could possibly do" to help further its own mission. Both sides were observed to be afflicted by a "failure of imagination."[3]

Institutions have to get to know each other much more deeply, gain a clearer sense of what others have to offer (for their own work and for young people), and come to understand others' priorities and preoccupations. In Washington State's high school preapprenticeship program, schools and apprenticeship sponsors clashed over access: schools wanted assurances that students who elected to pursue an apprenticeship would get placed, while employers and union training councils worried about changes in local labor market conditions wanted some discretion to decide placements.[4] At times, joint work will have to start with limited agreements. Sharing, access to, or contributions of physical resources—studios, laboratories, workshops, clinics, equipment, tools, and basic materials— can serve as a starting point for fuller relationships.

The joint attention and cooperation of two, three, or more institutions is inherent to some discrete learning experiences. For example, as discussed in chapter 4, making career and technical education work well requires close cooperation of state education authorities, local school staff, numerous employers, community colleges, and regional vocational-technical centers, among others. In such situations, particular institutions will have to work hard to reconcile different orientations toward and views of youth, different learning goals, time frames for young people's growth toward mastery, and timetables for their own work with youth. In a study of an apprenticeship initiative in Toronto, it was observed that community-based organizations, training centers, schools, employers, and trade unions each valued somewhat different aspects of the experience for youth, among them social inclusion, preparation for a particular trade or craft, alternative pathways to graduation and local labor market needs.[5] Employers wanted young people to prove themselves and their commitment to the trade by doing whatever was asked. Schools wanted young people to be trained for understanding so that they would know why they were being asked to work as they were. The training centers wanted young people to have some breadth of experience, to acquire a broader understanding of the occupation or trade at hand.

NEW LEARNING STRUCTURES

A broadened view of learning for young people means that learning settings will be decentralized, spread throughout the culture and across many sectors—qualities that make them hard to envision as a coherent whole. The task of rethinking learning for young people will have to include experimentation with new learning structures to address issues of visibility, coherence, and coordination among stakeholders. The development of such structures will have to be an organic as well as deliberate process. It will have to depend on local histories and institutional relationships that have already begun to develop. Different institutions and types of organizations are relevant in each city or county, be it charter school, career and technical education center, issue-focused intermediary, arts organization.

One strategy used in a handful of European countries is to define a particular geographic area of some size as a *learning region*. That concept has two purposes. It bounds the task of identifying learning resources and creating means for them to work together, and it simultaneously pulls in a variety of local institutions and sectors as potential resources for learning experiences. In that light, it also makes sense to think of the learning landscape as containing many *learning bases*, the settings in which young people link up with expert adults to nurture specific talents. These already exist in implicit form in numerous fields but receive too little attention as a deliberate means for nurturing the diverse population of youth. Learning bases can look and be organized very differently, as a studio or workshop, an ensemble, an apprenticeship or residency, and so forth. One example is math circles, which originated in Bulgaria and the Soviet Union and are organized so that young people with a serious interest in math can meet weekly with professional mathematicians.[6]

If more learning is going to take place outside of school, then young people will need to be helped to fully use nonschool settings as learning resources as well as to seek out such settings. Young people already view formal, school-based learning as only one element of their "life world," in part because they see themselves in a more multifaceted light than school sees them.[7] Yet young people still have to be able to—and be helped to—understand the interinstitutional context in which they might access learning experiences.[8] For example, they might be helped to see how coursework in English, history, and government provides an opening to involvement in journalism or work on a local political campaign and in turn to college-level courses available for dual credit. Helping young people see a bigger picture can only be accomplished if different institutions work together to paint that picture. Adults have to help young people see how the knowledge and experience acquired through individual experiences add up and fit together, how they constitute and signal a set of competencies recognizable in the adult world.

Young people, then, will need something like *a learning home*. This would be the place, setting, or organization that acts as the base for the full range of a young person's learning activities. Because developmental histories, interests, learning histories and learning styles are diverse, youths would find learning homes in different places. The importance of the idea is in raising adult awareness of their role in guiding young people's learning biographies. Adults in particular settings would have heightened responsibility for the logic of young people's learning experiences during the high school years; they would have some responsibility for gathering and sharing information about learning resources in the community at large and linking young people to those resources.

As described in previous chapters, institutions will have to collaborate to create *articulated pathways through and beyond high school.* These would be similar to but broader than the kinds of course-based maps and routes that have been created within career and technical education for different occupational clusters. Individual pathways would include nonschool learning experiences, personal explorations, and service experiences. Like the school-based concentrations discussed in chapter 3, they would still be rooted in specific fields or disciplines but could also be organized into problem areas or by interdisciplinary themes. For some young people, continuing to progress on a pathway beyond high school will require defined learning experiences between high school and postsecondary. Models exist, for example, in Youth Conservation Corps, Year Up (which provides six months of business skills training followed by a six-month corporate internship), and a variety of volunteer gap year programs that serve advantaged youth but need to be extended to more fields.

A critical set of structures needing to be created might best be described as *youth learning partnerships.* Partnerships create a sum greater than its parts, in effect making for a richer, more varied learning landscape for young people. They introduce institutions to each other, creating a structured dialogue that serves as a basis for those from different sectors share information and get to know one other. Partnerships allow for the strengths of one sector to be extended by the complementary strengths of others, adding value to each partner. In the Year Up program, the nonprofit itself gains access to a variety of corporate workplaces where the young people it serves can apply what they have learned in the classroom, and, in turn, employers gain access to a diverse population of youth who they might otherwise not consider for jobs. An administrator at Boston's Children's Hospital says that "the internship gives us an opportunity to work with interns, support their ongoing learning and see what they can do in our work environment. At the end of the internship we have a good sense of ability and fit, and we can hire the ones that we really like."[9]

Partnerships are often able to leverage resources or make implicit resources explicit and accessible to youth. For example, employers "typically do not have the time or resources to seek out youth on their own," but they might be willing to carve out a place for youth if they could trust referrals and help shape a planning and preparatory experience.[10] The Careers Through Culinary Arts Program, a nonschool learning provider based in New York City, places youth as apprentices in restaurants and food service operations.[11] It screens and selects the youth and prepares them with knowledge of food safety, knife skills, and other basics. Employers have come to trust the program's referrals and know that its staff are available to help with any problems.

A good example of the value of, and challenges in, youth learning partnerships is found in the work being done by the Center for Labor and Community Research with the Austin Polytechnical Academy, described chapter 4. This school provides a technical education in manufacturing operations and preengineering to youth from one of the most disenfranchised neighborhoods in Chicago. A local manufacturer, WaterSaver Faucets, provides funding for the purchase of a number of machines (and simulators) for students' applied learning at the center. Another small group of partners subsidize the salary of a machine shop instructor. A broad group of sixty partners, all local manufacturers, provides input on curriculum, one-week spring internships, and ten-week summer internship experiences to Academy juniors and seniors. The internship experience, which typically involves working on the shop floor alongside and under the guidance of an experienced machine operator, has proven to be a powerful vehicle for nurturing maturity, a more serious outlook, a better sense of strengths, and so forth. At the same time, some of these partners have struggled to accommodate young people with good basic machine operation knowledge but no experience in an adult work setting. School staff have worked with partners to put struggles into perspective and to encourage reluctant employers to stick with young people who were not meeting workplace expectations.

At a slightly broader level, *learning intermediaries* would play a role in bringing many kinds of resources together to create rich learning experiences. Intermediaries also can play different kinds of roles, depending on purpose and setting. They can operate across or within sectors and be directly or indirectly responsible for designing and providing learning experiences. MECHTECH USA, also described in chapter 4, is an example of a vocationally oriented intermediary that works across sectors to arrange good work-based learning experiences for young people.

After School Matters (ASM) in Chicago provides another good example of an intermediary operating within a specific sector, in this case non-school learning. ASM is a private organization whose mission is to foster apprenticeship-like experiences for high school–age youth. It recruits individual professionals, community-based organizations, and employers in a variety of fields to design and lead year-long apprenticeships overseeing a structured proposal-writing process, helping new instructors learn how to design apprenticeships, and giving instructors support for the youth development side of the work. It secures public and private funding; pays the instructors; buys needed tools, materials, and other physical resources; secures sites, negotiating with high schools and other organizations that serve as a base for apprenticeships. It oversees a structured formative and summative assessment process for tracking young people's growth in each particular field. Critically, ASM also makes young people in neighborhoods throughout Chicago aware of the apprenticeships available to them, gives them a concrete sense of what it would be like to participate in a particular apprenticeship, and manages the enrollment process.

In a less direct way, ASM also serves as a voice for the importance of good applied learning experiences for young people and as an example of the possibility of making such experiences available in disenfranchised communities that would seem to have few resources available to them. It has provided critical funding to resource-starved youth organizations working in the arts, design, media, and related fields. By locating many of its apprenticeships in school studios, workshops, kitchens, labs, and other spaces, it has helped school staff see a different side of youth who often reveal little of themselves during the school day. There have been a few tensions between ASM and its frontline providers. Individual professionals like to do things their way and have not always adjusted easily to the structure insisted on by ASM. In turn, individual youth-serving organizations are occasionally reluctant to submerge their distinct and often hard-won identity to the After School Matters common brand.

TOWARD A COMMON UNDERSTANDING OF LEARNING EXPERIENCES

Given the many tasks involved in creating a coherent framework for young people's learning, forging some common understanding of the criteria for good learning experiences and the metrics that define young people's growth will be among the most critical. As noted earlier, a broadened perspective on learning requires stakeholders to ask (and continue asking) what learning is for, in particular situations and over all. Stakeholders must work on the problem of knowing when something learned is useful, to whom and for which purposes (personal, cultural, civic, occupational, etc.). Stakeholders have to consider also what assessment is for. When an individual is of high school age, assessment makes particularly strong sense in the service of continued learning, in the service of recognizing and validating participation, and as an initial step toward mastery. It is also an important spur for reflection.

Stakeholders in young people's learning have to think about proficiency, mastery, and growth in new ways, less as internalized results of discrete experiences and more as a shared (individual and social) manifestation of a diverse mixture of learning, exploring, and contributing experiences. It is important as well to understand mastery, and therefore assessment and certification of it, as conditional in time and place. Stakeholders will have to agree on the kinds of indicators of knowledge and skill (and therefore assessment processes for these) to value. For example, there is sentiment even among those involved with school learning that mastery of concepts and information means ability to use them to solve authentic problems and that knowledge and skill are better understood as continuously developing, with many steps toward mastery, not as all or nothing (pass or fail) phenomena. The importance of knowledge is in its continuing use. That is why so much that is learned in school decays quickly.

Stakeholders will have to consider the types of certifications and level of aggregation of learning outcomes most appropriate for different audiences. They will have to consider whether, why, and how to distinguish between academic and applied learning. The question too often asked is how to make good applied learning experiences count for academic purposes (i.e., for high school, community college, or college credits). If we understand applied learning as distinctly valuable, traditional academic credits should not be the criterion for signaling knowledge or skill.

It is important to young people and society to broaden the kinds of learning experiences recognized as counting toward college and career readiness. Some of the most important outcomes of learning experiences during the high school years have received little or no attention in policy discussions and no concrete efforts to address assessment and certification. One prominent example is citizenship, both rights and responsibilities. (We do not even count registering to vote and voting as important outcomes of learning during the high school years, let alone many other expressions of citizenship.) We must work to find the right meaning of citizenship for young people of high school age: useful concerns, obligations, rights. If the role of service learning in the larger universe of good learning experiences were expanded, outcomes of these experiences would become more central to certifying different kinds of personal growth. It would also help with the needed reconceptualization of where to look for outcomes—that is, not just inside the individual but in the community surrounding her.

Figuring out what to assess, when, and how raises philosophical, practical, and, ultimately, political questions. Many philosophical questions are, after all, practical ones. For instance, what kinds of metrics are most appropriate when there is no one best solution to many learning tasks and problems? Who might certify knowledge and skill; for example, when might more experienced peers do so? What is the relative importance of the process of learning, described carefully, including sources, and the outcome of it? Is it possible and appropriate to measure personal change resulting from deep immersion in a field? If we are to use the knowledge and skills needed for twenty-first-century work as one touchstone for assessment of learning, which work should we use—good work, prevailing work, that is available to a few or that is available to the majority?

Stakeholders in young people's learning will have to acknowledge and wrestle with the specific and, especially, the embedded nature of much important knowledge, skill, and personal growth. Performance is often tied to its context and evoked by the demands of the setting. As a young person moves more deeply into a discipline, discrete knowledge and skills get linked together, and even similarly named proficiencies will look different. The meaning of broadly important skills, such as learning to work with care, will also be specific to the discipline or field. For the budding scientist, working with care may focus on careful measurement and recording, while for the apprentice electrician it may mean attention to local building codes, bundling wires behind a wall so others can get to them in the future, or even attending to personal safety. As one young apprentice notes, "It's a question of having an overview of the situation, before going for quick solutions and putting our fingers in the wrong place."[12]

Describing learning and growth will have to balance the general and the specific. Learning takes place largely within specific fields and disciplines, and assessment of mastery therefore should mostly be field/discipline specific. That would decrease the weight of very general markers like high school diplomas and content-free aptitude tests. Growth toward competence is about achieving levels of proficiency in relation to the standards of a discipline. That requires asking what aspects of a discipline's practices should be considered fundamental.[13] Some growth also occurs in important domains for which there is no metric for deciding when a young person is proficient. For instance, getting better at predicting or approximating, becoming more consistent in behavior and motivation, or developing capacity to cope with difficulties are not easily converted into standards.

Personal growth writ large is particularly difficult to capture. It is often not attributable to one discrete experience, making it more difficult to account for. A youth worker looking back on her own participation in a variety of nonformal education experiences observed that it is difficult to delimit, let alone measure, something that "encompasses both thoughts and emotions, knowledge and values, attitudes and behavior. It is hard to pass on the process of acquiring experience in its broad sense . . . experience which is like a universal tool, which can be used in a wide variety of your social, public, private, professional [lives]."[14] Participants in nonformal learning especially may need help identifying discrete clusters of knowledge and skill acquired but that seem too global to define let alone measure, such as a certain kind of confidence or perspective or sensitivity or a different understanding of family, community, or societal institutions.

MAKING A VARIETY OF LEARNING EXPERIENCES COUNT

If a greater variety of learning and working experiences during the high school years are to be recognized and made to count, vehicles for communication between different institutions will have to be developed: learning records, portfolios, signifiers such as digital badges, and youth learning "passports." A number of institutions in the United States, Canada, and the European Union have been experimenting with learning records, in the process clarifying challenges in making such records broadly usable. These include, for instance, deciding which evidence to include, creating accurate categories, finding the right level of detail, helping young people articulate what they have learned and mastered, and capturing cumulative growth over time in specific domains and overall.[15]

The MacArthur Foundation has been promoting the idea of digital badges, which are intended to reflect a combination of experience, knowledge, and skill in a specific field or discipline. The relevant evidence for meriting a badge in a field would be determined by those who teach, employ, and produce in that field, as well as by learners themselves. Badges would allow young people to convey the incremental, sometimes complementary, combinations of knowledge and skills young people acquire over numerous learning experiences. (They have also been criticized for fostering external motivation, for turning education into a kind of game, and for being idiosyncratic.)

Badges, or their equivalent, address an issue that has emerged as a result of the enormous growth in higher education, particularly for profit

education, but is just as relevant to high school. Even as college completion is held up as the key to personal and social futures, our society is
becoming less sure, employers have less confidence in, and young people
themselves are becoming insecure about the meaning of a diploma. Ann
Kirschner points out that "the value of the diploma is symbolic, backed
not by gold but by the graduate's sense of its worth and the employer's
willingness to accept it as the currency of competency. Sometimes sym-
bolism is just too expensive."[16] She hypothesizes a future in which learning
credentials are "disaggregated," in which competencies are acquired and
certified one by one. This possible future for certification is as relevant to
high school as it is for college.

The problems of expanding what counts and disaggregating certification of competence are complicated by the internally oriented focus of
institutions that serve young people. Institutional orientations have to be
turned outward and linked to broader developmental issues and contexts.
Stakeholders in young people's learning will have to expand or alter their
existing certification frameworks, developing at least some overlapping
metrics. Applied experiences in a specific discipline, located outside of
school or mentored by nonschool professionals, will have to translate in
some way to formal school credits. Schools would also have to recognize
assessment and certification of achievement by nonschool staff. For example young people who participate in ACME Animation (described in
chapter 5) through their high school fine or applied arts departments currently receive credits to be applied to graduation on demonstration of proficiency within ACME's own assessment scheme.

One approach to developing a cross-institutional framework is to think
of categories of certification in developmental terms. For instance, one can
imagine certification in personal, educational, and vocational skills and
dispositions. Alternatively, skills and dispositions acquired through a particular learning experience might best be viewed as foundational to formal
qualifications.[17] For instance, some might serve as first-level competencies
within a specific occupation. Many of the nonschool learning experiences
described in chapter 5 begin to build just those skills and dispositions—
part generic, part discipline/occupation specific—that are valuable to and

valued by employers. If that process and its results can be made explicit, it might serve the signaling function for employers that high school transcripts apparently do not, encouraging employers to find places for young people. Employers already recognize that certain applied learning experiences, such as preapprenticeships, foster the kinds of maturity they value, mitigating the common aversion to hiring young people.[18]

In a time marked by a narrow, instrumental view of learning and in which many social institutions are struggling to cope with internal concerns, it may seem counterintuitive to ask institutions to take on a new, as yet abstract set of tasks. I believe that the tasks discussed here will encourage institutions, not discourage them further. Working in isolation to educate and socialize young people is easier in an immediate sense but close to impossible in a larger one. When institutions find the means to work together, they reduce the partial and fragmented quality of young people's learning experiences. Such experiences, over the course of three or four years, do not have to fit together perfectly; in fact, they cannot do so if they are to meet young people's evolving needs and capacities. But if learning experiences can be connected and rationalized to some degree, if it feels to young people that different experiences have some relationship and some shared logic, this will provide them the beginnings of a learning story—a learning life, really—to carry into the postsecondary years.

Conclusions

The listeners are not merely being told the story but at the same time . . . growing into story tellers themselves.
—Tim Ingold, "Apprenticeship and Social Learning"

A society has to teach its young people to find pleasure in the right things.
—Eric Booth, "El Sistema's Open Secrets"

Young people are an unusual social force. The developmental work that preoccupies them is at once intensely personal and strongly collective. They take what is offered by their culture and their circumstances and run it through the mysterious filters that are the young heart and mind. They are a magnet for mentoring. A young person goes into a lab full of graduate students and post docs and the place is changed within a month; everyone has become a teacher and guide. Yet young people can seem difficult to reach. When they follow existing paths, they always seem be creating new ones while doing so. They are always becoming themselves and at the same time growing into something else. They are in so many ways the fulcrum on which society turns.

Because young people play a vital social role, the full range of social institutions have a responsibility for supporting their growth. When those institutions themselves are under pressure, as is the case now in the United States (and other countries), that creates a profound social problem. We do not know yet what precarious economic conditions—and adults' seeming inability to address critical societal problems—will do to young people's sense of the future, to their identities and identifications. Young people may well turn inward, losing interest, if not trust, in key institutions and the received wisdom of older generations. They will still strive for some stability in identity, but perhaps they'll expect less stability over the life course than have previous generations. They may have to continue throughout adulthood to make decisions about "what they should do and who they should be."[1] The role of occupational identity in conferring personal identity may well decline or acquire new meaning.

Social strain and a sense of crisis could induce adult institutions to refocus on young people, to reexamine assumptions about their support needs and potential contributions. Such a refocusing could be an enlivening experience for adult institutions if they focus on developmental potentials rather than market-related fears. A developmental perspective leads us to understand learning processes during middle adolescence as reciprocal, to understand young people as a potentially powerful resource in cultural renewal but also an inexperienced one. As Chris Higgins puts it, "The world needs the natality of the young to renew it and the young need the worldliness of the world to become human actors."[2]

The attributes of good learning described in this book, and in particular those embodied in nonschool learning settings, provide a basis for integrating the dual roles of learner and participant and for helping young people find a personal identity in these roles. These attributes foster engagement and commitment, provide the ingredients for actualizing new capacities, and attend to the psychological barriers to learning that emerge in adolescence. They serve also as means for young people to transcend societally imposed constraints, those encountered to due to social class or race or community of origin. Good learning experiences make a larger world that often seems distant and monolithic more differentiated and human.[3] Such experiences provide youth some first steps into the adult world, and they do so in a considered way. The education director of Chicago's Marwen Arts notes, "We send them out into the world to act as public agents, while they have the security of knowing there is support back here."[4] Good learning experiences communicate the message to young people that they are welcome and have a role in the adult world.

I have argued that schools, through no fault of their front-line staff, too rarely reflect attributes of good learning for high school–age youth. I focused on schooling, because in the United States we have located learning largely inside the comprehensive high school, an institution that John Rury calls "a peculiarly American cultural artifact."[5] By making schools the principal socializing agent for young people, we have cut off opportunity for the wider community to commit itself to young people's development. And our efforts to improve high school learning through standardization are the opposite of what is needed if we are to recognize and value heterogeneity among young people and within the larger culture. New approaches to schooling consonant with a broader understanding of learning are working mostly to expand the outer boundaries of schooling. Until we rethink the historic model of high school education, many youth will continue to be pushed toward its periphery.

Giving career and technical education a more prominent role in high school is one way to incorporate new assumptions, curricula, and pedagogy and to open school as an institution to the rich array of learning resources spread throughout communities. The international examples tell us that having a strong vocational-technical system goes some way to ensuring a place in the adult occupational world for a broad spectrum of youth. CTE also pushes educators to reconsider the distinction between academic and applied learning—though both need to be understood to support and feed each other. The idea that applied learning is mostly useful for those young people who cannot compete academically is destructive and represents a distorted understanding of human ability. Such learning is most useful to young people developmentally when it is normative.

In a dramatic statement addressed to the European context, Manuela du Bois-Reymond argues that a century-long epoch of mass schooling is drawing to a close.[6] European nations are entering a new learning epoch whose outlines are not yet clear but that will surely include greater heterogeneity in learning arrangements. This observation is probably true of the United States as well. We are certainly in a time of questioning, if not upheaval, with respect to learning. It is easy to see that the world outside of school is full of potentially rich learning opportunities for young people, but it is much less certain that American culture is as equipped as those in other nations to support a broad understanding of learning and of youth participation.

A prerequisite for moving American institutions toward a new learning framework and new social goals for youth is getting the "why" argument right. At this moment, with our civic culture in fragile condition, we have to ask whether we want market-related needs and fears to continue to be so central in defining rationales for investment in education. We have to ask also whether we want those with economic power to continue to have the central role in defining both the purpose and the desired outcomes of young people's learning experiences. We have to relearn how to debate what is important to know, and why.

Concern about the overriding influence of the marketplace in shaping our priorities as a nation, not to mention our common life, has special resonance when it comes to young people. James Gee wonders how any society can possibly "sustain equitable relations among its citizens when social cohesion and consent, even the minimal standards of human decency, are irrelevant to free markets."[7] Others argue that political and intellectual leaders have been in denial about the social and human damage caused by a commitment to neoliberal market theory.[8] If the executives of American corporations are willing to scour the world for the cheapest labor they can find, then they cannot expect America's young people to fall in line or even believe the promises made to them by society.

In their modest way, good learning experiences demonstrate that work and worklike experience can be developmentally rich, if supported as such. Workplaces provide ready-made and diverse communities of practice. But any effort to use work as a vehicle for learning and growth, and especially to nurture vocation in the deeper ways I have outlined, will also require attending to the steady disappearance of "good work." If this fundamental societal problem does not seem directly relevant to a book on learning during adolescence, it is actually central to it. If young people are to succeed with the critical developmental task of finding a pathway to occupation that is a good individual match, they need a labor market that supports this possibility.[9]

More fundamentally, when we abandon the idea of economies as local, as tied to place, when work and workplaces are not understood as underpinnings of communities, everything becomes contingent—where and in what to invest, who to hire, to whom and to what we are responsible. We inadvertently turn our attention away from those immediately around us, especially the rising generation. Among other effects, current patterns of production erode the notion of "a civic space in which different classes and groups of people share responsibility with and to each other."[10] These trends explain why some of the most thoughtful cultural observers in the United States have focused on the need to rethink what we value in and about work.

It is not far-fetched to argue that, while the idea of good learning experiences for young people may not be a counter to globalization, it does help with the critical task of deglobalizing our understanding of what young people—and their society—need to thrive. Good learning experiences for young people revitalize and renew the value of disciplines and fields of endeavor. They remind us that learning and work that are personally satisfying are also critical sources of societal continuity and renewal in an unstable time.

Notes

Introduction

1. Jerry Diakiw, "It's Time for a New Kind of High School," *Education Week*, May 19, 2012, 26–28.
2. Robert MacDonald, "Youth Transitions, Unemployment and Underemployment," *Journal of Sociology* 47, no. 4 (2011): 427–444.
3. Edward Gordon, *Winning the Global Talent Showdown: How Businesses and Communities Can Partner to Rebuild the Jobs Pipeline* (San Francisco, CA: Berrett Koehler, 2009).
4. *National Action Agenda for 21st Century Skills* (Washington, DC: Partnership for 21st Century Skills, 2011), 1.
5. Tim Ingold, *Learning Through Doing and Understanding in Practice* (Aberdeen, UK: Department of Anthropology, University of Aberdeen, 2005), 2.
6. Mark Pagel, *Wired for Culture: Origins of the Human Social Mind* (New York: W. W. Norton, 2012).
7. Erik Erikson and Kai Erikson, "The Confirmation of the Delinquent," in *A Way of Looking at Things: Selected Papers from 1930 to 1980*, ed. Stephen Schlein (New York: Norton, 1987), 636.
8. James Gee, "Communities of Practice in the New Capitalism," *Journal of the Learning Sciences* 9, no. 4 (2000): 515–523.
9. Ted Robinson, *Bring on the Learning Revolution*, video (New York: TED Conferences, 2010).
10. Abby Remer, *Welcome to Inside View* (New York: American Museum of Natural History, 2005), 2.
11. Ann Kirschner, "Innovation in Higher Education? Hah!" *Chronicle Review*, April 8, 2012, B8; Hilary Pennington, "For Student Success, Stop Debating and Start Improving," ibid., April 13, 2012, B8.
12. Richard Settersten and Barbara Ray, *Not Quite Adults: Why 20-Somethings Are Choosing a Slower Path to Adulthood, and Why It's Good for Everyone* (New York: Random House, 2010), 5.
13. Catherine Rampell, "More Young Americans Out of High School Are Also Out of Work," *New York Times*, June 6, 2012, B6, citing "Left Out, Forgotten? Recent

High School Graduates and the Great Recession" (survey, John J. Heldrich Center for Workforce Development, Rutgers University, New Brunswick, NJ, 2012).

14. Barry Down, "Schooling, Productivity and the Enterprising Self: Beyond Market Values," *Critical Studies in Education* 50, no.1 (2009): 51–64, http://www.informa world.com/smpp/title-db=all-content=t749441077-tab=issueslist-branches=50.

15. Guy Standing, *The Precariat: The New Dangerous Class* (New York: Bloomsbury USA, 2011).

16. Catherine Gewertz, "College for All Reconsidered: Are Four-Year Degrees for All?" *Education Week* 30, no. 34 (2011): 6.

17. Phillip Brown, Hugh Lauder, and David Ashton, *The Global Auction: The Broken Promises of Education, Jobs, and Incomes* (New York: Oxford University Press, 2011).

18. Standing, *The Precariat.*

19. Susan Robertson, Lois Weis, and Fazal Rizvi, "The Global Auction: The Broken Promises of Education, Jobs and Incomes," *British Journal of Sociology of Education* 32, no. 2 (2011): 293–311.

20. Alejandra Cancino, "Manufacturers Get Involved in Training Programs for Future Workers,"*Chicago Tribune*, February 26, 2012, 1.

21. Michael Peters, "Three Forms of the Knowledge Economy: Learning, Creativity and Openness," *British Journal of Educational Studies* 58, no. 1 (2010): 67–88.

22. David Hursh, "Assessing No Child Left Behind and the Rise of Neoliberal Education Policies," *American Educational Research Journal* 44, no. 3 (2007): 493–518.

23. Brown, Lauder, and Ashton, *The Global Auction*, 3.

24. Linda Camino and Shepherd Zeldin, "From Periphery to Center: Pathways for Youth Civic Engagement in the Day-to-Day Life of Communities," *Applied Developmental Science* 6, no. 4 (2002): 213–220.

Chapter 1

1. Christina Hinton, Kurt Fischer, and Catherine Glennon, "Mind, Brain, and Education" (working paper, Jobs for the Future, Washington DC, 2012), 13–14.

2. Mark Pagel, *Wired for Culture: Origins of the Human Social Mind* (New York: W. W. Norton, 2012).

3. Andrew Gonczi, "Advances in Educational Thinking and Their Implications for Professional Education" (working paper, UTS Research Center for Vocational Education and Training, Sydney, Australia, 2001).

4. Roy F. Baumeister et al., "How Emotion Shapes Behavior: Feedback, Anticipation, and Reflection, Rather Than Direct Causation," *Personality and Social Psychology Review* 11, no. 2 (2007): 167–203.

5. Lev Vygotsky, *Mind in Society* (Cambridge, UK: Cambridge University Press, 1978), 83.

6. Jerome Bruner, *The Culture of Education* (Cambridge, MA: Harvard University Press, 1996), 26.

7. Stephen Downes, *How the Net Works*, 2007, p. 1, www.downes.ca/cgi-bin/page .cgi?post=42068.

8. Barbara Rogoff, "Cognition as a Collaborative Process," in *Handbook of Child Psychology*. Vol. 2: *Cognition, Perception, and Language*, ed. William Damon (Hoboken, NJ: John Wiley & Sons, 1998), 679–744.

9. Jeanne Nakamura, "The Nature of Vital Engagement in Adulthood," *New Directions for Child and Adolescent Development* 2001, no. 93 (2001): 5–18.

10. Jerome Bruner, *The Relevance of Education* (New York: Norton, 1973), and *The Culture of Education*.

11. Kenneth Silseth and Hans Christian Arnseth, "Learning and Identity Construction Across Sites: A Dialogical Approach to Analysing the Construction of Learning Selves," *Culture and Psychology* 17, no. 1 (2011): 65–80.

12. Erik Erikson, *Childhood and Society* (New York: W. W. Norton, 1963), and *Identity: Youth and Crisis* (New York: W. W. Norton, 1968).

13. Douglas Kleiber, *Leisure Experience and Human Development: A Dialectical Interpretation* (New York: Basic Books, 1999).

14. David Kahn, "The Key Lessons of the Third Adolescent Colloquium," *NAMTA Journal* 31, no. 1 (2006): 1–25.

15. Seth Schwartz, "A New Identity for Identity Research," *Journal of Adolescent Research* 20, no. 3 (2005): 293–308.

16. Marlene Barajas, "Undecided," *Ampersand: High Tech High Student Journal* (2011): 33–34.

17. David Dobbs, "The Beautiful Teenage Brain," *National Geographic*, October 2011, 1.

18. Reed Larson and Natalie Rusk "Intrinsic Motivation and Positive Development," in *Advances in Child Development and Behavior: Positive Youth Development*, ed. Richard Lerner et al. (Oxford: Elsevier, 2011), 89–130.

19. Thomas Bailey, Katherine Hughes, and David Moore, *Working Knowledge: Work-Based Learning and Education Reform* (New York: Routledge, 2004), 159.

20. Reed Larson, "Positive Development in a Disorderly World," *Journal of Research on Adolescence* 21, no. 2 (2011): 317–334.

21. Belle Liang et al., "Mentoring Relationships from Early Adolescence through Emerging Adulthood: A Qualitative Analysis," *Journal of Vocational Behavior* 72, no. 2 (2008): 168–182.

22. Barajas, "Undecided," 33–34.

23. David Baker, "The Educational Transformation of Work: Towards a New Synthesis," *Journal of Education and Work* 22, no. 3 (2009): 163–193.

24. Robert Halpern, Reed Larson, and Paul Heckman, "Re-Thinking Learning in the High School Years" (unpublished manuscript, Erikson Institute, Chicago, 2012).

25. Larson, "Positive Development."

26. Bruner, *The Culture of Education*, 26.

27. Nicholas Farrar and Gillian Trorey, "Maxims, Tacit Knowledge and Learning: Developing Expertise in Dry Stone Walling," *Journal of Vocational Education and*

Training 60, no. 1 (2006): 35–48, http://www.informaworld.com/smpp/title-db=all -content=t716100716-tab=issueslist-branches=60-v60.

28. Larson, "Positive Development."

29. Theodore Lewis, "Vocational Education as General Education," *Curriculum Inquiry* 28, no. 3 (1998): 283–309.

30. Marsha Rehm, "Vocation as Meaning Making Narrative: Implications for Vocational Education," *Journal of Vocational Education Research* 24, no. 3 (1999): 145–159.

31. Erikson, *Identity*, 22.

32. Garnet Grosjean, "Alternating Education and Training: Students' Conceptualization of Learning in Co-op," in *Integrating School and Workplace Learning in Canada*, ed. Hans Schuetze and Robert Sweet (Montreal: McGill-Queen's University Press, 2003), 175–196.

33. Edna Szymanski, "Transition: Life-Span and Life-Space Considerations for Empowerment," *Exceptional Children* 60, no. 5 (1994): 402–410.

34. Joseph Renzulli, "The Definition of High-End Learning," p. 9, http://www.gifted .uconn.edu/sem/semart10.html.

35. Teresa Bolton and Esther Priyadharshina, "Boredom and Schooling: A Cross-Disciplinary Exploration,"*Cambridge Journal of Education* 37 no. 4 (2007): 579–595.

36. Dobbs, *The New Science.*

37. Manuela du Bois-Reymond, "Youth—Learning—Europe: Ménage à Trois?" *Young* 12, no. 3 (2004): 187–204.

38. Morena Cuconato et al., "Participation and Informal Learning in Young People's Transitions to Work" (working paper no. 3, vol. 3, Institut für Regionale Innovation und Sozialforschung, Tübingen, Germany, 2003), 30.

39. Mihaly Csikszentmihalyi and Barbara Schneider, *Becoming Adult: How Teenagers Prepare for the World of Work* (New York: Basic Books, 2000).

40. Michael Zuckerman, "The Paradox of American Adolescence," *Journal of the History of Childhood and Youth* 4, no. 1 (2011): 13–25.

41. Chris Higgins, "The Possibility of Public Education in an Instrumentalist Age," *Educational Theory* 61, no. 4 (2011): 451–466.

42. Lauren Resnick, "From Aptitude to Effort: A New Foundation for Our Schools," *Daedalus* 124, no. 4 (1995): 55–62.

43. Deborah Meier, "Undermining Democracy," *Dissent* 53, no. 4 (2006): 71–75.

44. Liang et al., "Mentoring Relationships from Early Adolescene through Emerging Adulthood: Qualitative Analysis," *Journal of Vocational Behavior* 72, no. 2 (2008): 168–182.

Chapter 2

1. Nell Daniel, "Sweat Equity Enterprises: The Convergence of Design Education, Youth Development and Situated Learning" (doctoral dissertation, New York University, 2007), 77.

2. Leon Botstein, "Let Teenagers Try Adulthood," *NSSE* 107, no. 2 (2008): 118–121.

3. Regine Grytnes, "Making the Right Choice! Inquiries into the Reasoning Behind Young People's Decisions About Education," *Young* 19, no. 3 (2011): 333–351.

4. Phil Cohen, "Apprenticeship a la Mode?" in *Apprenticeship: Towards a New Paradigm of Learning*, ed. Patrick Ainley and Helen Rainbird (New York: Routledge, 1999).

5. Erica Swinney, program coordinator, Austin Polytechnical High School/Center for Labor and Community Research, Chicago, in discussion with author, March and June 2012.

6. David Harding, "Rethinking the Cultural Context of Schooling Decisions in Disadvantaged Neighborhoods: From Deviant Subculture to Cultural Heterogeneity," *Sociology of Education* 84, no. 4 (2011): 322–339.

7. Erik Erikson and Kai Erikson, "The Confirmation of the Delinquent," in *A Way of Looking at Things: Selected Papers from 1930 to 1980*, ed. Stephen Schlein (New York: Norton, 1987), 649.

8. George Timmons, *Education, Industrialization and Selection* (London: Routledge, 1988).

9. Joseph Petraglia, *Reality by Design: The Rhetoric and Technology of Authenticity in Education* (New York: Routledge, 1998), ix.

10. Ken Roberts, "Opportunity Structures Then and Now," *Journal of Education and Work* 22, no. 5 (2009): 355–368.

11. Richard Lakes, "Work-Ready Testing: Education and Employability in Neoliberal Times," *Journal for Critical Education Policy Studies* 9, no.1 (2011): 317–340.

12. Theodore Sizer and Nancy Sizer, *The Students Are Watching* (Boston: Beacon Press, 1999), chap. 1.

13. Linda McNeil, *Contradictions of School Reform: Educational Costs of Standardized Testing* (Boca Raton, FL: Routledge, 2000), 118.

14. Robert Jones, "Vocational Education" (presentation at the International Seminar on Occupational Education, Hegeler Carus Foundation, Peru, IL, 2008); Christopher Swanson, "U.S. Graduate Rate Continues Decline," *Education Week* 29, no. 34 (2010): 22–23, 30; William Symonds, Robert Schwartz, and Ronald Ferguson, "Pathways to Prosperity: Meeting the Challenge of Preparing Young Americans for the 21st Century" (working paper, Pathways to Prosperity Project, Harvard University Graduate School of Education, Cambridge, MA, 2011).

15. Helen Marks, "Student Engagement in Instructional Activity: Patterns in the Elementary, Middle, and High Schools Years," *American Educational Research Journal* 78 (2000): 153–184; Robert McDonald and Jane Marsh, "Missing School: Educational Engagement, Youth Transitions, and Social Exclusion," *Youth and Society* 36, no. 2 (2004): 143–162; Deborah Stipek, *Engaging Schools: Fostering High School Students' Motivation to Learn* (Washington, DC: National Academy Press, 2004).

16. Marks, "Student Engagement"; Stipek, *Engaging Schools*; Shane Lopez, "2009 Gallup Student Poll: National Report," Gallup.org, www.gallupstudentpoll

.com/123173/survey-fall-2009.aspx; Dana Vedder-Weiss and David Fortuc, "Adolescents' Declining Motivation to Learn Science: Inevitable or Not?" *Journal of Research in Science Teaching* 48, no. 2 (2011): 199–216.

17. Kim Pierce, "Posing, Pretending, Waiting for the Bell: Life I High School Classrooms," *The High School Journal* 89, no. 2 (2006): 1–15.

18. Gad Yeir, "Educational Battlefields in America: The Tug of War over Students' Engagement with Instruction," *Sociology of Education* 3 (2000): 247–269.

19. Stephen Downes, *How the Net Works*, 2007, www.downes.ca/cgi-bin/page.cgi?post =42068.

20. Elliot Washor, "It's Deeper Than You Think," *Huffington Post*, February 2, 2012, http://www.huffingtonpost.com/elliot-washor/us-high-school-dropouts_b_1241670.html.

21. Janine Certo, Kathleen Cauley, and Carl Chafin, "Students' Perspectives on Their High School Experience,"*Adolescence* 38 (2003); John Smyth, "The Making of Young Lives with/against the School Credential," *Journal of Education and Work* 16, no. 2 (2003): 127–146; David J. De Wit et al., "Student Perceptions of Diminished Teacher and Classmate Support Following The Transition to High School: Are They Related to Declining Attendance?" *School Effectiveness and School Improvement: An International Journal of Research, Policy and Practice* 21, no. 4 (2010): 451–472.

22. Barbara Rogoff, Maricela Correa-Chavez, and Marta Cotuc, "A Cultural/Historical View of Schooling in Human Development," in *Developmental Psychology and Social Change*, ed. David B. Pillemer and Sheldon H. White (Cambridge, UK: Cambridge University Press, 2005), 227.

23. Michael Zuckerman, "The Paradox of American Adolescence," *Journal of the History of Childhood and Youth* 4, no. 1 (2011): 13–25.

24. Janine Certo et al., "Students' Perspectives on Their High School Experience," *Adolescence* 38, no. 152 (2003): 705–724.

25. Yeir, "Educational Battlefields."

26. Pierce, "Posing, Pretending," 3, 4.

27. Angela Valenzuela, *Subtractive Schooling: U.S. Mexican Youth and the Politics of Caring* (Albany: State University of New York Press, 1999).

28. McNeill, *Contradictions of School Reform*.

29. Martin Haberman, "The Ideology of Nonwork Learned in Urban Schools," *Phi Delta Kappan* 78, no. 7 (1997): 499–504.

30. Elliot Eisner, "The Misunderstood Role of the Arts in Human Development," in *Teaching for Intelligence*, ed. Barbara Pressisen (Arlington Heights, IL: Skylight, 1999), 107–117; Alberto Arenas "Connecting Hand, Mind, and Community: Vocational Education for Social and Environmental Renewal," *Teachers College Record* 110, no. 2 (2008): 377–404.

31. Giyoo Hatano and Yoko Oura, "Commentary: Reconceptualizing School Learning Using Insight from Expertise Research," *Educational Researcher* 32, no. 8 (2003): 26–29.

32. Noemi Waight and Fouad Abd-El-Khalick, "From Scientific Practice to High School Science Classrooms: Transfer of Scientific Technologies and Realizations of Authentic Inquiry," *Journal of Research in Science Teaching* 48, no. 1 (2011): 37–70.

33. Gail Richmond and Lori Ann Kurth, "Moving from Outside to Inside: High School Students' Use of Apprenticeships as Vehicles for Entering the Culture and Practice of Science," *Journal of Research in Science Teaching* 36, no. 6 (1999): 677–697.

34. Ruth Paradise, "What's Different about Learning in Schools as Compared to Family and Community Settings?" *Human Development* 41, no. 4 (1998): 270–278.

35. David Harding, "Rethinking the Cultural Context of Schooling Decisions in Disadvantaged Neighborhoods: From Deviant Subculture to Cultural Heterogeneity," *Sociology of Education* 84, no. 4 (2011): 322–339; Charles Blow, "Real Men and Pink Suits," *New York Times*, February 10, 2012.

36. Kai Schnabel, Corrine Alfeld, and Jacqueline Eccles, "Parental Influence on Students' Educational Choices in the United States and Germany: Different Ramifications-Same Effect?" *Journal of Vocational Behavior* 60, no. 2 (2002): 178–198.

37. Laura McCarger, cited in Chris Sturgis, *Black Holes in the Education Universe*, Connected by 25, Official Blog of the Youth Transition Funders Group, November 11, 2010, www.cby25.blogspot.com/2010/11/black-holes-in-education-universe.html.

38. David Yeager and Matthew Bundick, "The Role of Purposeful Work Goals in Promoting Meaning in Life and in Schoolwork During Adolescence," *Journal of Adolescent Research* 24, no. 4 (2009): 423–452.

39. Jeremy Staff et al., "Uncertainty in Early Occupational Aspirations: Role Exploration or Aimlessness?" *Social Forces* 89, no. 2 (2010): 659–684.

40. Lynn Gregory, "The 'Turnaround' Process: Factors Influencing the School Success of Urban Youth," *Journal of Adolescent Research* 10, no. 1 (1995): 136–154.

41. Daniel McFarland, "Curricular Flows: Trajectories, Turning Points, and Assignment Criteria in High School Math Careers," *Sociology of Education* 79, no. 3 (2006): 177–205.

42. Ronald Heck et al., "Tracks as Emergent Structures: A Network Analysis of Student Differentiation in a High School," *American Journal of Education* 110, no. 4 (2004): 321–352.

43. Walter Heinz and Alison Taylor, "Learning and Work Transition Policies in a Comparative Perspective: Canada and Germany," in *International Handbook of Educational Policy*, ed. Nina Bascia et al. (New York: Springer, 2005).

44. Jeylan T. Mortimer et al., "The Process of Occupational Decision Making: Patterns During the Transition to Adulthood" *Journal of Vocational Behavior* 61, no. 3 (2002): 439–465.

45. Yeager and Bundick, "The Role of Purposeful Work."

46. Lauren Resnick, "Getting to Work: Thoughts in the Function and Form of the School to Work Transition," in *Transitions in Work and Learning*, ed. Alan Lesgold, Michael, Feuer, and Allison Black (Washington, DC: National Academies Press, 1997), 249–263.

47. Moniek Kuijpers et al., "The Relationship Between Learning Environment and Career Competencies of Students in Vocational Education," *Journal of Vocational Behavior* 78, no. 1 (2011): 21–30.

48. Gilberto Conchas, *The Color of Success: Race and High-Achieving Youth* (New York: Teachers College Press, 2006).

49. Susan Phillips et al., "Preparation for the School-to-Work Transition: The Views of High School Students," *Journal of Vocational Behavior* 61, no. 2 (2002): 1–15.

50. Alison Taylor, "What Employers Look For: The Skills Debate and the Fit with Youth Perception," *Journal of Education and Work* 18, no. 2 (2005): 201–218; Andrew Helwig, "From Childhood to Adulthood: A 15-Year Longitudinal Career Development Study," *Career Development Quarterly* 57, no. 1 (2008): 38–50.

51. Jeylan T. Mortimer et al., "Tracing the Timing of 'Career' Acquisition in a Contemporary Youth Cohort," *Work and Occupations* 35, no. 1 (2008): 46.

52. Jen Ludwig, "Information and Inner-City Educational Attainment," *Economics of Education Review* 18, no. 1 (1999): 17–30.

53. Tom Hilliard, "Mobility Makers: A Study by the Center for an Urban Future" (working paper, Center for an Urban Future, New York, 2011).

54. Richard Pérez-Peña, "The New Community College Try," *New York Times*, July 22, 2012, A20.

55. Johanna Wyn and Rob White, "Negotiating Social Change: The Paradox of Youth," *Youth and Society* 32, no. 2 (2000): 165–183.

56. Jeremy Staff et al., "Uncertainty in Early Occupational Aspirations: Role Exploration or Aimlessness?" *Social Forces* 89, no. 2 (2010): 659–684.

57. Jocey Quinn et al., "'Dead End Kids in Dead End Jobs?' Reshaping Debates on Young People in Jobs Without Training," *Research in Post Compulsory Education* 13, no. 2 (2008): 185–194.

58. David Feiner, founding director, Albany Park Theater Project, Chicago, in discussion with author, June 2008.

59. Kenneth Gray, "The Gatekeepers," *Techniques: Making Education and Career Connections* 71, no. 9 (1997): 24–27; Nicholas Foskett and Jane Hemsley-Brown, *Choosing Futures* (New York: Routledge, 2001).

60. James Rosenbaum, "High School's Role in College and Workforce Preparation: Do College-for-All Policies Make High School Irrelevant? Spotlight on Student Success," in *The School to Work Movement: Origins and Destinations*, ed. William J. Stull and Nicholas M. Sanders (Hartford, CT: Praeger, 2003), 205.

61. Richard Settersten and Barbara Ray, *Not Quite Adults: Why 20-Somethings Are Choosing a Slower Path to Adulthood, and Why It's Good for Everyone* (New York: Random House, 2010), 5.

62. Tapan Monroe, "Can You Believe? A Shortage of Skilled Manufacturing Workers," Perspectives on the Economy blog, November 29, 2011, http://tmunroe.wordpress.com/2011/11/29/can-you-believe-shortage-of-skilled-manufacturing-workers.

63. Matt Sledge, "Maricopa Community Colleges Look to an Old Idea—Apprentice-ships—for New Workers," *Huffington Post*, August 7, 2012, http://www.huffington post.com/2012/08/07/maricopa-community-colleges-apprenticeship_n_1753633 .html.

64. Jonathan Meer, "Evidence on the Returns to Secondary Vocational Education," *Economics of Education Review* 26, no. 5 (2007): 559–573.

65. James Rosenbaum et al., "Beyond One-Size-Fits-All College Dreams," *American Educator* (Fall 2010): 2–8.

Chapter 3

1. Michael Powell, "A Brooklyn School Saved Lives, and Some Now Try to Return the Favor," *New York Times*, April 23, 2012, A17.

2. Melissa Gresalfi, "Taking Up Opportunities to Learn: Constructing Dispositions in Mathematics Classrooms," *Journal of the Learning Sciences* 18 (2009): 327–369.

3. Marion Brady, "Education Reform: An Ignored Problem and a Proposal" (unpublished manuscript, Truthout, June 2010).

4. William Johnson, "Confessions of a Bad Teacher," *New York Times*, March 4, 2012.

5. David Hursh, "Assessing No Child Left Behind and the Rise of Neoliberal Education Policies," *American Educational Research Journal* 44, no. 3 (2007): 493–518.

6. Michael Apple, "Introduction," in *Contradictions of School Reform: Educational Costs of Standardized Testing*, ed. Linda McNeil (New York: Routledge, 2000), xvi.

7. "How Do Students Learn Attitude at School?" (working paper, Citizen's League of Minneapolis, 2008), 2.

8. Marcus Raskin, *Being and Doing* (New York: Random House, 1971).

9. Hursh, "Assessing No Child Left Behind."

10. Sue Berryman, "Apprenticeship as a Paradigm of Learning," in *Education Through Occupations in American High Schools*, vol. 1: *Approaches to Integrating Academic and Vocational Education*, ed. Norton Grubb (New York: Teachers College Press, 1995).

11. John Rury, "Democracy's High School? Social Change and American Secondary Education in the Post-Conant Era," *American Educational Research Journal* 39, no. 2 (2002): 307–336.

12. Linda McNeil, *Contradictions of School Reform: Educational Costs of Standardized Testing* (Boca Raton, FL: Routledge, 2000).

13. Lesli Maxwell, "Los Angeles Schools Struggle with Curriculum Overhaul," *Education Week* 8, no. 6 (2012).

14. *Washington State Report Card* (Olympia, WA: Office of the Superintendent of Public Instruction, 2007), 5.

15. Jo Anne Kliefgen and Patricia Frens-Belken, "Problem Solving at a Circuit-Board Assembly Machine: A Microanalysis" (working paper, National Center for Research in Vocational Education, Berkeley, CA, 1996).

16. Mike Rose, "Blending Hand Work and Brain Work," in *Beyond Tracking: Multiple Pathways to College, Career, and Civic Participation*, ed. Jeannie Oakes et al. (Cambridge, MA: Harvard Education Press, 2008).

17. Norton Grubb, "The Richness of Occupational Instruction: The Paradox in U.S. Community Colleges" (paper presented at Teaching and Learning Within Vocational and Occupational Education and Training Conference, Göttingen, Germany, September 2001), 21.

18. Marty Nemko, "America's Most Overrated Product: Higher Education," *Chronicle of Higher Education*, May 2, 2008, B17.

19. Chris Asch, "The Inadvertent Bigotry of Inappropriate Expectations," *Education Week* 29, no. 35 (2010): 35.

20. Richard Rothstein, "A Blueprint That Needs More Work" (working paper, Economic Policy Institute, Washington, DC, 2010), 5–6.

21. Mike Rose, "Education for All: Unpacking the College for All versus Occupational Training Debate," *Teachers College Record Online*, September 10, 2010, www.mikerosebooks.blogspot.com.

22. L. Kaufman, "We Can Fix This One by Ourselves," letter to the editor, *Wall Street Journal*, January 27, 2011.

23. For some perspective, an educational profile of American adults finds that 2 percent have a professional degree, 7 percent a master's degree, 17.5 percent a bachelor's degree, and 7.5 percent an associate degree. See *Chronicle of Higher Education Almanac*, August 27, 2010.

24. Jean Johnson and Ann Duffett, "Life After High School: Young People Talk About Their Hopes and Prospects," Public Agenda, 2005, http://www.publicagenda.org/research/research_reports_details.cfm?list=3.

25. Kenneth Strike, "Community, the Missing Element of School Reform: Why Schools Should Be More Like Congregations Than Banks," *American Journal of Education* 110, no. 3 (2004): 215–227.

26. Linda Darling-Hammond, "The Right to Learn and the Advancement of Teaching: Research, Policy and Practice for Democratic Education," *Educational Researcher* 25, no. 6 (1996): 5–17.

27. Adam Davidson, "Making It in America," *The Atlantic*, January/February 2012, 58–70.

28. Kliefgen and Frens-Belken, "Problem Solving," 4.

29. Sasha Barab et al., "Our Designs and the Social Agendas They Carry," *Journal of the Learning Sciences* 16, no. 2 (2007): 263–305.

30. Darling-Hammond, "The Right to Learn," 5.

31. Gene Bottoms, *Crafting a New Vision for High School: How States Can Join Academic and Technical Studies to Promote More Powerful Learning* (Atlanta: Southern Regional Education Board, 2008), 17.

32. Norton Grubb and Jeannie Oakes, "Restoring Value to the High School Diploma: The Rhetoric and Practice of Higher Standards," Great Lakes Center for Education

Research and Practice, 2007, http://epsl.asu.edu/epru/documents/EPSL-0710–242-EPRU.pdf.

33. William Symonds, Robert Schwartz, and Ronald Ferguson, "Pathways to Prosperity: Meeting the Challenge of Preparing Young Americans for the 21st Century" (working paper, Pathways to Prosperity Project, Harvard University Graduate School of Education, Cambridge, MA, 2011), 11.

34. Jerry Diakiw, "It's Time for a New Kind of High School," *Education Week* vol. 31, no. 30 (May 19, 2012): 26–28.

35. Ron Brandt, *Powerful Learning* (Alexandria, VA: ASCD, 1998), 9.

36. Tony Monfiletto, "We Need All Hands," video filmed at TEDx Front Range, Denver, CO, June 8, 2012, available on YouTube.

37. Rob Riordan et al., *Seeing the Future: A Planning Guide for High Schools* (Providence, RI: Big Picture, 1999).

38. Jane Atkinson, "A Crisis of Relevance" (working paper, North Carolina Department of Education, 2009), p. xx. North Carolina is a leader in promoting the Early College High School.

39. Chris Sturgis, "Customizing Without Computers," Connected By 25: Official Blog of the Youth Transition Funders Group, September 21, 2011, www.cby25.blogspot.com.

40. Yrjo Engstrom, "*Non ScolaeSed Vitae Discimus*: Toward Overcoming the Encapsulation of School Learning," *Learning and Instruction* 1, no. 3 (1991): 243–259.

41. Deborah Parizek cited in "A Design-Thinking Approach to Public Schools," IDEO Blog, 2009, www.idea.com/work/a-design-thinking-approach-to-public-school.

42. Eliot Levine, *One Kid at a Time: Big Lessons from a Small School* (New York: Teachers College Press, 2002), 44.

43. Kristin Olson, "Passion at the Center of New Education," Pedagogies of Abundance, May 22, 2012, http://oldsow.wordpress.com/2011/09/19/passion-at-the-center-of-new-education-model.

44. Olson, "Passion at the Center."

45. Tina Barseghian, "Napa New Tech High: 5 Reasons This Is the School of the Future," Huffington Post Education Blog, January 7, 2011, www.huffingtonpost.com/tina-barseghian/napa-new-tech-high-5-reas-b-805972.html.

46. Sturgis, "Customizing Without Computers," 1.

47. Dennis Littky, *The Big Picture: Education Is Everyone's Business* (Alexandria, VA: Association for Supervision and Curriculum Development, 2004), 123.

48. Michael F. Shaughnessy, "Interview with Deborah Parizek," *Education News*, September 17, 2009.

49. Shaughnessy, "Interview."

50. Jack Chin, "All at a Place: Connecting Schools, Youth, and Community" (report by Bay Area School Reform Collaborative, San Francisco, 2001), 16.

51. Barseghian, "Napa New Tech High," 201.

52. Morgan Barrett, "Carpe Diem," *Ampersand: High Tech High Student Journal* 3 (2011): 35–37.

53. Malia Bence, "The Georgie in Me," *Ampersand: High Tech High Student Journal* 3 (Spring 2011): 47–49.

54. Janine Certo et al., "Students' Perspectives on Their High School Experience,"*Adolescence* 38, no. 152 (2003): 725–754; Kim Pierce, "Posing, Pretending, Waiting for the Bell: Life I High School Classrooms," *The High School Journal* 89, no. 2 (2006): 1–15.

55. Theodore Sizer and Nancy Sizer, *The Students Are Watching* (Boston: Beacon Press, 1999), chap. 1.

Chapter 4

1. Jonathan Meer, "Evidence on the Returns to Secondary Vocational Education," *Economics of Education Review* 26, no. 5 (2007): 559–573.

2. Theodore Lewis, "Vocational Education as General Education," *Curriculum Inquiry* 28, no. 3 (1998): 283–309.

3. National Center for Education Statistics, *High School Data, Student Participation CTC* (Washington, DC: U.S. Department of Education, 2009), table H122.

4. Linda Darling-Hammond, "The Right to Learn and the Advancement of Teaching: Research, Policy and Practice for Democratic Education," *Educational Researcher* 25, no. 6 (1996): 5–17.

5. Institute for a Competitive Workforce, "The Skills Imperative: How Career and Technical Education Can Solve the U.S. Talent Shortage" (report by U.S. Chamber of Commerce, Washington, DC, 2008), 3.

6. William Symonds, Robert Schwartz, and Ronald Ferguson, "Pathways to Prosperity: Meeting the Challenge of Preparing Young Americans for the 21st Century" (working paper, Pathways to Prosperity Project, Harvard University Graduate School of Education, Cambridge, MA, 2011), 11.

7. Sara Goldrick-Rab, "Following Their Every Move: An Investigation of Social Class Differences in College Pathways," *Sociology of Education* 79, no. 1 (2006): 61–79.

8. Anthony Carnevale et al., "Help Wanted: Projections of Job and Education Requirements through 2018" (report, Georgetown Center on Education and the Workforce, Washington, DC, 2010).

9. Ibid.

10. Cynthia Mester, "Health Science and Technology: State of the Art" (working paper, CTE Curriculum Revitalization Initiative, Illinois Department of Education, Office of Educational Services, Springfield, 2005), 6.

11. Catherine Gewertz, "College for All Reconsidered: Are Four-Year Degrees for All?" *Education Week* 30, no. 34 (2011): 6.

12. Jeremy Roschelle et al., "Eight Issues for Learning Scientists about Education and the Economy," *Journal of the Learning Sciences* 20, no. 1 (2011): 3–49.

13. Carnevale et al., "Help Wanted."

14. Joel Kotkin, "The U.S. Desparately Needs a Strategy to Attract the Right Skilled Immigrants," blog posting, June 26, 2012, www.joelkotkin.com; Ania Monaco, "Are Engineers Really in Demand?" Institute for Electrical and Electronics Engineers, February 10, 2012, http://theinstitute.ieee.org/ieee-roundup/opinions/ieee-roundup/are-engineers-really-in-demand?goback=.gde_3968449_news_5573633689029451791.

15. Dan Swinney, *Building the Bridge to the High Road* (Chicago: Midwest Center for Labor Research, 2000).

16. Adam Davidson, "Making It in America," *The Atlantic*, January/February 2012, 58–70.

17. David C. Bjorkquist, Review of *Shop Class as Soulcraft: An Inquiry into the Value of Work* by Matthew B. Crawford, *Journal of Industrial Teacher Education* 47, no. 1 (2010): 128–133.

18. Kyle Stone et al., "Closing the Gap: Education Requirements of the 21st Century Production Workforce," *Journal of Industrial Teacher Education* 45, no. 3 (2009): 5–32.

19. Peter Whoriskey, "U.S. Manufacturing Sees Shortage of Skilled Factory Workers," *Washington Post,* February 19, 2012.

20. Ibid., 2.

21. Theodore Lewis, "Social Inequality in Education: A Constraint on an American High Skills Future," *Curriculum Inquiry* 37, no. 4 (2007): 329–349.

22. James Gee, "Communities of Practice in the New Capitalism," *Journal of the Learning Sciences* 9, no. 4 (2000): 515–523.

23. Swinney, *Building the Bridge*, 10.

24. Elisabeth Muhlenberg, "Who Benefits? A Comparison of School-Firm Partnerships in Chicago and Berlin" (doctoral dissertation, University of Illinois, Chicago, 2011), 150.

25. Meer, "Evidence on the Returns."

26. John Bishop and Ferran Mane, "The Impacts of Career-Technical Education on High School Labor Market Success," *Economics of Education Review*, 23, no.4 (2004): 381–402.

27. Robert Lerman, "Are Skills the Problem? Reforming the Education and Training System in the United States" (working paper, Upjohn Institute for Employment Research, Kalamazoo, MI, 2008).

28. Thomas Bailey, "Can Youth Apprenticeship Thrive in the United States?" *Educational Researcher* 22, no. 3 (1993): 4–10.

29. Mike Rose, "Blending Hand Work and Brain Work," in *Beyond Tracking: Multiple Pathways to College, Career, and Civic Participation*, ed. Jeannie Oakes et al. (Cambridge, MA: Harvard Education Press, 2008), 27.

30. Meer, "Evidence on the Returns," 568.

31. Robert Harreveld and Michael Singh, "Contextualising Learning at the Education-Training-Work Interface," *Education and Training* 51, no. 2 (2009): 92–107.

32. David Beckett and Paul Hager, *Life, Work and Learning: Practice in Postmodernity* (London: Routledge, 2002).

33. Marcia Gentry et al., "Professionalism, Sense of Community and Reason to Learn: Lessons from an Exemplary Career and Technical Education Center," *Career and Technical Education Research* 30, no. 1. (2005): 47–85.

34. Alison Fraser, "Vocational Technical Education in Massachusetts" (white paper no. 42, Pioneer Institute, Boston, 2008).

35. Anthony Chow et al., "A Catalyst for Educational Change: The Role of Career and Technical Education in Georgia's Statewide Educational Improvement Efforts," *The Online Journal* 9, no. 1 (2011): 1–8; Amy Detgen and Corinne Alfeld, "Replication of a Career Academy Model: The Georgia Central Education Center and Four Replication Sites" (working paper, Regional Education Lab Southeast, Atlanta, 2011).

36. Robert Halpern, *The Means to Grow Up: Reinventing Apprenticeship as a Developmental Support in Adolescence* (New York: Routledge, 2009). For an exception to the lack of apprenticeship opportunity in high school, see my case study of the Wisconsin Youth Apprenticeship Program.

37. Etienne Wenger, *Communities of Practice* (Cambridge, UK: Cambridge University Press, 1998), 102.

38. Linda McNeil, *Contradictions of School Reform: Educational Costs of Standardized Testing* (Boca Raton, FL: Routledge, 2000), 37, 38.

39. Amy Ryken, "Content, Pedagogy, Results: A Thrice Told Tale of Integrating Work-Based and School-Based Learning" (doctoral dissertation, University of California, Berkeley, 2001), 75.

40. Ibid.

41. Fischer and Rauner, "The Implications of Work Process Knowledge."

42. James R. Stone III et al., "Rigor *and* Relevance: Enhancing High School Students' Math Skills Through Career and Technical Education," *American Educational Research Journal* 45, no. 3 (2008): 767–795.

43. Thomas Bailey et al., *Working Knowledge: Work-Based Learning and Education Reform* (New York: Routledge, 2004).

44. Amy Johnson, Ivan Charner, and Robin White, "Curriculum Integration in Context: An Exploration of How Structures and Circumstances Affect Design and Implementation" (working paper, Academy for Educational Development, National Institute for Work and Learning, Washington, DC, 2003); Donna Person et al., "Capitalizing on Context: Curriculum Integration in CTE" (working paper, National Research Center for Career and Technical Education, Curriculum Integration Work Group, University of Louisville, KY, 2010).

45. James Stone and Oscar Aliaga, "Career and Technical Education and School-to-Work at the End of the 20thCentury: Participation and Outcomes," *Career and Technical Education Research* 30, no. 2 (2005): 125–144; Stone et al., "Rigor *and* Relevance."

46. Johnson et al., "Curriculum Integration in Context."

47. Ibid.

48. Marsha Silverberg et al., "National Assessment of Vocational Education: Final Report to Congress" (working paper, U.S. Department of Education, Washington, DC, 2004), 85.

49. Gilberto Conchas, *The Color of Success: Race and High-Achieving Youth* (New York: Teachers College Press, 2006), 47.

50. Cathy Stasz et al., "Teaching Generic Skills," in *Education Through Occupations in American High Schools*, Vol. 1: *Approaches to Integrating Academic and Vocational Education*, ed. Norton Grubb (New York: Teachers College Press, 1995), 169–191; Gentry et al., "Professionalism, Sense of Community."

51. Grubb, "The Richness of Occupational Instruction," 26.

52. Ibid., 9.

53. Lerman, "Are Skills the Problem?" 26.

54. Ryken, "Content, Pedagogy, Results."

55. Stephen Hamilton, *Apprenticeship for Adulthood: Preparing Youth for the Future* (New York: Free Press, 1990), 16.

56. Bonalyn Nelsen, "Should Social Skills Be in the Vocational Curriculum? Evidence from the Automotive Repair Field," in *Transitions in Work and Learning: Implications for Assessment*, ed. Alan Lesgold et al. (Washington, DC: National Academies Press, 1997), 85.

57. Bishop and Mane, "The Impacts of Career-Technical Education"; Stone and Aliaga, "Career and Technical Education."

58. Silverberg et al., "National Assessment."

59. Morgan Lewis, "Effectiveness of Previous Initiatives Similar to Programs of Study: Tech Prep, Career Pathways, and Youth Apprenticeships," *Career and Technical Education Research* 33, no. 3 (2008): 165–188.

60. Lauren Resnick, "Getting to Work: Thoughts in the Function and Form of the School to Work Transition," in *Transitions in Work and Learning* (Washington, DC: National Academies Press, 1997), 249–263.

61. Carnevale et al., "Help Wanted," 15.

62. Fischer and Rauner, "The Implications of Work Process Knowledge."

63. Martin Fischer, "Work Experience as an Element of Work Process Knowledge," in Boreham et al., *Work Process Knowledge*, 118–133.

64. Beckett and Hager, *Life, Work and Learning*.

65. John Halliday, "Critical Thinking and the Academic Vocational Divide," *Curriculum Journal* 11, no. 2 (2000): 159–175.

66. Richard Lakes, "Work-Ready Testing: Education and Employability in Neoliberal Times," *Journal for Critical Education Policy Studies* 9, no.1 (2011): 317–340.

67. Halpern, *The Means to Grow Up*.

68. Gene Bottoms and Marna Young, *Lost in Transition: Building a Better Path from School to College and Careers* (Atlanta: Southern Regional Education Board, 2008), 3.

69. Stone and Aliaga, "Career and Technical Education"; Ross Edmunds and Sheryl Freeman, "New Demands and Dimensions for Apprenticeship in the New Economy School Work Partnerships," www.umanitoba.ca/unevoc/2002conference/text/papers/freeman.pdf.

70. Kenneth Gray, "The Role of Career and Technical Education in the American High School: A Student Centered Analysis," *Journal of Vocational Special Needs Education* 24, no. 1 (2001):15–25; Richard Kazis, "Re-Imagining Career and Technical Education for the 21st Century: What Role for High School Programs?" (working paper, Jobs for the Future, Boston, 2005); David Stern and Roman Stearns, "Evidence and Challenges," in *Beyond Tracking: Multiple Pathways to College, Career, and Civic Participation*, ed. Jeanine Oakes and Marisa Saunders (Cambridge, MA: Harvard Education Press, 2008).

71. Bishop and Mane, "The Impacts of Career and Technical Education."

72. Ryken, "Content Pedagogy, Results," 79.

73. L. Allen Phelps et al., "The Wisconsin Youth Apprentices Go to College: Access, Persistence, and Achievement" (paper presented at the American Educational Research Association Annual Meeting, Montreal, April 22, 1999).

74. Ryken, "Content, Pedagogy, Results," 57.

75. Gentry et al., "Professionalism, Sense of Community," 70.

76. Bailey et al., *Working Knowledge*, 164.

77. Ryken, "Content, Pedagogy, Results," 71.

78. Ibid., 120.

79. Gilberto Conchas, "Structuring Failure and Success," *Harvard Educational Review* 71, no. 3 (2001): 475–504.

80. Bailey et al., *Working Knowledge*.

81. Cheryl Evanciew and Jay Rojewski, "Skill and Knowledge Acquisition in the Workplace: A Case Study of Mentor-Apprentice Relationships in Youth Apprenticeship Programs," *Journal of Industrial Teacher Education* 36, no. 2 (1999): 24–53.

82. Amy Ryken, "Goin' Somewhere: How Career Technical Education Programs Support and Constrain Urban Youths' Career Decision-Making," *Career and Technical Education Research* 31, no. 1 (2006): 49–71.

83. Theodore Lewis, "Vocational Education as General Education," *Curriculum Inquiry* 28, no. 3 (1998): 283–309.

84. Ibid.

85. J. D. Hoyt and Chris Sturgis, "A Framework for Dropout Reduction and Recovery" (working paper, The Alternative Pathways Project, San Francisco, 2005).

86. Katherine Oliver, "Prepared Remarks for the American Youth Policy Forum Workshop on Career Pathways to Employment," Washington, DC, November 14, 2011.

87. Erica Swinney, program coordinator, Austin Polytechnical High School/Center for Labor and Community Research, Chicago, in discussion with author, March and June 2012.

88. Grubb, "The Richness of Occupational Instruction," 1.

89. Mike Rose, "Education for All: Unpacking the College for All versus Occupational Training Debate," *Teachers College Record Online*, September 20, 2010.

90. Donna Person et al., "Capitalizing on Context: Curriculum Integration in CTE" (working paper, National Research Center for Career and Technical Education, Curriculum Integration Work Group, University of Louisville, KY, 2010), 3.

91. Stone and Aliaga, "Career and Technical Education," 4.

92. Grubb, "The Richness of Occupational Instruction."

93. Ryken, "Content, Pedagogy, Results,"53.

94. Marlene Barajas, "Undecided," *Ampersand: High Tech High Student Journal* (2011), 33–34.

95. Fischer and Rauner, "The Implications of Work Process Knowledge," 165.

96. Silverberg et al., "National Assessment of Vocational Education," 60; Jeremy Staff et al., "Uncertainty in Early Occupational Aspirations: Role Exploration or Aimlessness?" *Social Forces* 89, no. 2 (2010): 659–684.

97. Jeylan T. Mortimer et al., "The Process of Occupational Decision Making: Patterns during the Transition to Adulthood," *Journal of Vocational Behavior* 61, no. 3(2002): 439–465.

98. Ryken, "Content, Pedagogy, Results," 79.

99. John Smyth, "The Making of Young Lives With/Against the School Credential," *Journal of Education and Work* 16, no. 2 (2003): 127–146.

100. Staff et al., "Uncertainty in Early Occupational."

101. Symonds et al., "Pathways to Prosperity," 23.

102. Nelsen, "Should Social Skills Be in the Vocational Curriculum?" 84.

103. Lene Tanggaard and Claus Elmholdt, "Assessment in Practice: An Inspiration from Apprenticeship," *Scandinavian Journal of Educational Studies* 52, no. 1 (2008): 97–116.

104. Ryken, "Content, Pedagogy, Results," 132.

105. Norton Grubb, "Vocational Education and Training: Issues for a Thematic Review" (report prepared for the Organisation for Economic Co-operation and Development "Learning for Jobs" project, Paris, 2006).

106. Robert Schwartz, "The German Dual System: Impressions of a U.S. Observer" (unpublished paper, Harvard Graduate School of Education, 2010), 7.

107. Roschelle et al., "Eight Issues."

108. Irena Grugulis and Dimitrinka Stoyanova, "The Missing Middle: Communities of Practice in a Freelance Labour Market," *Work, Employment and Society* 25, no. 2 (2011): 342–351.

109. Prue Huddleston and Su-Ann Oh, "The Magic Roundabout: Work-Related Learning within the 14–19 Curriculum," *Oxford Review of Education* 30, no. 1 (2004): 83–103, http://www.informaworld.com/smpp/188472500-29314795/title-db=all-content=t713440173-tab=issueslist-branches=30 - v30.

110. Alberto Arenas, "Connecting Hand, Mind, and Community: Vocational Education for Social and Environmental Renewal," *Teachers College Record* 110, no. 2 (2008): 377–404.

111. John Rogers, Joseph Kahne, and Ellen Middaugh, *Multiple Pathways, Vocational Education, and the Future of Democracy* (Los Angeles: Institute of Democracy, UCLA, 2007).

Chapter 5

1. Barbara Rogoff, Maricela Correa-Chavez, and Marta Cotuc, "A Cultural/Historical View of Schooling in Human Development," in *Developmental Psychology and Social Change*, ed. David B. Pillemer and Sheldon H. White (Cambridge, UK: Cambridge University Press, 2005), 227.

2. David Feiner, founding director, Albany Park Theater Project, Chicago, in discussion with author, June 2008.

3. Nell Daniel, "Sweat Equity Enterprises: The Convergence of Design Education, Youth Development and Situated Learning" (doctoral dissertation, New York University, 2007), available at www.sweatequityeducation.org.

4. Leon Botstein, "Let Teenagers Try Adulthood," *NSSE* 107, no. 2 (2008): 118–121.

5. Abby Remer, *This Is Inside View* (New York: American Museum of Natural History, 2005), chaps. 4, 10.

6. John Dewey, *Democracy and Education* (1916; repr. New York: The Free Press, 1997).

7. Jerome Bruner, "The Culture of Education," in *Social Construction: A Reader*, ed. M. Gergen and K. Gergen (Thousand Oaks, CA: Sage, 2003), 21.

8. Jerome Bruner, *The Culture of Education* (Cambridge, MA: Harvard University Press, 1996).

9. Magnus Bryn, teaching artist, Free Street Theater, Chicago, in discussion with author July 2008.

10. Zanna Chase, mentor, Apprenticeship in Science and Engineering, Portland, OR, in discussion with author, June 2007.

11. Magnus Bryn, teaching artist, Free Street Theater, Chicago, in discussion with author, July 2008.

12. Maria Gaspar, teaching artist, Marwen Arts, Chicago, in discussion with author, July 2007.

13. F. Smith, "Learning from the Pros," p. 1, 2006, http://www.edutopia.org/learning-from-the-pros.

14. Ibid., 2.

15. Padraig Nash and David Shaffer, "Epistemic Trajectories: Mentoring in a Game Design Practicum," *Instructional Science* online, September 29, 2012, 9.

16. Vivian Chávez and Elisabeth Soep, "Youth Radio and the Pedagogy of Collegiality," *Harvard Educational Review* 75, no. 4 (2005); Elisabeth Soep et al., "Social

Justice Youth Media," in *Handbook of Social Justice in Education*, ed. William Ayers et al. (Mahwah, NJ: Lawrence Erlbaum, 2007), 10.

17. Daniel, "Sweat Equity Enterprises."

18. Steve Strauss, mentor, Apprenticeship in Science and Engineering, Portland, OR, in discussion with author, May 2007.

19. Julie Quiroz-Martinez et al., "Changing the Rules of the Game: Youth Development and Structural Racism" (working paper, Philanthropic Initiative for Racial Equity, Washington, DC, 2004), 22.

20. Chris Sturgis, "The Youth Transition Funders Group," 2012, http://www.metisnet.net/relationships5.htm.

21. Steve Goodman, "Educating for Democracy," *EVC Newsletter* 3, no. 1 (2010): 1–3.

22. Linda Camino and Shepherd Zeldin, "From Periphery to Center: Pathways for Youth Civic Engagement in the Day-To-Day Life of Communities," *Applied Developmental Science* 6, no. 4 (2002): 213–220.

23. Tine Radinja, "From Practice to Theory and Back Again," in *The NFE Book: The Impact of Non Formal Education on Young People and Society*, ed. Maria Nomikou (Brussels: AEGEE Europe, n.d.), 2–3.

24. Deborah L. McKoy and Jeffrey M. Vincent, "Engaging Schools in Urban Revitalization," *Journal of Planning Education and Research* 26, no. 4 (2007): 389–403; Deborah L. McKoy et al., "Trajectories of Opportunity for Young Men and Boys of Color: Built Environment and Place-Making Strategies for Creating Equitable, Healthy, and Sustainable Communities," in *Changing Places: How Communities Will Improve the Health of Boys of Color*, ed. Christopher Edley Jr. and Jorge Ruiz de Velasco (Berkeley: University of California Press, 2010).

25. Ibid.

26. Camino and Zeldin, "From Periphery to Center."

27. Claudia Vicin, teaching artist, Artists for Humanity, Boston in discussion with author, January 2007.

28. Eric Booth, "El Sistema's Open Secrets" (unpublished manuscript, 2010), 11, available at www.arts.virginia.gov/resources/artworks/EricBoothReadingList2.pdf.

29. Soep et al., *Social Justice Youth Media*, 10.

30. Magnus Bryn, teaching artist, Free Street Theater, Chicago, in discussion with author, July 2008.

31. Alvin Keith, teaching artist, Roundabout Theater, New York City, in discussion with author, April 2007.

32. Gibbs, painting teaching artist, Artists for Humanity, Boston, in discussion with the author, December 2006.

33. Mark Graham, "How the Teaching Artist Can Change the Dynamics of Teaching and Learning," *Teaching Artist Journal* 77, no. 2 (2009): 85–94.

34. Liz Millmn, Joffrey Ballet, Chicago, in discussion with author, August 2008.

35. Denise Zaccardi, founder and director, CTVN, in discussion with author, July 2008.

36. Steve Strauss, mentor, Apprenticeship in Science and Engineering, Portland, OR, in discussion with author, May 2007.

37. Phil Wenger, instructor, Urban Boat Builders, St. Paul, MN, in discussion with author, June 2007.

38. Priscilla Block, executive director, St. Louis Artworks, in discussion with the author, August 2006.

39. Steve Goodman, founder and director, Educational Video Center, New York City, in discussion with author, January 2007.

40. Robert Halpern, "A Qualitative Study of After-School Matters: Final Report" (working paper, Erikson Institute, Chicago, 2006).

41. Constant Albertson and Miriam Davidson, "Drawing with Light and Clay: Teaching and Learning in the Art Studio as Pathways to Engagement," *International Journal of Education and the Arts* 8, no. 9 (2007).

42. Ibid.

43. David Feiner, founding director, Albany Park Theater Project, Chicago, in discussion with author, June 2008.

44. Booth, "El Sistema's Open Secrets," 2.

45. Denise Zaccardi, founder and director, CTVN, in discussion with author, July 2008.

46. Nicholas Farrar and Gillian Trorey, "Maxims, Tacit Knowledge and Learning: Developing Expertise in Dry Stone Walling," *Journal of Vocational Education and Training* 60, no.1 (2006): 35–48.

47. Margaret Riordan, "Discovering the Core of Experiential Education: How Big Picture School Students Learn Through Internships" (doctoral dissertation, New York University, 2006), 255.

48. Morena Cuconato et al., "Participation and Informal Learning in Young People's Transitions to Work" (working paper no. 3, Institut für Regionale Innovation und Sozialforschung, Tübingen, Germany, 2003), 23.

49. Simon Yu, mentor, Marwen Arts/Art at Work, Chicago, in discussion with author, June 2007.

50. Steve Strauss, mentor, Apprenticeship in Science and Engineering, Portland, OR, in discussion with author, May 2007.

51. Gail Richmond and Lori Ann Kurth, "Moving from Outside to Inside: High School Students' Use of Apprenticeships as Vehicles for Entering the Culture and Practice of Science," *Journal of Research in Science Teaching* 36, no. 6 (1999): 677–697.

52. Zanna Chase, mentor, Apprenticeship in Science and Engineering, Portland, OR, in disussion with author, June 2007.

53. Chávez and Soep, "Youth Radio."

54. Elizabeth Thomas, "Student Engagement and Learning in a Community-Based Arts Classroom," *Teachers College Record* 109, no. 3 (2007): 770–796.

55. Booth, "El Sistema's Open Secrets," 7.

56. Gee cited in Brian Cambourne, "Conditions for Literacy Learning," *The Reading Teacher* 55, no. 8 (2002): 758–762.

57. Chris Higgins, "The Possibility of Public Education in an Instrumentalist Age," *Educational Theory* 61, no.4 (2011): 451–466.

58. Kathleen Cushman, *What's Essential About Learning in the World of Work*, 1997, www.essentialschools.org/resources/107.

59. Jane Kroger, *Identity in Adolescence: The Balance Between Self and Other* (London: Routledge, 1996).

Chapter 6

1. Manuela du Bois-Reymond, "Youth—Learning—Europe: Ménage à Trois?" *Young* 12, no. 3 (2004): 187–204.

2. Andreas Walther, "Risks and Responsibilities: The Individualization of Youth Transitions and the Ambivalence between Participation and Activation in Europe," *Social Work and Society* 3, no. 1 (2005): 116–127.

3. Anna Beling, "Unemployment, Mental Health and Well-Being in Youth" (bachelor's thesis, Maastricht University, Netherlands, 2011).

4. Guy Standing, *The Precariat: The New Dangerous Class* (New York: Bloomsbury USA, 2011), 1.

5. Beling, "Unemployment."

6. Regine Grytnes, "Making the Right Choice! Inquiries into the Reasoning Behind Young People's Decisions about Education," *Young* 19, no. 3 (2011): 333–351.

7. Ken Roberts, "Opportunity Structures Then and Now," *Journal of Education and Work* 22, no. 5 (2009): 355–368.

8. Andrew Morrison, "I Can't Do Any More Education: Class, Individualisation and Educational Decision-Making," *Journal of Vocational Education and Training* 60, no. 4 (2008): 350–351.

9. Hannu Raty, "What *Comes after* Compulsory Education? A Follow-Up Study on Parental Expectations of Their Child's Future Education," *Educational Studies* 32, no. 1 (2006): 1–16.

10. Grytnes, "Making the Right Choice," 340.

11. Walter Heinz, "Structure and Agency in Transition Research," *Journal of Education and Work* 22, no.5 (2009): 391–404.

12. Ross McKibbin, "Will We Notice When the Tories Have Won?" *London Review of Books*, September 24, 2009, 9–10.

13. Aaron Benavot, "The Diversification of Secondary Education: School Curricula in Competitive Perspective" (working paper, UNESCO: International Bureau of Education, Geneva, 2006).

14. Elisabeth Muhlenberg, "Who Benefits? A Comparison of School-Firm Partnerships in Chicago and Berlin" (doctoral dissertation, University of Illinois, Chicago, 2011); Justin Powell and Heike Solga, "Why Are Higher Education Participation

Rates in Germany So Low? Institutional Barriers to Higher Education Expansion," *Journal of Education and Work* 24, nos. 1–2 (2011): 49–68.

15. Norton Grubb, "Vocational Education and Training: Issues for a Thematic Review" (report prepared for the Organisation for Economic Co-operation and Development "Learning for Jobs" Project, Paris, 2006).

16. Morena Cuconato et al., "Participation and Informal Learning in Young People's Transitions to Work" (working paper no. 3, vol. 3, Institut für Regionale Innovation und Sozialforschung, Tübingen, Germany, 2003).

17. Ibid., 23.

18. Jane Higgins et al., "Vocational Imagination and Labor Market Literacy: Young New Zealanders Making Education-Employment Linkages," *Journal of Vocational Education and Training* 62, no. 1 (2010): 13–25.

19. Willibrord de Graaf and Kaj van Zenderen, "Segmented Assimilation in the Netherlands? Young Migrants and Early School Leaving," *Ethnic and Racial Studies* 32, no. 8 (2009): 1470–1488.

20. Bettina Haidinger and Roland Atzmuller, "The Vocational Placement Guarantee: European Commission: Educational, Vocational, and Policy Landscapes in Europe" (final report, Work Able Projects, Brussels, 2011).

21. Eric Hanushek and Ludger Woessmann, "Does Educational Tracking Affect Performance and Inequality? Differences-in-Differences Evidence Across Countries" (discussion paper no. 1901, Institute for the Study of Labor, Bonn, Germany, 2005).

22. Gerald K. LeTendre et al., "What Is Tracking? Cultural Expectations in the United States, Germany, and Japan," *American Educational Research Journal* 40, no. 1 (2003): 43–90.

23. Powell and Solga, "Higher Participation Rates," 55.

24. Pasi Sahlberg, *Finnish Lessons: What Can the World Learn from Educational Change in Finland?* (New York: Teachers College Press, 2011).

25. Lisa O'Donnell et al., *Evaluation of the Increased Flexibility for 14 to 16 Year Olds Programme* (London: National Foundation for Educational Research, Report No. 790, 2006); Jacky Lumby, "14–16 Year Olds in Further Education Colleges: Lessons for Learning and Leadership," *Journal of Vocational Education and Training* 59, no. 1 (2007): 1–18.

26. Gunilla Bergstrom, "General Presentation on the Swedish Educational Regime and Basic Statistical Overview of the Main Educational Data at the National Level" (final report, Work Able Projects, European Commission: Educational, Vocational, and Policy Landscapes in Europe, 2011); Arthur Morgan et al., "Community Consortia and Post-Compulsory Education: A Local Approach to Local Problems," *Journal of Vocational Education and Training* 56, no. 2 (2004): 227–244.

27. Holger Ziegler, "Outline of Insights European Commission: Educational, Vocational, and Policy Landscapes in Europe" (final report, Work Able Projects, Bielefeld, Denmark, 2011), 7.

28. Ewart Keep, "Where Next for Vocational Education?" *British Journal of Sociology of Education* 33, no. 2 (2012): 315–322.

29. Gunter Walden and Klaus Troltsch, "Apprenticeship Training in Germany—Still a Future-Oriented Model for Recruiting Skilled Workers?" *Journal of Vocational Education and Training* 63, no. 3 (2011): 305–322; Haidinger and Atzmuller, "The Vocational Placement Guarantee."

30. Robert Schwartz, "The German Dual System: Impressions of a U.S. Observer" (unpublished paper, Harvard Graduate School of Education, 2010).

31. Ibid.

32. Linda Clark and Georg Herman, "The Institutionalization of Skill in Britain and Germany," in *The Skills That Matter*, ed. Chris Warhurst et al. (London: Palgrave, 2004), 128–147.

33. Tim Oates, "Parity of Esteem Between Academic and Vocational Qualifications: Time to Abandon a Misguided Notion" (working paper, Gatsby Charitable Foundation, London, 2007), 4.

34. Schwartz, "The German Dual System," 1.

35. Walden and Troltsch, "Apprenticeship Training."

36. Robert Glover, "The German Apprenticeship System: Lessons for Austin, Texas," *Annals of the American Academy of Political and Social Science* 544, no. 1 (1996): 83–94.

37. Muhlenberg, "Who Benefits?"

38. Powell and Solga, "Higher Participation Rates," 53.

39. Walter Heinz and Alison Taylor, "Learning and Work Transition Policies in a Comparative Perspective: Canada and Germany," in *International Handbook of Educational Policy*, ed. Nina Bascia et al. (New York: Springer, 2005).

40. Muhlenberg, "Who Benefits?"

41. Haidinger and Atzmuller, "The Vocational Placement Guarantee," 138.

42. Alison Taylor, "What Employers Look For: The Skills Debate and the Fit with Youth Perception," *Journal of Education and Work* 18, no. 2 (2005): 201–218; Robert Harreveld and Michael Singh, "Contextualising Learning at the Education-Training-Work Interface," *Education and Training* 51, no. 2 (2009): 92–107.

43. Robert Harraveld and Michael Singh, "Contextualizing Learning at the Education-Training-Work Interface," *Education and Training* 51, no. 2 (2009): 92–107.

44. Taylor, "What Employers Look For," 212.

45. Susan Waite et al., "Work-Related Learning for Students with Significant Learning Difficulties: Relevance and Reality," *Cambridge Journal of Education* 36, no. 4 (2006): 579–595.

46. Keep, "Where Next for Vocational Education?" 318.

47. Andrea Laczik and Carolyn White, "Employer Engagement Within 14–19 Diploma Development," *Research in Post-Compulsory Education* 14, no. 4 (2009): 399–413.

48. Helen Colley et al., "Informality and Formality in Learning" (report for the Learning and Skills Research Centre, London, 2003), 480, 482.

49. Micheala Brockman, "Identity and Apprenticeship: The Case of English Motor Vehicle Maintenance Apprentices," *Journal of Vocational Education and Training* 62, no. 1 (2010): 63–73.

50. Robert MacDonald, "Youth Transitions, Unemployment and Underemployment," *Journal of Sociology* 47, no. 4 (2011): 427–444.

51. Ann Hodgson and Ken Spours, "The Organization of 14–19 Education and Training in England: Beyond Weakly Collaborative Arrangements," *Journal of Education and Work* 19, no. 4 (2006): 325–342.

52. Alison Taylor and Laura Servage, "Perpetuating Education-Jobs Mismatch in a High School Internship Programme: An Ecological Model," *Journal of Education and Work* 25, no. 2 (2012): 163–183; Alison Taylor and Sheryl Freeman, "Made in the Trade: Youth Attitudes Toward Apprenticeship Certification," *Journal of Vocational Education and Training*, 63, no. 3 (2011): 345–362.

53. Grubb, "Vocational Education and Training."

54. Alison Taylor, "The Challenges of Partnership in School-to-Work Transition," *Journal of Vocational Education and Training* 58, no. 3 (2006): 319–336.

55. Wolfgang Lehmann, "I'm Still Scrubbing the Floors: Experiencing Youth Apprenticeships in Canada and Germany," *Work, Employment and Society* 19, no. 1 (2005): 107–129.

56. Ibid., 109.

57. Ibid., 120.

58. Ibid.

59. Ross Edmunds and Sheryl Freeman, "New Demands and Dimensions for Apprenticeship in the New Economy School Work Partnerships" (paper, International Conference on Technical and Vocational Education and Training, Manitoba, Canada, October 2002), 5, available at www.umanitoba.ca/unevoc/2002conference/text/papers/freeman.pdf.

60. Taylor, "The Challenges of Partnership."

61. Cuconato et al., "Participation and Informal Learning," 24.

62. Grubb, "Vocational Education and Training."

63. Keep, "Where Next for Vocational Education?" 318.

64. Anita Harris et al., "Beyond Apathetic or Activist Youth: 'Ordinary' Young People and Contemporary Forms of Participaton," *Young* 18, no. 9 (2010): 9–32.

65. Haidinger and Atzmuller, "The Vocational Placement Guarantee," 123.

66. Walden and Troltsch, "Apprenticeship Training in Germany."

67. Landon Thomas, "For London Youth, Down and Out Is a Way of Life," *New York Times*, February 15, 2012, A3.

68. du Bois-Reymond, "Youth—Learning—Europe: Ménage à Trois?" *Young* 12, no. 3 (2004): 187–204.

Chapter 7

1. Robert Halpern, *The Means to Grow Up: Reinventing Apprenticeship as a Developmental Support in Adolescence* (New York: Routledge, 2009).

2. National Collaborative on Workforce and Disability, "Strategies for Youth Workforce Programs to Become Employer-Friendly Intermediaries" (information brief no. 12, National Collaboration on Workforce and Disability, Washington, DC, 2005).

3. Elisabeth Muhlenberg, "Who Benefits? A Comparison of School-Firm Partnerships in Chicago and Berlin" (doctoral dissertation, University of Illinois, Chicago, 2011), 139.

4. "Running Start for the Trades: A Report to the Governor and Legislature" (report, Washington State Apprenticeship and Training Council, 2007).

5. Alison Taylor, "The Challenges of Partnership in School-to-Work Transition," *Journal of Vocational Education and Training* 58, no. 3 (2006): 319–336.

6. Francis Schrag, "Nurturing Talent: How the U.S. Succeeds," *Education Week* 29, no. 25 (2010): 22.

7. Sarojni Choy and Brian Delahaye, "Some Principles for Youth Learning" (paper, Australian VET Research Association, Brisbane, April 13–15, 2006).

8. Wolfgang Lehmann, "I'm Still Scrubbing the Floors: Experiencing Youth Apprenticeships in Canada and Germany," *Work, Employment and Society* 19, no. 1 (2005): 107–129.

9. Terry Grobe, Elyse Rosenblum, and Todd Weissman, *Dollars and Sense: How Career First Programs Like Year Up Benefit Youth and Employers* (Boston: Jobs for the Future, 2010), 9.

10. National Collaborative on Workforce and Disability, "Strategies for Youth Workforce."

11. Richard Grausman, founder, Careers Through Culinary Arts, New York City, in discussion with the author, December 2006.

12. Lene Tanggaard and Claus Elmholdt, "Assessment in Practice: An Inspiration from Apprenticeship," *Scandinavian Journal of Educational Studies* 52, no. 1 (2008): 97–116.

13. Michael Ford and Ellice Forman, "Redefining Disciplinary Learning in Classroom Contexts," *Review of Research in Education* 30, no. 1 (2006): 1–32.

14. Zara Lavchyan, "Spiral Learning," in NFE Book: The Impact of Nonformal Education on Young People and Society, ed. Maria Nomikov (Brussels: Association des Estats Generaux des Etudiants de'l Europe, n.d.), 14.

15. Kathryn Barker, "Innovations in Workforce Management: The Electronic Learning Record, Prior Learning Assessment, and Human Capital Accounting" (working paper, Workshop on Public Sector Innovation, University of Ottawa, Canada, 2002).

16. Ann Kirschner, "Innovation in Higher Education? Hah!" *Chronicle Review*, April 8, 2012, B8.

17. *European Guidelines for the Validation of Non-Formal and Informal Learning* (Berlin: European Center for the Development of Vocational Training, 2008).

18. Robert Lerman, "Helping Disconnected Youth by Improving Linkages between High Schools and Careers" (working paper, the Urban Institute, Washington, DC, 1996).

Conclusions

1. David Buckingham, "Introducing Identity," in *Youth, Identity, and Digital Media*, ed. David Buckingham (Cambridge, MA: MIT Press, 2008), 9.

2. Chris Higgins, "The Possibility of Public Education in an Instrumentalist Age," *Educational Theory* 61, no. 4 (2011): 451–466.

3. Nell Daniel, "Sweat Equity Enterprises: The Convergence of Design Education, Youth Development and Situated Learning" (doctoral dissertation, New York University, 2007).

4. Scott Lundius, education director, Marwen Arts, Chicago, in discussion with author, July 2007.

5. John Rury, "Democracy's High School? Social Change and American Secondary Education in the Post-Conant Era," *American Educational Research Journal* 39, no. 2 (2002): 307–336.

6. Manuela du Bois-Reymond, "What Does Learning Mean in the Learning Society?" in *Trading Up: Potential and Performance in Non-Formal Learning*, ed. Lynne Chisholm et al. (Strasbourg, France: Council of Europe, 2005).

7. James Gee, "Communities of Practice in the New Capitalism," *Journal of the Learning Sciences* 9, no. 4 (2000): 515–523.

8. Susan Robertson et al., "The Global Auction: The Broken Promises of Education, Jobs and Incomes," *British Journal of Sociology of Education* 32, no. 2 (2011): 293–311.

9. Walter Heinz, "Structure and Agency in Transition Research," *Journal of Education and Work* 22, no.5 (2009): 391–404.

10. James Gee et al., *The New Work Order* (Boulder, CO: Westview Press, 1996), 41.

Acknowledgments

The author gratefully acknowledges the support of Jeffrey and Toby Herr, through the Herr Foundation, for providing a grant to fund time for research and writing. He also thanks the Joyce Foundation and the Lloyd Frye Foundation for support on career and technical education research that helped with the writing of chapter 4.

About the Author

Robert Halpern is a professor at the Erikson Institute for Graduate Study in Child Development in Chicago. His research focuses on the nature of good learning and developmental experiences during the high school years. He is the author of *The Means To Grow Up: Reinventing Apprenticeship As A Developmental Support in Adolescence* (Routledge, 2009); *Making Play Work: The Promise of After-School Programs for Low-Income Children* (Teachers College Press, 2003); *Fragile Families, Fragile Solutions: A History of Supportive Services for Families in Poverty* (Columbia University Press, 1998); and *Rebuilding the Inner City: A History of Neighborhood Initiatives to Address Poverty in the United States* (Columbia University Press, 1995), among many other works.

Index